BUILDING EXPERIMENTS IN

PsychoPy

JONATHAN PEIRCE & MICHAEL MacASKILL

BUILDING EXPERIMENTS IN
PsychoPy

Los Angeles | London | New Delhi
Singapore | Washington DC | Melbourne

Los Angeles | London | New Delhi
Singapore | Washington DC | Melbourne

SAGE Publications Ltd
1 Oliver's Yard
55 City Road
London EC1Y 1SP

SAGE Publications Inc.
2455 Teller Road
Thousand Oaks, California 91320

SAGE Publications India Pvt Ltd
B 1/I 1 Mohan Cooperative Industrial Area
Mathura Road
New Delhi 110 044

SAGE Publications Asia-Pacific Pte Ltd
3 Church Street
#10-04 Samsung Hub
Singapore 049483

Editor: Becky Taylor
Editorial assistant: Katie Rabot
Production editor: Imogen Roome
Copyeditor: Neville Hankins
Proofreader: Neil Dowden
Marketing manager: Lucia Sweet
Cover design: Wendy Scott
Typeset by: C&M Digitals (P) Ltd, Chennai, India
Printed in the UK

Library of Congress Control Number: 2017958160

British Library Cataloguing in Publication data

A catalogue record for this book is available from
the British Library

ISBN 978-1-4739-9138-5
ISBN 978-1-4739-9139-2 (pbk)

At SAGE we take sustainability seriously. Most of our products are printed in the UK using responsibly sourced
papers and boards. When we print overseas we ensure sustainable papers are used as measured by the PREPS
grading system. We undertake an annual audit to monitor our sustainability.

CONTENTS

ACKNOWLEDGMENTS

This book wouldn't have been possible without the help and support of many people.

Jon is very grateful to the support he has had from his family who have at times been left holding the baby (literally) while he has spent his evenings and weekends writing this book. Shiri Einav, in particular, has often had to fill in the bits of life that he hasn't been doing while working on this endeavor! Michael thanks Sarah Kirk and Paige MacAskill for putting up with his absences on the home front. He'd also like to thank Jon himself, for creating PsychoPy in the first place, but also setting the tone for the good-natured and enthusiastic community that has grown up around it. Our respective institutions (University of Nottingham and New Zealand Brain Research Institute) have paid us throughout this period and allowed us to work on these projects, for which we are also grateful.

It hasn't just been about the writing of the book though. The book couldn't have been written without PsychoPy and there are many more people involved in that project that must all be thanked. PsychoPy is a community project, driven by people volunteering their time, in between running experiments and teaching students in their universities. These volunteers are helping in various ways: some are writing the software itself and fixing bugs they find; others are helping out on the forum so that new users can get their questions answered. The people *asking* those questions also contribute, by showing where software features aren't obvious or need improvement, and what sorts of areas need to be covered in a book like this.

A few of the contributors need special mention because of the vast number of hours they have put into the project. Jeremy Gray and Sol Simpson have both put in ridiculously large amounts of time in both development and user support. Some very notable features are theirs entirely (like the Rating Scale and the ioHub) but they have contributed to code across the entire project. They, and their families, have sacrificed a lot for the sake of this project, for no financial gain, solely to help users run experiments.

Richard Höchenberger, Hiroyuki Sogo, Jonas Lindeløv, Damien Mannion, Daniel Riggs, Oliver Clark, Yaroslav Halchenko, Jan Freyberg and Eric Kastman have each contributed hundreds of hours to the project, either in programming or in the support forum, and a huge number of additional people have contributed their time to some level (apologies if we failed to include your name here).

We are very grateful to the entire community for their support of the project and each other. Working with this team of committed, selfless individuals has given us a great deal of pleasure. The open-source, open-science community, which we see constantly growing, is a great testament to what people can achieve working together.

HOW TO USE YOUR BOOK

PsychoPy is an open-source (free) software package for creating rich, dynamic experiments for psychology, neuroscience and linguistics. *Building Experiments in PsychoPy* is the first textbook to cover the use of PsychoPy with relevant examples and content from psychology, neuroscience or linguistics. This textbook provides a detailed guide on how to use PsychoPy, supporting the learning of undergraduates, postgraduates and research professionals. The unique learning features guide you throughout your PsychoPy journey.

WHAT YOU'LL FIND

Divided into three parts, this textbook is suitable for teaching practical undergraduate classes on research methods, or as a reference text for the professional scientist.

UNIQUE LEARNING FEATURES

Pro Tips are for the perfectionists – using these will help you become more efficient.

Info topics for the curious reader provide further information and background.

Warnings are for the skim readers, crucial for learning, and point out common mistakes.

EXERCISES

In-text and online exercises help you test your understanding.

ONLINE RESOURCES

You can find the relevant learning resource online at

https://study.sagepub.com/psychology

These resources include learning objectives, links to the PsychoPy website and forum, and additional demonstrations for each chapter.

'This book has all the tips and tricks you need to get the most out of using PsychoPy! There's something for researchers at every stage, from learning to build simple experiments to more advanced tricks to fulfil those niche experimental requirements. I wish I had this book when I started my PhD!'

Rebecca Hirst, PhD student, University of Nottingham

'This book provides everything you need to know, covering the basics of the GUI all the way through to advanced debugging/programming skills. Whether you're an undergraduate student or seasoned researcher this book will have something for you.'

Joshua Henk Balsters, Lecturer, Department of Psychology, Royal Holloway University of London

1

INTRODUCTION

This book is designed to get you up and running with experiments in the PsychoPy software package. We hope it will help you, whether you're a student, an educator or a research scientist. Some people perceive computers, and anything technical, as somewhat challenging. We hope to convince you that you can create experiments in PsychoPy even if you think of yourself as 'not very technical'. You might not get to the point of using the more advanced features but most standard experimental designs should be possible for you even if you hate computers.

For those of you that are quite technically competent we hope to provide you with some advanced features as well. Hopefully we'll convince you that PsychoPy provides a pretty easy way to get the boring stuff done (saving data files and tracking randomization) while allowing you to create some neat effects (like presenting live video from a webcam or making your stimulus 'throb').

To meet the needs of such a varied target audience we've split the book into three parts.

Part I aims to teach you all the basic skills you need (and some more advanced tips along the way) to design experiments in behavioral sciences. Each chapter will introduce some new concept but we'll do so by creating a series of working experiments that you can build on. For instance, we'll teach you about how to present and manipulate image files by creating an experiment looking at the face inversion effect.

Part II presents more of the details, which are important if you are a professional scientist intending to use PsychoPy for published research. This part is recommended reading for science professionals in any discipline.

Part III covers a range of specialist topics that only some people will need, such as those doing fMRI research, or those studying visual perception, so this is something that could be read selectively.

1.1 CREATING EXPERIMENTS

There was a time when psychologists needed engineering staff in order to run experiments. A professor would go down to the workshop and ask the engineer to construct some electronics box that would allow a light to be flashed at a very precise rate, or to buy a tachistoscope (a device like a camera shutter that would present stimuli for a very brief period) from a specialist company and arrange for a PhD student to run around changing the stimulus (e.g. a photograph) that would appear behind the shutter on each trial.

Then computers came along and a lot of the hardware and electronic approaches to running experiments became obsolete. Most departments no longer have workshops for building experimental hardware. Instead, computer programmers were needed in order to control the computer in the way that was needed. A program was written for each individual experiment that the professor wanted to run and when the experiment was changed the programmer had to be called back to make the necessary changes.

As time has gone by the programming languages used to create experiments have gradually become easier to use (assembly language was replaced by C, which, in turn, has been supplanted by interpreted scripting languages like Python, MATLAB and Java). Those changes made it possible for the technically minded to write their own experiment even if they didn't have a PhD in computer science.

The final step was when some software packages allowed you to create a wide range of experiments without even 'programming', or at least not in the traditional sense of writing lines of code. This development opened the door for you to create studies yourself, even though you might not know how to program and, possibly, find the suggestion a little terrifying! This book shows you how to construct basic experiments yourself, using one of the possible options called PsychoPy. We'll also show you how to extend these graphically built experiments with a little bit of programming for those of you who need something more advanced. You might find that a little bit of programming isn't as bad as you imagine. You might even get some sort of satisfaction from it (we'll get on to that later).

By the way, although we might be teaching you how to create experiments yourself, we aren't suggesting that you sack your departmental programmer or tech support! It really helps to have someone around with good tech/programming skills, to provide local help when things go wrong or when you want to do something a bit more advanced. Having someone around who understands the nitty gritty is always good. On the other hand, they'll appreciate it if you take the experiment as far as you can to being ready so they just have to make the final tweaks!

1.2 BUILDING VERSUS CODING

Some experimental design software packages require you to write lines of text (code) to create your experiment. The Psychophysics Toolbox (http://psychtool box.org/) and Presentation (https://www.neurobs.com/) are examples of that.

They can be very powerful but they do require that you know how to program and, even if you can program, creating an experiment can be quite time consuming and often leads to errors.

Others, such as E-Prime (https://www.pstnet.com/), PsyScope (http://psy. cns.sissa.it/) and OpenSesame (http://osdoc.cogsci.nl/), allow you to create your experiment visually using a graphical user interface (GUI). These tools are generally easier to use when creating simple experiments, but more complex experiments may not be possible or may require you to create such a complex visual representation in order to get the result you want that you would have been better off learning to program instead! You may get annoyed that a graphical package can't handle the particular form of experiment you have in mind, or the particular form of 'random with a few exceptions' that you want for your stimuli, but bear in mind that a graphical interface capable of handling all possible experiments would probably be so complicated that you wouldn't be able to learn it in the first place!

PsychoPy, the software package we're focusing on throughout this book, provides interfaces for creating experiments by either means: programmers can use the *Coder* interface and those that prefer to use graphical interfaces can use the *Builder* view. Coder was designed to allow moderately competent programmers to achieve any conceivable design they like – maximum flexibility and power in a language that's as user-friendly as possible. Conversely, Builder was designed to be simple enough that undergraduate students in psychology (many of whom are not fans of programming) can get up and running with experiments that they created themselves. The aim is to allow most 'standard' experiments to be possible with minimal fuss. It has actually worked well with that aim in mind and, indeed, has allowed much more complicated experiments than we ever really envisaged. Many universities now use it for their undergraduate teaching but also many fully fledged scientists, even those who are perfectly capable of writing the code manually, use Builder to run the bulk of their experiments. We wrote PsychoPy itself, so we seem to be moderately competent programmers, but we also use Builder to create most experiments because it's just quicker to get something up and running without lots of bugs to fix!

When you do find that the Builder interface can't handle the experiment you have in mind, all is not lost. You can also add code to it to run more advanced studies. Maybe you have a hardware device that isn't supported by the graphical interface. Maybe you need a particular type of stimulus sequence that isn't simply 'random' or 'sequential', such as a random sequence but with *Stimulus A* never appearing twice in a row; all possible variants of that structure would be hard to create in a GUI but writing them in code is usually possible. (We'll be covering those in the chapter on randomization and counterbalancing.)

Beyond that, many users (including ourselves) use a combination approach, whereby they construct the bulk of the experiment in the Builder view (because the nature of one trial and the saving of data are usually fairly straightforward) and then simply add *Code Components* to handle aspects that aren't easy to construct graphically (like the randomization method).

For a number of users, adding a little code here and there to improve their study has led them to learn the basics of Python programming as well. Some people have found that programming is not the scary beast that they once thought it to be (or possibly they don't realize that 'programming' is what they're doing!). Some people have found it's actually quite enjoyable. It's problem solving, like playing Sudoku, but with the added bonus that you get something useful when you've finished. Ultimately, programming is also a more general tool than using Builder. With code you can manage your files, automate tasks, analyze data and even produce the final visualizations of your results, as well as running the experiments themselves.

Although it's great to be able to write code, the *fastest* way to construct most experiments with fewest mistakes is to use the PsychoPy Builder.

1.3 PROS AND CONS OF OPEN-SOURCE SOFTWARE

The rise of open-source software is something of an enigma to many people. The idea that someone would write code without getting paid for it and then give it away for free is a little strange. People are also somewhat suspicious that the software is presumably poor quality, or doesn't have many features (if it was any good you'd sell it, right?!). Others assume that this is a trick and sooner or later you'll start charging for the software once there is a big enough market attached to it. Neither of these are necessarily true. For instance, look at the Mozilla suite (Thunderbird mail client and Firefox web browser). It's amazingly powerful and professional. The Python programming language, the R stats package and the Linux operating system are more great examples of open-source software that have proven to be bug-free, sustainable, powerful products that never cost you a cent!

So, what is the deal here? Why do they do this? Well, often, open-source software is written by fanatics in some particular topic, who felt that the existing products didn't meet their needs and so started writing their own. Put yourself in their shoes. If the aim is simply to make the product awesome (remember, you're a fanatic), rather than making money from it, then one way to make it better is to allow everyone access to the code. This might encourage other people to get involved and help you fix bugs and add features. Yes, it means you probably can't sell it, because you gave everyone the code, but if you're not in it for the money that won't matter. It is the underlying drive behind many open-source products.

So how does this compare with the traditional approach in which a company charges for its software and pays professional programmers to write the code? Well, it's true that open-source software *can be* buggy. As you didn't pay the programmers they don't feel indebted to you and are under no obligation to fix the bug you care about. They want the software to be awesome but they have limited time. Commercial software companies won't want to release software with any bugs and will invest a lot of time testing all aspects first, for fear of being sued. Another *potential* downside is that many open-source projects collapse after a short period with just a few die-hard supporters; many keen programmers start a project and then get bored and stop. You don't want to invest your time learning a package that disappears a few years later. Both of these issues are biggest for young open-source projects, however. As projects grow in users they also typically grow in contributors and that means that there are more people fixing bugs and adding features, as well as less chance of the project dying on its feet.

When open-source projects take off they're pretty great! First, there's the fact that these fanatics go off and write software for you for free. But the added advantage is that the people *writing* the software are the people *using* the software. In the case of experimental design software this means people who actually run experiments themselves are writing the software to run them. Hopefully they have a really good sense of how other scientists think and what they will want.

The last advantage is that because you have access to all the code (a) you get to change the software yourself if it doesn't do exactly what you want; and (b) you can inspect the code to see exactly what is happening if you're the sort of scientist who likes to feel nothing was hidden from you. 'Open' scientists like to know what they're getting.

1.4 UNDERSTANDING YOUR COMPUTER

To some this may be an obvious statement but, if you care about the precision of your study, it's important to have a reasonable understanding of your computer when you learn to run experiments. Very often experiments are made imprecise, not by the software being used, but because the user didn't really understand their computer. Here are three examples of common misunderstandings that could lead you to have a 'less-than-precise' experiment.

Your computer screen updates at a precise and fixed rate. Most flat-panel computer screens refresh at 60 Hz. You can only update your stimulus (e.g. turn it on or off) during a screen update and that means there are only certain durations that your stimulus can have. We'll call those update cycles *frames*. For instance, you can present your stimulus for 200 ms (0.2 s) because at 60 Hz this is given by exactly 12 frames (0.2 × 60 = 12) and you can present your stimulus for 250 ms by presenting 15 frames (0.25 × 60 = 15), but 220 ms is not a valid duration because it would require your stimulus to be presented for 13.2 frames and that just isn't possible. There are various other things that are worth knowing about your monitor, like the fact that it draws the screen from the top line downwards in a process that takes around 10 ms, so stimuli at the top of your screen are always presented up to 10 ms before stimuli at the bottom of the screen!

Your keyboard has poor timing. When you were told that your software package provides sub-millisecond timing, this glossed over the fact that you generally aren't getting that level of precision. Computer keyboards have latencies in detecting keypresses in the region of 30 ms and variability on the order of 15 ms. It might well be true that the software package has 'submillisecond' timing in that it can access a very precise clock on the computer, but what use is that claim if it doesn't apply to every situation (for no software does this apply to all situations)?

 Info: Origins of PsychoPy

The PsychoPy project was first registered in March 2002 on sourceforge.net, although it was initially called PsychPy and the 'o' was added a little later. It was originally written by Jon Peirce as a proof of principle that Python could be a useful tool to deliver stimuli in real time using hardware-accelerated graphics (OpenGL) routines. In 2003 Jon started as a Lecturer in Psychology at the University of Nottingham and decided to develop the project further to run the experiments in his lab. The project then was just a library of functions written in Python to make programming more convenient.

It has run all the experiments in Jon's lab since 2004, and features that were added fastest were because they were needed by him and his PhD students. Support for users was minimal: it was done for Jon's lab and if you found it useful that was fine, but if not then you should just not use it. Gradually people started saying 'I like that library you wrote but I wonder if it could…'. Well, Jon enjoys a challenge and some of the features people were requesting seemed interesting, so he added them piece by piece.

A few years later Jon added the Standalone 'application', rather than just a library, including a code editor with a big green 'run' icon to launch the script. As it was easier to install and try out, more users started trying it. In 2007 the first paper describing the package was written (Peirce, 2007). By 2009 there were a few hundred users who were all programming enthusiasts and who were willing to live with PsychoPy's little 'quirks' (aka bugs). Gradually those users (notably Jeremy Gray and Michael MacAskill) started getting involved in fixing bugs, adding features and helping each other on the users' forum.

> Around the same time Jon became frustrated with teaching EPrime to his undergraduates and started thinking about the next major step, which was to write a graphical interface that students would understand sufficiently for his classes. The idea was that this graphical interface would essentially write the Python script that he would otherwise have to write for them. 'Builder' was ready for basic use in 2010 and has been used in many undergraduate lab classes since 2011.
>
> With the addition of Builder, the number of users, and also contributors to the software, increased dramatically. At the time of writing this book (2017) there were over 16,000 users (measured by the unique IP addresses launching the application each month) and over 70 contributors to the package (with varying degrees of commitment).
>
> In short, PsychoPy was never really *designed* to be this big. It just kind of grew. But we're glad to see such a lovely community growing around it and proud to be a part of the work that has brought it this far.

Loading an image from disk is not instantaneous. If you have, say, a 5 megapixel camera (small by modern standards) and each pixel is specified as a red, green and blue value (actually there's usually an *alpha* channel as well), then that means 15 million numbers have to be loaded from the disk, processed and sent to your graphics card. Although computers are incredibly fast at processing and moving around numbers these days, they can't do that instantly and so some delays will occur, particularly at the stage where you load files from the disk.

The above problems all have solutions that work in most scenarios: you can present stimuli in multiples of frame intervals, you can buy button boxes that allow for more precise timing of responses (although more likely, you don't need the level of precision that you think you do) and image files can be preloaded and can be much smaller than you might think, with no loss of quality. The point is that you need to be aware of these issues in order to understand how to avoid them.

1.5 WHAT IS PSYCHOPY?

PsychoPy is several things. As explained in the *Origins of PsychoPy* topic, they were developed gradually and fairly independently as the following:

- A library for the Python programming language.
- A distribution of the Python programming language (the *Standalone* installers install Python and many dependent libraries so that you don't need to and your own installation of Python won't be affected).

- A code editor (cunningly called 'Coder') that, as it happens, was also written in the Python programming language.
- A graphical interface (called 'Builder') for converting visual representations of experiments into computer code.

As you can see from the list above, this 'Python programming language' comes up a lot. In case you haven't heard of Python, it's a general-purpose, high-level, interpreted scripting language. 'General purpose' simply means it can be used for many things; OS X and most Linux distributions provide it as part of the operating system because it's such a useful little beastie! 'High level' indicates that you can achieve a lot with a few simple commands and that these might be quite easy to read, compared with some languages (although that does depend on who writes the code). 'Interpreted' indicates that you don't have to 'compile' the code into 'machine code' after you've written it, and also that it should run on most types of computer. If you've spent any time compiling C code and trying to get it to run the same way on different computer platforms you might be pleased about this!

Python itself doesn't do an awful lot, but it has very many libraries written by enthusiasts to do different jobs. The reason this is useful is that the developers of PsychoPy didn't have to write code to do all these different things. To load an image we could use the Python Imaging Library (*PIL/PILLOW*, written by some image-processing junkies) and to manipulate it we could use the numerical Python library (*numpy*, written by people who do a lot of number crunching). All these libraries are freely available and written by enthusiasts in their fields. So PsychoPy's job, to some extent, is to knit those various libraries together and provide a coherent application so that the user doesn't have to know too much about each of the underlying packages.

1.6 GETTING STARTED

You obviously need to have a working copy of PsychoPy on your computer in order to get maximum use from this book. If you go to the PsychoPy web page (www.psychopy.org) you should see a link on the right of the page to 'Download', but when you get to that page you find a whole list of different options. Most beginners should probably select one of the files labelled 'StandalonePsychoPy _____'. At the time this book was written the current version was 1.85 but we recommend you use the most recent version where possible.

When you first start PsychoPy you might find it launches a 'Start Up Wizard' that will inspect your system and see what your computer is like, but you can also just skip that option.

Then you'll probably see a pair of windows appear. The *Builder* view is going to be the main focus of this book, but the *Coder* view will crop up at times as well when we look at some Python code (we have to do that, but it really isn't so bad!).

1.7 GOING FURTHER

If after reading this book you still have questions you'll find a lot of information on the users forum (https://discourse.psychopy.org). Or just Google the question and/or error message to see if Google knows the answer (it's amazing how often it does!).

Please be understanding on the forum. Most people answering questions there are simply volunteers helping each other out. They are doing this in addition to their own jobs so it isn't appropriate to ask them for help to create your entire experiment. If the help you need is more generally about computers (e.g. installing software) then you might want to talk to your local tech support staff instead of using the list. If your question is too broad then you might be better off talking to someone local (e.g. an academic supervisor). Also, if you feel that you know the answer to someone else's question, it would be great if you'd jump in there and answer it!

But for specific questions the user forum is an excellent place to get information.

 Pro Tip: Updating PsychoPy

The Standalone packages provide their own copy of Python and all the 'dependencies' needed for PsychoPy to work, as well as providing the code that provides the PsychoPy application and library itself. (We hope we haven't lost you there; you might want to re-read that sentence.) Now, when you want to update PsychoPy to the latest version, with (hopefully) fewer bugs and (probably) more features, you generally don't need to download/install the whole Standalone package (which is several hundred mega-bytes); you can usually either tell PsychoPy to auto-update to the latest version or download one of the files labelled PsychoPy-_.__._.zip to install a specific version from the same `Tools>Update` dialog box.

You may need to launch the application as an administrator in order to be able to perform an update. In Windows, right-click the PsychoPy icon in the Start Menu and select 'Run as Admin'.

Pro Tip: Using the forum

If you post a message on the PsychoPy users forum, asking for help, it's a really good idea to state:

- whether you're using Builder or Coder view
- what you tried to do
- what exactly happened when it failed (saying 'it didn't work' doesn't help)
- what operating system you use and what version of PsychoPy.

1.8 CONVENTIONS OF THIS BOOK

During the book most text will be written in this font but some text will refer to code that you might need to type in PsychoPy windows and that will have a font like this: `event.getKeys()`. We typically use italics to indicate technical terms, and terms specific to PsychoPy often have initial capitals like the *Routine* and the *Flow*.

PsychoPy runs on Windows, Mac and Linux operating systems and the keyboard shortcuts may differ slightly between those. We tend to report the Windows keyboard shortcut (e.g. `Ctrl-L` to switch views) and hopefully you will remember that on the Mac this usually equates to the `Cmd` key (⌘). While we're talking about keys we might mention the `<return>` key at times. A lot of people call the `<return>` key the `<enter>` key but technically the `<enter>` key is different and is usually on the number pad. The `<return>` key has the arrow pointing down and to the left. It is derived from 'carriage return', which is a name stemming from the times when you had to push the carriage of a typewriter back to the beginning of the line.

In addition to those typographical conventions, there are some specific blocks of text as shown below that provide tips, warnings, topics and exercises so you can ignore or pay particular attention to these as you see fit.

Pro Tip: For the perfectionist

Tips show you how the 'pro' tends to work. They aren't necessary but if you learn to use them they'll probably help you to be more efficient in your work. Or at least you'll earn kudos with your more geeky friends.

Info: For the curious

Information topics provide information that isn't strictly needed for you to understand how to build your study, but which you might find interesting. Some of these provide background information about the field and others provide information about scientific techniques that may already seem obvious. Feel free not to read any of these boxes if they don't interest you!

 Warning: For the skim reader

Even if you don't read anything else in the book, make sure you look out for the warnings. These indicate common mistakes or things that could lead you to do something very bad without realizing.

OK, hopefully you now understand at least how to read the book! Now let's go and learn how to build some studies!

PART I
FOR THE BEGINNER

This first part of the book is designed to get you up and running. We will help you to develop a variety of experiment designs with the emphasis very much on the practicalities of getting going. We hope it will be a useful resource for all users, with minimal experience of designing experiments, such as Psychology undergraduate classes.

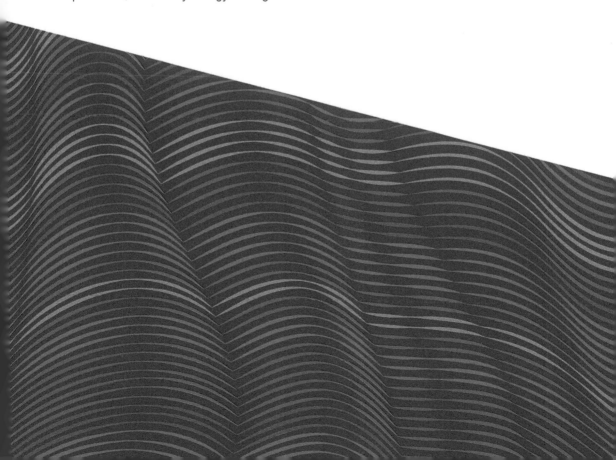

2

BUILDING YOUR FIRST EXPERIMENT

Learning objectives: This chapter will teach you all the basic aspects of the PsychoPy Builder interface while creating a simple experiment; the Stroop task.

You might be thinking, 'How on Earth do I create an experiment from start to finish?' You might be thinking, 'I'm not very good with computers; this is going to be difficult.' Hopefully we'll be able to show you that you can absolutely create experiments of your own. Even the least 'technical' of users can get up and running.

One of the first things to realize is that you don't have to build the whole study in one go. Work on a piece at a time, save the study and see if it worked. That way you'll (a) feel like each chunk is manageable and (b) you'll narrow down what might have gone wrong if your experiment stops working, because it's probably related to what you just did. So we'll go through a series of steps thinking about how to define the structure of a single trial in your study (including how to present stimuli and how to collect responses), then how to set that trial to repeat several times and how to make it vary on each repeat, and how to extract the data that you just collected. The study we create here will be basic – there are lots of ways you could extend and improve it – but this will be enough to measure an effect.

Before we get started, though, let's take a quick look at the PsychoPy Builder view.

2.1 THE BUILDER INTERFACE

The PsychoPy Builder interface is designed to allow quick visual construction of a wide range of studies. OK, let's take a look at what makes a Builder experiment. If you start up PsychoPy and the Builder view isn't immediately visible then you might be in the Coder view instead. Go to the menu `View` and select `Builder` or press `Ctrl-L` (`Cmd-L` on a Mac).

An experiment in Builder has three panels showing you:

- a single *Flow*
- one or more *Routines* that can be combined in the *Flow*
- several *Components* that are combined in each *Routine*.

Info: Why can't Builder do my experiment?

You may find yourself wishing that Builder had more features, but it was designed deliberately to be simple and handle most experiment designs easily. If the interface contained all the necessary controls for all possible experimental designs then, for a beginner seeing it for the first time, it would look much more scary than it does!

COMPONENTS

Components are the basic items that can be combined to create an experiment. They typically represent either stimuli (e.g. Image or Text Components), or methods of responding (e.g. Mouse or Keyboard Components), but can also represent points at which your experiment should perform other actions, like connecting with external hardware. Your experiment can include as many Components as you like and different Components can interact with each other however you choose. The right-hand panel of the Builder interface shows you all the different Components available to you, arranged by category (Figure 2.1).

Pro Tip: Adding favorite Components

If you expect to use one of the Components a lot you can right-click it and add it to the Favorites category so you can find it more easily in future.

When you click on one of these Component buttons a dialog box will appear for you to set various variables for that Component, and if you press 'OK' the Component will be added to the currently selected Routine.

ROUTINES

These define how *Components* interact in time. A typical Routine would be the definition of a trial, presenting one or more stimuli and getting a response, but it might be something else like the presentation of instructions, or feedback, or some other message. Also, a trial could comprise multiple Routines.

Let's take a look at the `trial` Routine for the Stroop task (Figure 2.2).

You can see that the Routine has a time view, like a track editor for movie/audio editing software, so Components can be controlled independently in time.

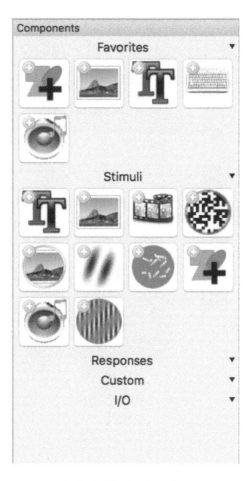

FIGURE 2.1   The Components panel in the Builder interface. Components are arranged by groups, which can be opened or collapsed with a mouse click. Note that the set of available Components and the appearance of this panel can differ according to your computer and the version of PsychoPy you have installed.

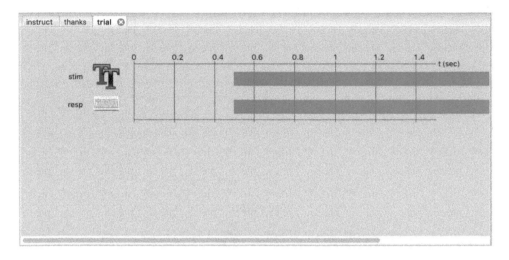

FIGURE 2.2 The 'trial' Routine in the basic Stroop task. You can see there are just two things comprising the trial, a `Text Component` and a `Keyboard Component`.

A fixation point might stay on for your entire trial but the stimulus would just appear for a short period.

In the Stroop demo the stimulus and keyboard both start at 0.5 s after the beginning of the Routine. They both last an infinite duration (the time bar extends beyond the screen).

THE FLOW

The *Flow* is at the bottom of the Builder view. When you first create an experiment it simply has a red box on the timeline indicating the (default) 'trial' Routine. The Flow is just a flow chart (Figure 2.3) and controls the order of things and whether or not they repeat in Loops. It cannot control how long things last in time and

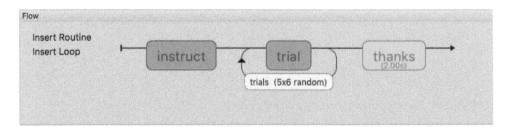

FIGURE 2.3 The *Flow* of the Builder view provides a flow chart of how the different parts of the experiment are combined and in what order. In the case of the Stroop task we have three Routines that run in turn and the `trial` Routine is repeated a number of times in a Loop.

does not contain information about what happens within a Routine. Each item on the Flow simply continues until it ends and then we continue to the next item (or around a Loop).

As many Routines can be added to the Flow as you choose (you can also make the Flow icons larger or smaller from the **View** menu if you have too many to be able to see clearly), although if you have an awful lot of Routines in your Flow it *might* suggest that your experiment could be organized more efficiently. Also a single Routine can be added multiple times at different parts of your Flow. For instance, your study might have some practice trials preceding some main trials, in which case you could have a single Routine called 'trial' that appeared twice, surrounded by two different loops.

LOOPS

Loops are used to control repetition and also to allow things to vary from one repeat to the next. They are attached to the Flow and can wrap around one or more Routines, but also around any other object on the Flow, including other loops!

Loops can be used to select random or sequential presentation of conditions (Figure 2.4) or to create 'staircase' procedures whereby the next condition is determined by responses to the previous one (Figure 2.5).

FIGURE 2.4   A design with a `practice` Loop containing a `trial` Routine and a `feedback` Routine and another loop controlling the main `trials` (which don't have any feedback).

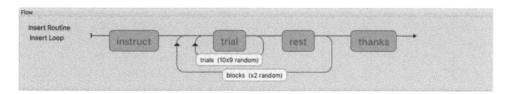

FIGURE 2.5   A block design in which two blocks of 90 trials are conducted with a rest occurring after each block.

THE TOOLBAR

The first few icons are probably obvious (New experiment, Open, Save, Undo, Redo). With the others, if you hover you get a tool tip telling you what they do.

The first two icons concern the overall application settings:

- ✗ Alters the preferences for the application.
- ⬛ Controls monitor calibrations and tells PsychoPy about sizes.

The remaining four icons control the current experiment:

- ▣ Changes settings about this experiment, such as whether it should run fullscreen and what the opening dialog should contain.
- ✎ Builder is ultimately going to create a (slightly complicated) Python script. This button allows you to view the Python code that it will run.
- ⊙ Launches your current experiment.
- ✖ Force-quits the running current experiment.

 Warning: The red STOP button aborts with no data saved

In general PsychoPy will attempt to save data for you and is generally successful at that, even if your participant aborts with the escape key or if your experiment has an error right at the end. If you press the red stop button that will not happen. This is a very forceful exiting of the experiment and typically results in no data being saved

---

2.2 BUILDING THE STROOP TASK

We'll build a task to measure the Stroop effect (Stroop, 1935) in which color names are presented on the screen either in colored letters that match the word being spelled (a congruent condition) or with letters that differ in color from the word.

The task for the participants is simply to read out the color of the letters, ignoring the word itself, but, it turns out, that's extremely hard to do.

2.3 DEFINE YOUR CONDITIONS

The key to understanding how to set up your study in PsychoPy is to think about what **differs** from one trial to the next and what **stays the same**. Things that **stay the same** (e.g. the fact that an image is presented or that a response is recorded) will be controlled within the structure of the *Routine* that determines the trial (which we look at next), whereas things that **differ** from one trial to the next need to be controlled by a conditions file.

For example, in the Stroop task, we always present a text stimulus (a word) and collect a response from the keyboard so those things stay the same. What changes on each trial is the word that the text stimulus presents, the color of its letters and what the correct answer is. Those things are `variables` and we need to create a conditions file to determine what values they can have on different trials.

 Info: The Stroop effect (Stroop, 1935)

John Ridley Stroop (doesn't that name have a nice ring to it? Well done J. Ridley Stroop's parents!) first demonstrated a very simple but very robust effect of mental interference when people are reporting the color of a word when the letters of that word actually spell another color. He ran his studies before computers could do this sort of thing and simply asked participants to read out loud from a set of cards and timed them with a stopwatch. His control condition, in which there was no interference between ink and word, was just to present a block of ink, with no word at all. Most modern variants of his task use letters that are different from the word (incongruent) and compare reaction times with letters that are the same as the word (congruent).

The effect was discovered in 1935, as a part of Stroop's PhD dissertation, and is still used widely in psychology and linguistics research. The paper he wrote on it has over 10,000 citations. In particular, it has been used a great deal to study 'executive function' and attention. The fact that most people find it hard to ignore the letters of the written word makes it an interesting tool to study individual differences, asking whether certain groups of people show more or less Stroop-type interference. See MacLeod (1991) for a (slightly outdated) review of those studies.

Others have claimed that this is good training for your brain. A Google search for `brain training Stroop` results in 140,000 pages, most of which suggest you play their game based on the Stroop effect. We do not wish to express any public opinion on whether the Stroop task will increase the longevity of your intellectual abilities!

You can create your conditions file in any spreadsheet application, like Microsoft Excel, OpenOffice Calc or Google Sheets. (Some applications provide dialog boxes for you to create the conditions files yourselves, but since there are many very powerful spreadsheet applications it seems silly not to make use of them.) All you need is something that can save either a 'comma-separated value' (csv) file or a Microsoft Excel (xlsx) file.

Your file should be organized with a column for every variable (each thing that needs to change from one trial to the next) and with a row for each type of trial that you intend to run. For the Stroop task that might look something like this:

word	letterColor	corrAns	congruent
red	red	left	1
red	green	down	0
green	green	down	1
green	blue	right	0
blue	blue	right	1
blue	red	left	0

The word variable is obviously the word that will be presented on each trial whereas the letterColor represents the color of the letters on the screen. Half the time these variables have the same value and half the time they don't.

Then we have the corrAns column. The participants in the task have to respond by pressing the left button (i.e. the arrow keys near to the number pad here, but you could use any set of keys you choose) when they see red *letters*, press the down key when they see green letters and press the right key when they see blue letters. (Remember, red, green, blue, in that order for the three keys. Remembering the keys is the hardest part of this task!) By specifying in this file what the correct answer is on each trial (the corrAns variable) we can get PsychoPy to check whether the participants got the answer right each time.

The final column isn't really necessary but it makes it easier to perform an analysis in the data file. Remember, our aim is to test whether reaction times are different for congruent trials than for incongruent ones and by including a column like this we'll be able to simply sort by this variable to make it easier to compare the trials where this was true and false (1 and 0).

There are a few very important rules to follow in creating names of variables (and also of Components):

- **Variables in your conditions file must have unique names.** That means unique from each other and unique from all other aspects of your experiment. If you have a variable called word but also a Component called word then PsychoPy cannot know which one you're referring to.
- **Variables cannot contain spaces, punctuation or accents.** Apologies to the non-English speakers out there, but these names are going to be converted into variables in a Python script and variables can only have names using

ASCII letters. Underscores (_) are allowed and numbers can be used anywhere except as the first character of the name, but that's about all.

- **All columns with values in them need a variable name at the top.** Don't be tempted to have an extra column that contains some information 'just for your benefit' where you didn't need a heading. It is really confusing for PsychoPy ('You've got values here but I don't know what to call them. Help!')
- **Naming of variables/conditions is case-sensitive.** This means that the names `Stimulus` and `stimulus` would count as unique names (though you might struggle to remember which was the one you intended to refer to if you use both!).

 Warning: Watch out for spaces in your conditions file

If you add a space character in one of your headers (e.g. at the end of a variable name) it can be really hard to spot but it will count as one of those forbidden characters in your variable names.

2.4 DEFINING THE TRIAL STRUCTURE

To define how each of trials will run we need to think about what **stays the same** on each trial. In the Stroop task each trial consists of a text stimulus being presented and a response being recorded on the keyboard. We can do all this in a single *Routine* but in some experiments your trial might need more than one *Routine*.

Open the PsychoPy Builder view and make sure you have an empty (New) experiment so that you are starting with a clean state. Save it straightaway, next to the conditions file, in the folder you created. You might call it something like `stroop.psyexp` although the .psyexp extension should be added automatically if you don't add it yourself. The extension .psyexp always denotes a PsychoPy experiment and is distinct from the .py files which indicate (Python syntax) script files. Do keep in mind the location of the folder and experiment file. This may seem obvious but it seems quite common that we say that the data are in a folder 'next to the `experiment file`' and it turns out the user doesn't know where their experiment file was saved.

Create your stimulus: The first thing we need to add for each trial is a *Text Component* to present the stimulus. Create a new Text Component by clicking the **T** button in the Components Panel (on the right of the Builder view). Note that the buttons in the Components Panel create new Components, but you can edit an existing Component by clicking on its icon or timeline in the Routine panel.

You can remove a Component by *right*-clicking its icon in the Routine panel. (If you have an Apple Macintosh computer you may find that right-click isn't enabled because Apple seems to think that using two buttons on a mouse is too confusing for the average user! You can/should turn this on in the System Settings because your mouse almost certainly does actually contain two buttons.)

All Components need to be given a name and the names follow the same rules as for the variables (unique, no punctuation, case-sensitive). For instance, we can't call our component `word` because we already used that name as a variable in the conditions file. Let's call it `stim` instead.

 Pro Tip: Use good names

It's really worth thinking carefully about the name you give your Component, especially if your experiment has many Components and variables. When you come back to your experiment in a year's time and find three Components called `image_1`, `image_2` and `image_3`, then you might not remember what each of the images was for. If you called them `target`, `flank_left`, `flank_right` it would have been more obvious. For response objects (like the Keyboard Component) the name also appears in the header of the data output, so if you name them clearly it will be much easier to tell later which column you need to analyze and which one was caused simply by the participant advancing to the next block of trials (both of which might have been driven by keyboard events).

If the stimulus comes on at the very beginning of the Routine it will appear immediately after the participant responded to the previous trial. For a participant that's surprisingly stressful; they'll complain that your study is 'running too fast'. We can create an **inter-trial interval** (ITI) simply by delaying the start of our stimulus until `0.5 s` (`500 ms`) into the Routine. Set the **start** time in your Text Component dialog to be 0.5 (PsychoPy refers to all times in units of seconds but that doesn't mean it's less precise than other packages that refer to time in `ms`). We could present the stimulus for any **duration** really, but let's delete all the contents of the **duration** box, which will cause the `stim` to be presented indefinitely. Lastly, set the **Text** box to have the value `red`. Your dialog box should look something like Figure 2.6.

Note that we changed the following settings from their default entries:

- the *start* time to `0.5` (seconds after Routine started)
- the *stop* (duration) was set to be blank, but it could also be shorter if you prefer
- the *text* became `red`.

Several of the properties of Text Components are common to many Components. We encountered **Start and Stop** already but note that there are several ways they can be set:

- So far we simply used seconds, which is the most intuitive way to time stimuli, but not always the most precise.
- We could also have used number of frames instead of seconds which is generally more precise for brief stimulus presentations.
- We could also have used a condition, which would be a Python expression. Often this is used to yoke one stimulus to another. For instance, you could set a condition that `distractor.status==FINISHED` to make something start/stop when the `distractor` stimulus stopped, even though that time might not be known in advance.

FIGURE 2.6 Presenting the word 'red' in white letters, starting at 0.5 s and lasting for ever.

- For start times and durations where the time in seconds isn't known in advance (because it is based on a variable or condition or computed using frames which can differ from one computer to another), these don't automatically appear on the timeline of the Routine, but you can set the `Expected duration` in seconds if you wish to make them more visible. The `Expected duration` has no effect on the actual experiment.

Colors can be defined for most visual stimuli and these can also be set using a variety of ways: names (any of the X11 colors), hexadecimal values like #00FFC0 as well as a triple of values in various color spaces (RGB, RGB255, DKL, HSV, etc.). These are covered in more detail on page 166.

Position, for most stimuli, refers to the center of the stimulus, although for Text Components it depends whether the Component is set to align on the left, right or center; these define how position is defined. The coordinates of the position are controlled by the **units** that have been set for that stimulus (or for the experiment as a whole). PsychoPy supports various units for its coordinates, explained more fully starting on page 160. In all cases the center of the screen is (0,0) and, fairly obviously, the first coordinate runs negatively to the left and positively to the right, whereas the second runs negatively to the bottom and positively to the top. By default, and for our purposes here it's fine, the units are 'normalized' in which the left of the screen is −1, the right is +1, the bottom is −1 and the top is +1. Beware of confusions between units. Also, using units incorrectly is one of the very common ways for a stimulus that 'doesn't appear' because you've accidentally tried to draw it 4 m to the right of your monitor, say, or 1/100th the size of a pixel. So do go and read the section on units (page 160) carefully at some point!

While we're talking about units, there's also a Text Component parameter called 'Letter Height'. It sets, well, the letter height, but there's a caveat as well, which is that the *height* refers to the maximum height of any character in the font. Obviously a letter like 'e' doesn't go near the top or bottom, so its height will be a lot smaller than this. 'E' goes quite near the top and 'g' goes near the bottom for many fonts but there are often still gaps: 'É' obviously goes higher than 'E'. If you want a very precise size of letter you need either to measure its height in the specific font you wish to use, or to create a bitmap image of the text and present that image instead.

You can find out about the other parameters of the Text Component by hovering your mouse over their entry boxes, or by pressing the `Help` button at the bottom of the dialog box, which will take you to online help for any dialog. Note that there are additional parameters in the `Advanced` tab, like the **Opacity** (most visual stimuli can be made semi-transparent so that you can see things behind them, or with `opacity=0` they can be made to disappear altogether).

COLLECTING A KEYBOARD RESPONSE

Given that we just set the text stimulus to last for ever we better make sure we can end the trial somehow. Very often a trial will be set to end when the participant responds to the stimulus and that will work fine for the Stroop task.

Let's add a Keyboard Component (click on the keyboard icon in the Components Panel). The structure of this is similar to the above. We need to give our Keyboard Component a name; let's **call it resp**. Now, we don't want participants to respond before the stimulus appears, but we're happy for them to respond as soon as it does. We'll set the keyboard to **start** at 0.5 s (i.e. we'll begin polling it for keypresses at the same time as the stimulus. The Keyboard Component will measure the reaction time from its *start* time so this will mean that the reaction time is relative to the start of the stimulus as well.

Make sure you set the Keyboard to last forever as well (set the **stop** value to be blank). If we leave the stimulus on the screen but stop checking the keyboard it can look as though the experiment has 'crashed'. It's actually still running but hasn't been told how to get out of the stimulus presentation cycle.

We can set the keys that are **allowed** by inserting a list of key names. To do this each key name must be in quotes (either the " character or the ', though they must match) and separated with a comma from the others. On this occasion we use the keys `'left'`, `'down'`, `'right'` so type the key names in this box. Alternatively you could set the box to contain nothing (meaning any key is allowed) but if you've given your participant instructions to use the arrow keys and then they press something else, you don't want that to count as a response.

> ### 💡 Pro Tip: But why do I need to type in quotes and commas in the keys list?
>
> It might seem unnecessary but there are two reasons. The first is that this allows PsychoPy to know the difference between `"left"` and `"l"`,`"e"`,`"f"`,`"t"` whereas if we just wrote `left` it would be ambiguous which thing we meant. The second reason is that this is actually valid Python code and that makes it very easy for PsychoPy to interpret.

OK, the last thing we need to do with the keyboard (for now) is to check that 'Force end of Routine' is ticked on. This is turned on by default but just check it hasn't accidentally been switched off. That is going to end this Routine and advance the Flow to whatever comes next.

SAVE AND RUN

Once you've saved the file you can run it by pressing the lovely green running man (or press `Ctrl-R` on Win/Linux or `Cmd-R` on a Mac). With any luck a dialog box came up asking you to provide a participant ID and a session number. Neither are important right now so you can just press `OK`. You should see your stimulus appear on the screen and you should be able to end the trial (and the entire experiment so far) by pressing one of the `left`, `down or right` arrow keys. If you got stuck with your stimulus word on the screen then **pressing the `<esc>` key (top left corner of most keyboards) will quit the experiment**. If this was needed then go and check you Keyboard Component; did you remember to clear its duration to be blank (so it lasts for ever)? Did you set the 'allowed keys' correctly?

2.5 ADDING A LOOP TO REPEAT TRIALS

Technically you could create a large number of Routines, one for each of your trials, and add them sequentially to your Flow, but that would be very inefficient and also wouldn't allow your trial Routines to be presented in different order. We can do this more efficiently and more flexibly using a *Loop*.

Click ONCE on `Insert Loop` in the Flow panel, as shown in Figure 2.7.

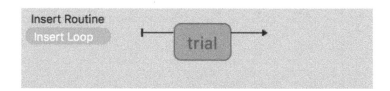

FIGURE 2.7 Clicking the `Insert loop` button on the Flow panel (don't double-click it!).

This will cause a dot to appear on the timeline of the Flow. You can move the dot to any location to signify the start or end of the loop (it doesn't matter which). Click ONCE to insert the end of the loop *just before* the trial Routine on the Flow as in Figure 2.8.

Then click the start and the end points for your loop (it doesn't matter which you do first). If there is only one remaining valid place for your loop to go the other point will be added automatically.

Usually you need to insert both the start and end points of your Loop but, on this occasion, there is only one valid place for the end to go once the start has been decided (and vice versa) so this time PsychoPy will insert the other end of the Loop automatically for you.

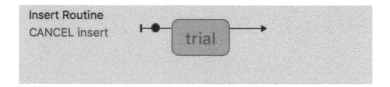

FIGURE 2.8 Hover over where you want the loop to start and/or finish and click the mouse once (don't double-click it!).

When the start/end points are added a dialog will appear to allow you to control the settings (see Figure 2.9). As with the Components that you added to the Routine, you can *edit* the properties of an existing Loop by clicking on its name/ icon later, and you can remove it by *right*-clicking the name or icon.

FIGURE 2.9 The Loop dialog box allows you to set parameters, controlling how many repeats of conditions the have and how they are randomized.

As with Components, the Loop needs a name and it also follows the same rules of needing to be unique and not contain punctuation or spaces. In our case the default name of 'trials' seems sensible, but if you intend to have practice trials and main trials then it would be best to distinguish between them in the loop name.

The next parameter determines what *type* of Loop will be inserted. This is most often **random** in which case the lines of your conditions file will be chosen at random for each repeat of the Loop (there's also a **full random** option; the difference between this and **random** is covered in Section 10.2). You can also have a `sequential` loop where the lines of your conditions file are used in the same order as you had specified. Lastly there are options for using the staircase procedures discussed on page 232.

The next tick-box parameter, with the label 'Is trials', might seem strange. It effectively indicates whether each entry should be on a new line in the data file.

The reason for this parameter is that a loop might not indicate a trial. You could have an inner loop in which 10 stimuli are presented and these 10 stimuli represent one trial. You wouldn't want a new line for each stimulus, just a new line for the next *trial* of 10. Or you might have an outer loop to indicate blocks around an inner loop of trials (see Chapter 8).

For now let's just make our trial repeat five times without changing any stimuli, just to check it works. To do so all the existing properties can be left as they are. Now when you save and run your experiment you can see five 'trials' (albeit identical each time) running and you can end each one by 'responding' (of sorts) using the arrow keys.

2.6 VARYING YOUR STIMULI ON EACH TRIAL

So far so good, except that this experiment doesn't achieve a whole lot, on account of the stimuli never changing. The remaining piece of the puzzle is simply to take the variables from the conditions file that we created and connect them to the parameters of our Components.

Click on the label of your `trials` Loop that you already created to edit its properties. Press the `Browse...` button next in the dialog to find your conditions file ('conditions.xlsx'). If all went well when you created that file you should now see the conditions file location show up in the box and a message underneath reminding you that you have specified six conditions with four variables. If that message doesn't appear then your file has not been read in correctly, which might indicate an error in the file (e.g. a space somewhere or a missing column heading). Your Loop settings should now look like Figure 2.10. Your five repeats will now refer to five repeats of all six conditions, so 30 trials in total. Each time around the loop a new line of the file will be randomly selected. Press OK to accept your changes.

Your Flow should now look something like Figure 2.11. If you have other Loops or Routines, or if your Loop doesn't go around your Routine, then you may need to remove it by *right*-clicking on the erroneous entry.

UPDATE THE TEXT ON EVERY TRIAL

Now that PsychoPy 'knows' about the different variables and trial types in your experiment we can connect those things to the stimulus and the keyboard. Go and edit the Text Component you added to the `trial` Routine. Rather than present the word **red** as the text on every trial, we want to present the **word** variable from our conditions file. Obviously we can't just write **word** into this box; that would present the word 'word' as a stimulus! We want it to present the *contents of the variable* named 'word'. To do this we add a $ symbol to the box to indicate that PsychoPy should treat this as code, not as literal text. Note that some boxes (like 'Position') are always treated as code because they would make no sense to be interpreted as text. These boxes have a $ next to them always so you don't *need* to add one, but it shouldn't hurt to do so, to be on the safe side. So go ahead and delete the word **red** from your text and add **$word** making sure you spell it **exactly** as you did in the conditions file, with the same case of letters, etc.

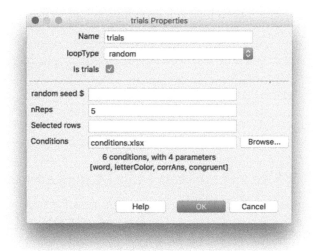

FIGURE 2.10 Completed dialog for your Loop. Note that the dialog tells you about the conditions file that you imported (indicating that it was imported successfully). The five repeats will result in a total of 30 trials.

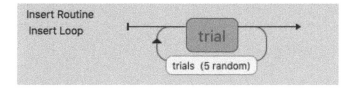

FIGURE 2.11 The Flow of the basic Stroop experiment after the Loop is added.

For most parameters that are set as a variable you also need to tell PsychoPy when to update those variables with a new value. The choice box to the right of the value allows you to select options like 'constant', 'set every repeat' and 'set every frame'.

In this study you also need to set the 'Color' of your text to be $letterColor so that it also uses the value of your letterColor variable in each trial. Set this to be 'set every repeat' as well.

At this point you could run your experiment again to see if it still works and if the stimulus is correctly changing its text and its letter color on each trial.

UPDATE THE CORRECT ANSWER ON EVERY TRIAL

You also need to update your Keyboard Component because the correct answer was also changing using a variable in your conditions file. Click on your Component (it was called 'resp' if you stuck carefully to the instructions) to edit its parameters. You need to tick the box that says 'Save correct response' and this will cause a new box to appear in which you can tell PsychoPy what the correct response is. Based on your conditions file you want this to be $corrAns. Again, it's really important that you use the $ symbol here or PsychoPy will look for the key literally called $corrAns and won't find one, so all your responses will appear to be 'incorrect'.

At this point your stim settings and your resp settings should look like those in Figures 2.12 and 2.13.

 Pro Tip: Save and run often while creating a study

You may notice we've been saving and rerunning the study rather often. The advantage of doing this is that if something doesn't work, you've got a relatively small number of things to check in order to work out what broke your experiment (i.e. only the things since it was last working).

While running your experiment for debugging you might want to set the number of repeats to fewer than normal so it doesn't take 15 minutes to test each time. Also, if there are sections that you don't want to run (e.g. the training or adaptation period) you can set a Loop to have zero repeats and that will cause the contents of that Loop not to run at all.

2.7 ADD SOME INSTRUCTIONS

By the time your experiment is running, with the stimulus being updated correctly on each repeat and the keyboard signaling the end of the trial, you are almost finished. That is, your experiment is fully capable of running and demonstrating the Stroop effect. It could be made a lot nicer, though. For instance, it really helps to have some text at the beginning to remind you of the keys to press and enable you to get ready before you start the trials (if you press OK to the dialog box and it goes straight to the first trial it can be off-putting).

FIGURE 2.12 The final state of the `stim` Text Component. Note the $ symbols where we've inserted variable names and the `set every repeat` option for most of the variable parameters.

FIGURE 2.13 The Keyboard Component in its final state. Note the quote marks around the key names (these can be single- or double-quote symbols but they must match). Also make sure you insert $corrAns and not simply corrAns or PsychoPy will check whether the participant pressed the key with the name 'corrAns' and there is no such key!

Just click `Insert Routine` in the Flow panel and select the option called (`new`). You'll be asked to provide a name for the new Routine. Call it `instructions` and then you can set it to appear on the Flow just before the trials loop starts (Figure 2.14). Alternatively you can do this in two steps: the `Experiment` menu has an entry called `create new Routine` and you can use the Flow to insert a Routine that you previously created (including one that is already somewhere else on the Flow).

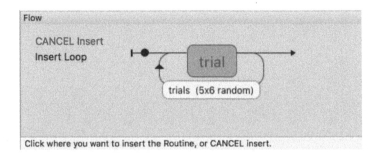

FIGURE 2.14 Adding another Routine just before the trials loop, to hold our instructions.

Now click on that Routine (either in the Flow or in the Routine tabs at the top) so we switch to editing it.

As you did in the trial Routine you need to add a Text Component to the `instructions` Routine. Of course, it can't have the same name as the Routine `instructions` so you'll have to call the Text Component something else, like `instrText`. You also want to let your participants read the text in their own good time and then press a button when they're ready to get started. So set the duration to be infinite. For the text itself, it helps to tell your participants what to do and what keys to press, but also tell them to 'Press a key when ready to start'. So for this Component these are the key things to change:

- name = `instrText`
- start = 0
- duration = `<blank i.e. infinite>`
- text = `<something useful here about the keys to press>`

Of course, because we made the text last for ever we need to provide something to end the Routine or we'll never get to the main experiment!

Add a Keyboard Component with parameters like these:

- name = `ready`
- save = `nothing`

- duration = `<blank i.e. infinite>`
- forceEndRoutine = `True`
- allowedKeys = `<blank i.e. any keys>`

Again, make sure the duration of your keyboard is blank. If the keyboard stops being checked after 1 second then PsychoPy will never spot that the key has been pressed. The user will have to press the escape key and quit the study.

2.8 ADD A THANK-YOU SLIDE

A similar touch that isn't *strictly* necessary is to add something at the end of your study to say thanks. Partly this is just a nice thing to do, but also, if at the end of the study there is no message and the screen suddenly disappears, your participants will be surprised and may think the experiment 'crashed'. You'll get lots of concerned participants thinking they broke your study! A message that says 'Thank you for taking part' reduces this.

This time you probably don't have so much to say and you don't need to leave your participants unlimited time to read the brief text, so you could just put it on screen for 2 or 3 seconds and not bother with a Keyboard Component to end the thanks screen.

So go ahead and try to do these tasks:

- add a new Routine called **thanks** that comes after your **trials** Loop
- go to that Routine and add a Text Component called **thanksText** with a simple thank-you message
- set the Text Component to start immediately and last for 2 s.

2.9 CHANGING YOUR INFO DIALOG

In the Experiment Settings you can alter the information you collect at the beginning, as well as a variety of other options. For instance, the value called 'session' in the dialog box at the beginning of your study could be used to study which session someone was in if you run your study on different days, but if you only run your study once per participant then it seems unnecessary. We don't care (do we?) about the 'session' number for this study so we could remove that row, but we do care about storing the participant's gender so that later on we can report how many of our participants were male/female.

Click on the Experiment Settings icon ▨ and rename the field called **session** so that it is called **gender (m/f)**. If you like, you can provide a default value (e.g. **f**) which shows the participant what format you expect. **Do keep the participant setting** (it is used in creating the data filename for each participant).

You could add a row for participant age if you like (Figure 2.15). Just click one of the 'plus' symbols to add a row. Anything you put into these fields is stored with your data file. Is there anything else you want to be kept alongside the data? The order of the entries doesn't matter (it will be alphabetical anyway)

FIGURE 2.15 Experiment Settings for the Stroop task with no 'session' information but with a gender field and an age field added

The Experiment Settings dialog also allows you to control other aspects of the screen, such as:

- whether or not the mouse is visible
- what color the background of the screen should be
- whether it should be full-screen mode or shown in a window.

 Pro Tip: Debug your experiment in window mode, not full-screen

When the experiment is in full-screen mode it can be hard to escape if something goes wrong (e.g. your experiment gets stuck in a cycle that it can't get out of or loads a file that is taking a lifetime). You can usually force-quit the application using your computer's 'task manager' but that's annoying. If you stay in window mode until your experiment is definitely working then you can always hit the red stop button to force it to quit.

2.10 ANALYZE YOUR DATA

DATA FILE TYPES

The Experiment Settings dialog box also allows you to control the data file outputs. The main file output is the trial-by-trial csv file and this is all you generally need (it opens in Excel or it can be imported into R or most other statistics packages).

- **Don't** bother about **summarized** formats and Excel (native) files. They don't add information and can slow things down.
- **Do** keep the `log` file and the `psydat` file. You might not need them but they're a safety net in case things go wrong. They exist in PsychoPy for historical reasons.

The format of the filename (and folder to which it is saved) can also be changed but that's a little easy to break if you don't know what you're doing. You can read about that on page 214.

When we run the experiment, PsychoPy will create a folder called **data** next to your .psyexp experiment file. It will contain three files for each run of the study:

- csv file. This is what you'll most likely use for analysis. The data are stored in columns of values and with rows representing the trials as they occurred (in chronological order). It can be opened in any spreadsheet application, like Excel, and this is what we'll focus on in the analysis below.
- `log` file (a text file). This is a file containing lots of detail. Every time something changes in the experiment it sends a message to the log file with a time-stamp and in chronological order. This is handy for checking that your stimuli had good timing or to find data that you didn't think you would need, but isn't easy for normal analysis because it has far too much information.
- `psydat` file. This is a file for doing analyses in Python scripts. This isn't a file you can easily 'read'. It doesn't double-click to open in an application (currently) but it contains a great deal of information, including all the data to recreate the `csv` file if you accidentally lose/damage it, or a copy of the experiment you originally ran. Unfortunately, it currently requires that you write Python code in order to load/use the file. Keep these files – they potentially rescue you if other things go wrong.

Pro Tip: Applications for opening the log file

The log file is simple text (tab-delimited). On a Mac by default it opens in the Console, which works fine. In Windows it opens in the `Notepad` application by default, which is horrible. `Notepad` doesn't recognize the line-end characters in the log file, which makes it unreadable by most humans! You could install `Notepad++` instead, as a much better free alternative (https://notepad-plus-plus.org/) to `Notepad`, or you could open the file in a spreadsheet package like Excel.

ANALYZING THE CSV FILE

Let's open the most recent `csv` file that you saved. If you gave yourself a participant name when you started the experiment it will now show up in the filename. Otherwise you may need to simply choose the most recent file. You could actually get rid of all the earlier files from when you were simply testing whether the experiment ran properly and didn't really run any trials. (For the future you might want to give the participant name as `test` or just leave it blank when testing the experiment so that it's easy to see which data files really contain data and which are from debugging your experiment.)

You could try double-clicking it and hopefully it will open directly in your spreadsheet application. We analyze this assuming you have Excel but all the features we will use (sorting by column and calculating an average) should be available in any package.

Once you've opened your data file in Excel the first thing to do is **save it straightaway as an Excel Workbook**. The csv format is useful in that it's very simple and can be used by many software applications, but `xlsx` files in Excel are more powerful in the things they can store, like graphs. Using this method (starting with a csv file but then analyzing with an `xlsx` file) has the advantages that:

- Excel will not keep asking if you want to change the format
- you can add things like graphs and formulae and they will get saved
- if you mess up your analysis here the original `csv` file will still be there for you to go back to.

Let's look at the data, with an example file shown in Figure 2.16. Each row represents one trial, organized chronologically, and each column represents a different variable. Some of these variables (the first four in this experiment) came from your conditions file, telling you in each trial what the letter color and word were. Next come some columns containing information about the loop and trial number:

- **trials.thisRepN**: how many of the five repeats in the **trials** Loop have finished (starts at zero)
- **trials.thisTrialN**: how may trials have occurred within this 'repeat', starting at zero
- **trials.thisN**: how many trials have completed in total, starting at zero
- **trials.index**: which line in the conditions file this condition came from and, yes, this also starts at zero!

 Pro Tip: Expanding columns in Excel

In Excel, if you cannot see all of the data in the heading then you may need to expand the width of the column. If you double-click on the line between a pair of columns it will expand that column to the width of the widest cell.

In some data sets you may find cells, or often an entire column, that appear to be ########. Don't panic, your data are probably still there – this isn't a PsychoPy bug or a mistake on your part. This is what Excel does when it has a number that's too long to display in a column. Again, try expanding the column and seeing if the real numbers appear.

After those Loop information columns we have three columns referring to the participant's responses:

- **resp.keys**: the key the participant pressed in the **resp** Keyboard Component (or keys if we allow multiple keypresses). This will be empty if no response was detected.
- **resp.corr**: stores whether or not that answer was considered 'correct' according to your conditions file. Hopefully this will have mostly ones (correct) in it with maybe the occasional zero (incorrect). If it shows up as all zero then check you used **$corrAns** rather than simply **corrAns** in your Keyboard Component.
- **resp.rt**: the time in seconds since the beginning of the Keyboard Component which, for most purposes, indicates response time.

Lastly there are some columns that are recorded from the information dialog box at the beginning of the run (age, gender, participant, etc.) and some additional information about the computer (e.g. the frame rate of the monitor).

For this particular analysis all you would need to do is calculate the average reaction time of the congruent and incongruent trials. You could do that with a calculator, but it will be easier using Excel's **average** function.

First, sort your data by whether the condition was a *congruent* one, which we conveniently stored in our file. To do this make sure you select all the data first (if you accidentally sort your data while only a few columns are selected then those columns will no longer match up with the order of the others). You can select all by pressing `Ctrl-A` (`Cmd-A` on a Mac) or by pressing the square in the top left of the spreadsheet table, as in Figure 2.16.

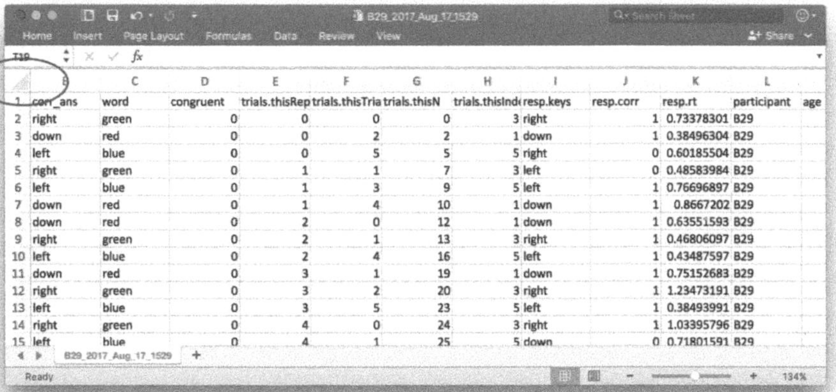

	corr_ans	word	congruent	trials.thisRep	trials.thisTria	trials.thisN	trials.thisInd	resp.keys	resp.corr	resp.rt	participant	age
2	right	green	0	0	0	0	3	right	1	0.73378301	B29	
3	down	red	0	0	2	2	1	down	1	0.38496304	B29	
4	left	blue	0	0	5	5	5	right	0	0.60185504	B29	
5	right	green	0	1	1	7	3	left	0	0.48583984	B29	
6	left	blue	0	1	3	9	5	left	1	0.76696897	B29	
7	down	red	0	1	4	10	1	down	1	0.8667202	B29	
8	down	red	0	2	0	12	1	down	1	0.63551593	B29	
9	right	green	0	2	1	13	3	right	1	0.46806097	B29	
10	left	blue	0	2	4	16	5	left	1	0.43487597	B29	
11	down	red	0	3	1	19	1	down	1	0.75152683	B29	
12	right	green	0	3	2	20	3	right	1	1.23473191	B29	
13	left	blue	0	3	5	23	5	left	1	0.38493991	B29	
14	right	green	0	4	0	24	3	right	1	1.03395796	B29	
15	left	blue	0	4	1	25	5	down	0	0.71801591	B29	

FIGURE 2.16 An example data file from the Stroop task. You can select all the data (important if you plan to sort them) by pressing this lesser known button at the top left (circled in red).

Hopefully all your data will move into position with the top half being incongruent trials and the bottom being congruent (or vice versa). Now we can simply take the average of the `resp.rt` column for the top half and compare it with the bottom. Click on a cell somewhere in the spreadsheet where you want to store the average of the incongruent trials and create an average function there. There are a few options of how to do this. The first may seem appealing because they involve clicking on buttons rather than typing, but from one version of Excel to another the items never seem to stay in the same place, so you might do better learning the third (typing) option:

- Go to the 'Ribbon' tab named `Formulas`, hit the button to `Insert` (probably on the left-hand edge) and select `Average` in the Statistical category. In the dialog that comes up you should be able to enter the cells whose average you want to find by dragging your mouse around them.
- OR go to the menu item `Insert` and find the option `Function`. This should bring up roughly the same dialog as above and, again, you should select the cells you want to include in the average.

- OR, if you can't find those options because Microsoft keeps moving them, you could simply type =average (then select the cells you want to include — or type them in if you prefer — and finally type the ending bracket) to complete your function.

Repeat this process for the *congruent* trials and see if the reaction time is faster (or shorter) for these trials than for the *incongruent* trials.

That's it: one study created, run and analyzed!

EXERCISES AND EXTENSIONS

EXERCISE 2.1: PRACTICE TWEAKING THINGS

Just for practice try and change the color of the screen (for the entire experiment) to be black instead of gray. Also for practice set the color of the instructions text to red instead of white.

Solution: Page 285

EXERCISE 2.2: ALTER THE LANGUAGE OF THE ENTIRE STUDY

You could test how much the Stroop effect depends on the stimuli being in your first language. You could create a variant of the task in French, say, so the **word** variable would have values like **rouge, vert** and **bleu**. Does it still interfere? (Of course if English *isn't* your first language then you could now test in your first language!)

Solution: Page 285

EXERCISE 2.3: MEASURE THE REVERSE STROOP EFFECT

You could run a similar study to look at the reverse effect. You've probably seen here that the meaning of the word interfered with your ability to report the letter color, but is there an equivalent effect in which the letter color interferes with your ability to read? Stroop's original paper suggested a lack of effect in this direction but, then again, he was running his study with paper ink and asking participants to call out the answers while he timed them on a stopwatch. Maybe with the somewhat more precise timing of modern computers we can reveal such an effect.

Solution: Page 285

(Continued)

EXERCISE 2.4: CHECK OUT THE FULL EXPERIMENT

There is also an extended version of this task included in the PsychoPy demos, which adds a feedback routine and some training trials, with the feedback being used only in the training period. Trying to create this from scratch is probably too much right now, but you might find it useful to take a sneak peak at what you'll be learning in the future!

Solution: Page 285

3

USING IMAGES: A STUDY INTO FACE PERCEPTION

> **Learning objectives:** In this chapter you'll learn more about image files and how to use them in PsychoPy. You'll also develop a better understanding of pathnames (using relative paths) and image sizes.

Users often don't realize how easy it is to create a study where an image file changes, rather than the contents of some text. This chapter will create another study from scratch, focusing on loading images and manipulating them in each trial.

We'll study the face inversion effect: it's really hard to recognize faces upside-down. To start with, we'll recreate a version of the Glasgow Face Matching Task (Burton et al., 2010) and then adapt it so that the faces are shown twice: once the right way up and once upside-down.

Although that sounds a lot more complex than simply changing some text, it really isn't! We'll hopefully also reinforce many of the skills learned in the previous chapter because we need to create conditions files, and set up a trial, in much the same way as before.

3.1 ACCURACY VERSUS REACTION TIME

The other thing that's different in this chapter is that, rather than measuring reaction time as a measure of performance, we're going to measure accuracy: the percentage of correct answers. In many tasks participants will get the answer correct nearly all the time, so measuring accuracy doesn't make any sense. In the Stroop task most people are able to report correctly any of the letter colors; they simply take longer in the conflicting than the congruent condition. In other tasks participants' reaction time may not vary at all, either because participants are responding so fast, or because they are taking so long that differences in speed are not noticeable. In those cases we might be able to measure differences in accuracy instead. In the test we generate in this chapter, participants can spend as long as they like looking at the stimuli but most will still make some mistakes, so we can investigate the nature of those mistakes.

Of course, in some studies the speed **and** accuracy are compromised by one of the conditions, and this is the most luxurious position for the experimenter. If the reaction time gets longer and the accuracy gets lower in one of your conditions then you can be sure that this condition is, in some way, hard!

 Info: Speed-accuracy tradeoffs

In some studies you might find that there is a 'speed-accuracy tradeoff' and this is always something to watch out for. If in some conditions participants are trying to respond more quickly but do so by reducing accuracy, then the results will always be hard to interpret. Between participants you can often also see different strategies: in a task where participants are told 'Please respond as quickly and accurately as possible', it turns out that some participants will focus more on being accurate whereas others will focus on being as fast as possible and you can usually see the results of those different strategies in their performance. That needn't affect your study in a negative way, but you should be aware that the exact words you use in instructions may alter your participants' strategies.

3.2 TESTING FACE RECOGNITION

We start off by creating a task to test accuracy in recognizing faces, based on the Glasgow Face Matching Test (Burton et al., 2010). In this task two images are presented and the participant is asked whether the images are of different individuals or of the same individual on two different occasions. It's a surprisingly hard task.

 Info: The Glasgow Face Matching Test

We feel that we're rather good at recognizing faces. It's true that recognizing friends and family is an easy task for humans. It's effortless and fast and we can do it under very difficult conditions, like in a crowded nightclub. On the other hand, it turns out that we're relatively poor at recognizing faces that we don't know. In particular, deciding whether two photographs are of the same person is surprisingly hard when we don't know this individual. That task is the focus of this test. Whereas you might feel that you can always recognize a face, and laugh at the poor face-recognition abilities of computer programs, in the Glasgow Face Matching Test the average score was 89.9%, meaning that the average participant got a match wrong on one trial in every ten!

MATERIALS AND CONDITIONS FOR THE TEST

The materials for the study are available for you to download at (https://study. sagepub.com/psychology). Save them all to a folder somewhere.

Open the Builder view in PsychoPy and create a new experiment. Let's save the experiment straightaway. From the **File>Save** menu select the folder where you downloaded the materials and save the file right next to the folders 'different' and 'same' that contain the images for the experiment. Give your experiment file the name **GFMT** for 'Glasgow Face Matching Test' (in case that wasn't obvious what it stood for!).

The materials you downloaded should contain an Excel file specifying the conditions for your test already, to save your having to type in all the names of the files. You're welcome. Open that file in your spreadsheet application (e.g. Excel). It will look something like the image in Figure 3.1. Note that the image files are also there, in folders labelled 'same' and 'different'. Lastly there's a fully working PsychoPy experiment file, but we strongly recommend you follow the steps to recreate that yourself. The more you actually do these things the better you learn them.

	A	B	C	D	E
1	imageFile	corrAns	sameOrDiff		
2	same/020_C2_DV.jpg	left	same		
3	same/025_C2_DV.jpg	left	same		
4	same/068_C2_DV.jpg	left	same		
5	same/069_C2_DV.jpg	left	same		
6	same/074_C2_DV.jpg	left	same		
7	same/075_DV_C2.jpg	left	same		
8	same/081_C2_DV.jpg	left	same		
9	same/085_C2_DV.jpg	left	same		
10	same/092_C2_DV.jpg	left	same		
11	same/102_C2_DV.jpg	left	same		
12	same/108_DV_C2.jpg	left	same		
13	same/115_C2_DV.jpg	left	same		
14	same/120_DV_C2.jpg	left	same		
15	same/129_C2_DV.jpg	left	same		
16	same/136_C2_DV.jpg	left	same		
17	same/139_DV_C2.jpg	left	same		
18	same/168_C2_DV.jpg	left	same		

FIGURE 3.1   A section of the conditions file for the Glasgow Face Matching Test.

Pro Tip: Correctly specifying image paths

Take a look at the conditions file. Note the way the files are specified using file paths like this: `same/020_C2_DV.jpg`.

Note that this path is written **relative to the experiment file**. Next to the experiment file that we just saved is a folder called 'same' and within that is a file called '020_C2_DV.jpg'. We could have written the full path of the file ('C:/Documents and settings/. . .') but if we then move the experiment to a new folder (or to a different computer) the path will change and we'll have to change all the entries in the conditions file, which can be painful.

SETTING UP YOUR TRIAL DEFINITION

OK, so we've got a conditions file and an experiment file. How do we get started?

As with the Stroop task in Chapter 2 we next need to determine how the timing of a single trial will work. In the Glasgow Face Matching Test (let's stick to calling it the GFMT) the faces were presented for an unlimited period and the key to the test was whether or not the participant got the answer right. The way the materials have been prepared (by Burton et al., 2010) is that we have a pair of faces already inserted into a single image file, with a white background between them. That means that, on this occasion, we only need to include one image in our trial (containing both faces). If this had been organized with two images (left and right) then adding a second image, at a different location, would have been trivially easy as well, using the image position attributes for the two images and having a conditions file that had a column for each image.

So let's go ahead and create an Image Component called `faces` in our `trial` Routine by clicking on the icon in the Components Panel. Set up the Component as in Figure 3.2.

Next we need to create a Keyboard Component so that participants can respond. This is just the same as in the Stroop task, except that in this task we only need two valid keys for the participant, one to indicate that the faces are matched (let's use the left cursor key to indicate a match and the right arrow to indicate the pictures are different).

As in the Stroop task we saved the correct answer for each trial in the column called `corrAns` in the conditions file, so we'll need to set the correct answer in

FIGURE 3.2 Settings of the `faces` Image Component for the GFMT. Note that the 'Image' is set to be `$imageFile` and the timing is set to start at 0.0 and never end.

the Keyboard Component to be **$corrAns**. The Keyboard Component should look like Figure 3.3.

LOADING THE CONDITIONS FILE

Now we need to tell PsychoPy about repeating the files and also about the variables that we've used in our stimulus and our response components. As in Chapter 2, we need to add a loop to the Flow (using the **Insert Loop** button). Call it **trials** and set the values as in Figure 3.4. Press **Browse...** to load the conditions file, which should be right next to your experiment file. If it loads correctly then you'll see a summary of the conditions that have loaded.

If not, then it might be that the conditions file is incorrectly formatted. On this occasion, you downloaded it, so did you accidentally change it afterwards? Maybe download another copy?

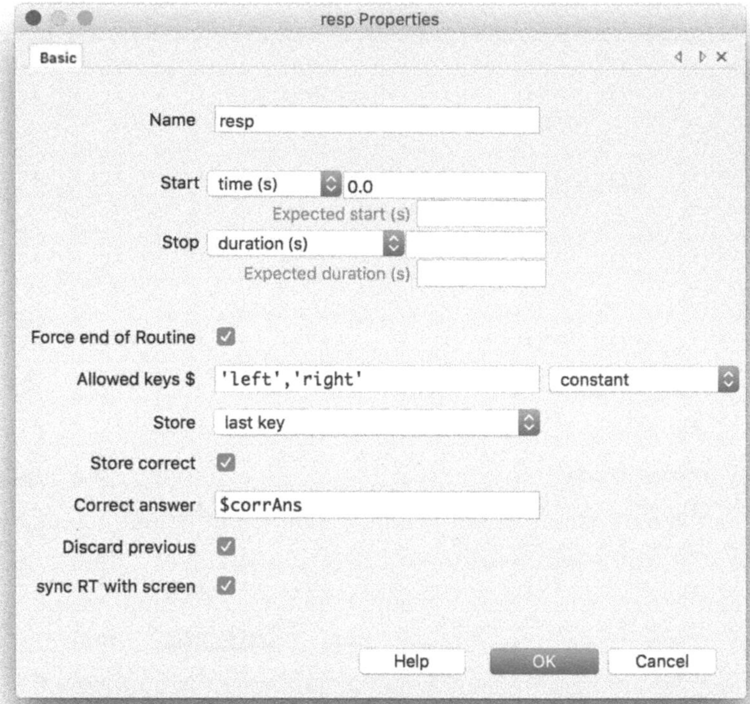

FIGURE 3.3 Parameters for the Keyboard Component in the GFMT. Remember, the correct answer variable needs to be $corrAns. If you accidentally type just corrAns then PsychoPy will look for a key literally called corrAns (and won't find one!).

RUNNING THE STUDY

At this point your study should run and present a different pair of faces on each trial and you just need to press the left and right arrow keys to indicate 'same' or 'different' individuals. Of course, for a real experiment you'd want to add some instructions to the beginning of the study telling participants what to do, which you would add as a new Routine at the beginning of the experiment. You might also add a reminder, while the stimuli are presented, of which key is for 'same' and which is for 'different'. To do this you could add two new Text Components to your **trial** Routine, one at the bottom left of the screen saying 'same' and another at the bottom right saying 'different'.

Once the experiment has run you can take a look at how you did by opening the 'csv' file (with an Excel icon) that has been stored in your 'data' folder. You'll be able to see how many times you got the answers right and wrong, but

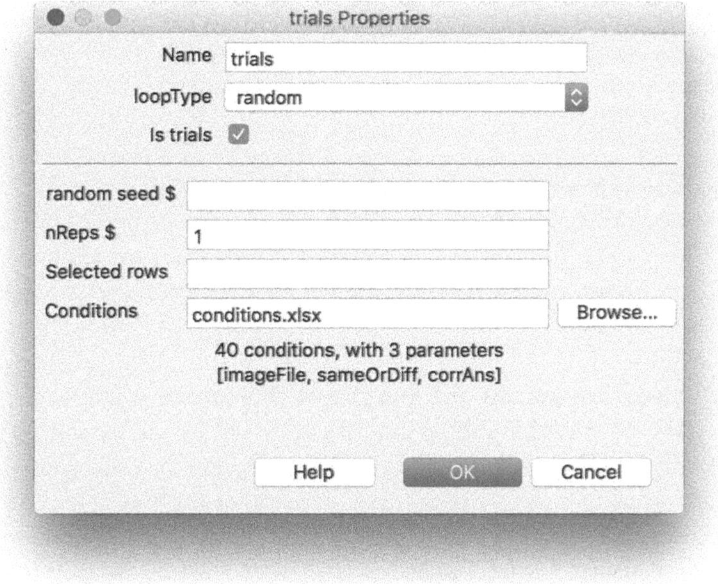

FIGURE 3.4   Parameters for the `trials` loop in the GFMT study.

you might also want to separate these by whether there was actually a match or not. Burton et al. found marginally better performance when the faces did actually match than when they didn't (the rate for hits was greater than the rate for correct rejects).

3.3 IMAGE SIZES IN DIFFERENT UNITS

So far we've presented the image without specifying the size. When we do this it will simply be presented at whatever size the raw image was (in pixels). That's fine if your images are all the right size already and, particularly, if you don't need to worry about presenting images on different screens.

On the other hand, it doesn't matter if your images are actually different sizes; PsychoPy can set your image to a specific size when the experiment is run. If you specify a value in the 'size' setting for the image, then, whatever size it was on the disk, the image will be stretched or compressed to the size you specify. Size values take a pair of numbers for the *width* and *height* but you can also specify a single value that will be applied to both dimensions.

What the size setting does depends on the **units** setting for the stimulus as well. These have already been discussed in relation to positioning your stimulus and are covered in more depth in Chapter 11. In brief, if you want a stimulus to be the same fraction of the screen on all computers then you should use either 'normalized' or 'height' units. If you want it to be the same size to the participant, and **not** scale with the screen, then you should use cm or deg. Here are some common scenarios:

- **For a full-screen image** you can set the units to be **norm** and set the size to be [2,2] (in **norm** units the screen goes from −1 to +1 in both directions so the full *width* and *height* of 2). Bear in mind that screens can differ in their aspect ratio; some are wider and some are more square, and if you use normalized units the screen aspect ratio will alter the shape of the stimulus.
- **For a square image the full height of the screen** (on all screens) then set the units to be **height** and set the size to be [1,1]. This will mean that the image will be the height of the screen and square, but the gaps on the sides will vary from one screen to another depending on how wide the screen is.
- **For a constant size in cm** irrespective of the physical screen size, then you might want to set the image size in cm.
- **For a constant size at the participant's eye** you should use deg (degrees of visual angle).

For the latter two options you need to remember to calibrate your monitor using Monitor Center (see Section 13.3). PsychoPy also needs to know which monitor calibration you intend to use. In the Experiment Settings for your study go to the Screen tab and add the name of your monitor, making sure it matches exactly the name in Monitor Center.

When you change the units of your stimulus, that change affects all the relevant aspects of this stimulus (e.g. the size as well as the position and, for Grating Stimuli, it affects the spatial frequency).

 Warning: Make sure your units and your sizes match

One of the most common reasons that 'my image doesn't appear', but with no error message provided, is that the size or position of the stimulus don't make sense for the specified units. A size of 0.5 makes sense for 'normalized' units but if you set your units to be pixels then the image will try to draw smaller than a pixel and you won't see it! Or if you set the position to be (100, 0) then in pixels this would be sensible, but in normalized units it would be about 30 m to the right of your screen!

So check your units carefully if your stimulus doesn't appear.

3.4 COMPARING INVERTED AND CORRECTLY ORIENTED FACES

If we wanted to use the GFMT to measure the 'Face inversion effect' then we could very easily run the same task but with half the trials turning the faces upside-down. In PsychoPy, this step of turning them upside-down is really easy. There's a setting for orientation in the Image Component, taking the orientation in degrees. If we want to compare performance on the face recognition task according to whether the faces are presented the correct way up then all we need to do is set the orientation. We could, of course, create two copies of our experiment, one with the stimulus orientation set to be 0 (original orientation) and one with it set to be 180 (inverted). Alternatively we could run all the conditions twice, upright and inverted, and make this a part of a single experiment using our conditions file.

To do this you simply need to copy and paste the rows of the conditions file so that all the image conditions appear twice. Then create a new column in our conditions file called something like `ori` and set this to be 0 for half the trials and 180 for the other half. Don't worry that all the '0' trials are at the top and all the '180' trials are below; PsychoPy is going to randomize the trial order by default anyway so these will be shuffled.

Pro Tip: Parameters that are always code

Some parameters in the Component dialog boxes don't actually need to have the $ symbol inserted in order to provide a variable name. In the case of the orientation parameter, for instance, you could type the variable without needing $. This is usually the case for parameters where the input is usually a number and text input doesn't make sense. For the color field, the entry could be `black`, meaning literally the color, or `txtColor`, meaning a variable, so we needed the $ sign to indicate which one we wanted. On the other hand, in the orientation field no text makes any sense, so if we see text here we can safely assume it's a variable name. When a field will *always* be treated as a variable/code it has the $ sign next to it in the dialog box.

On the other hand, it doesn't hurt to put the symbol in on every occasion; PsychoPy will simply ignore it. So maybe it's a good thing to do, just to maintain the habit.

Lastly, you need to go and change the stimulus in your trial so that it uses this new information. To do that, open your `stimuli` Component in your `trial` Routine (remember to click on the one you already created – don't click on the icon in the panel on the right). You don't technically need to reload the conditions file into the loop; although it won't show quite the right information in the dialog box (it doesn't currently mention the `Orientation` parameter) this should be loaded correctly when the experiment runs. If you want to be extra thorough then click on the icon for the `trials` Loop in the Flow and press the `Browse` button again to reload the conditions file.

3.5 ADDITIONAL OPTIONS FOR IMAGES

As with any Builder Component you can get a brief description of all the parameters that the Component supports online by pressing the `Help` button in the relevant dialog box. We won't discuss them all here but the following are some of the parameters whose behavior might not be very obvious.

3.6 USING OPACITY

The Image `Opacity` setting controls how your image combines with the background. In many systems and applications it is known as `alpha`.

Imagine your image is printed onto a sheet of glass. The opacity determines how strong the ink is and whether you can see what is 'behind'. In our case, what is 'behind' the image is the color that we set the window (in Experiment Settings) and any other visual Components that have been drawn already. Components that are higher up in the Routine are drawn earlier on each screen refresh so they are effectively 'behind' the Components that are lower down. If the image is opaque (opacity = 1.0) then it fully occludes the background. If it is transparent (opacity = 0.0) then it is invisible and the background is completely visible. If it has an intermediate value then it is semi-transparent and you can see both the image and the things that are 'behind'. This is the case where the ink on your glass can be seen through and the effect is a combination of the scene and the background.

 Pro Tip: Uses for opacity

Although opacity can be used to create semi-transparent stimuli it is most often used simply to make a stimulus 'disappear' on trials where it isn't needed. You can also use it to make a stimulus appear gradually by setting the opacity to be controlled as a function of time (see Chapter 5 on dynamic stimuli for more information on this).

Technically, the effect is caused by a weighted average of the pixel colors in the image versus the background; other 'blending rules' are possible as well and these are discussed in Section 16.2.

3.7 USING MASKS

In the `Advanced` properties of the Image Component there is also the possibility to set a value for a `Mask` which can determine an alpha mask applied to your image. The mask is what technical folk call an 'alpha' mask and is exactly like setting the opacity value, as described above, but doing so for each pixel individually. The neat thing here is that this can be used to give the impression that you're seeing your stimulus through a window and the shape of the window can be controlled. The mask parameter can be set to one of a few built-in options like `circle`, `gauss` or `raisedCosine` (these are discussed in detail in Chapter 16) or it can be another image if you want to specify a custom mask of your own.

If you set the mask to be an image of your own then this will be forced into grayscale on loading (if it isn't already grayscale) and the luminance of each pixel will then be used as the opacity at that point. White pixels will be fully opaque and black pixels will be fully transparent.

Note that the shape of the mask is also affected by the size parameter for the stimulus; if you specify a circular mask but then specify a rectangular size then the stimulus will ultimately appear as an ellipse.

 Pro Tip: Changing the color of images

In the Advanced properties of the Image you can see a setting to control the color of the image. That works just as it does for the other stimuli, such as the Text Component described in the previous chapter, but you may not have expected to see this option for an image stimulus. The problem for many people is that the color parameter you set is multiplied by the value of each pixel and, because of PsychoPy's signed color values, very dark pixels are given the negative of the color you specify (see the tip on page 166 for an explanation of why this is the case). For most people that isn't expected or desirable.

There is an alternative way to achieve the expected result, however, which is to use the mask to control the shape of the image. It actually also has the advantage that parts of your image that you want to be the background will be made transparent, rather

(Continued)

than being black. So how do you do this? Imagine you want to provide a shape (say an apple) and make it appear in different colors on different trials. What you need to do is set your `image` parameter to be simply `color` (rather than the name of any actual image) and then set the `mask` parameter to be an image of the shape you require (e.g. a grayscale image of an apple). As discussed in the main text, when an image is a mask, any white areas are visible and any black areas disappear, so this is effectively showing only the apple area. Then that area is simply a color because of the `image` setting. The last step is to connect the actual `color` parameter (in the Advanced panel) to the variable in your conditions file, which is just the same as in other parameters using the $ symbol. Now you have a color-changing stimulus using the image to control its shape (and with transparency on the edges)! Cool huh?

3.8 PRESENT A MOVIE INSTEAD OF AN IMAGE

Presenting movie stimuli is really very similar to presenting images. The size and position parameters work just the same. You need to provide a filename, which works just the same (see the tip about using *relative paths* on page 46). What is dissimilar, obviously, is that the image is constantly changing and there is (optionally) audio in the movie as well. Often in experiments you want to mute the audio so the Movie Component has a tick-box to do that as well, which means PsychoPy has less work to do too!

There are several different libraries that can be used to load movies from the disk, which PsychoPy refers to as the 'backend'. For simple purposes the default (`moviepy`) should be sufficient, but if you find your movie is jerky or poor quality in some other way you might want to try a different option.

 Warning: Don't use AAC for your movie audio

You might need to get your movie files in a format that PsychoPy can understand. File types `mov`, `mkv`, `mp4` and `ogg` are all supported but one issue is that the audio 'stream' within these files might not be. Often movie audio is in a format called AAC, which is a proprietary format that we would have to pay for in order to decode. This might mean that, to play your audio in the movie, you will need to recode the movie to use 'linear' or 'uncompressed' audio. Recoding movies can be done for free using open-source software like HandBrake but is also possible from most video editing suites.

For the video stream (within the video file), the most common CODEC is called H.264 and that is supported, so you probably won't have problems there.

EXERCISES AND EXTENSIONS

EXERCISE 3.1: ADD INSTRUCTIONS

It really helps to add instructions to any study and also to add a thank-you message at the end of the study. Your instructions page also gives participants a chance to settle and get ready to start the trials in their own time, so remember to make the instructions last indefinitely, and give the option to 'Press a key when you're ready to begin'.

You could try out the option to copy and paste these Routines from your existing Stroop task (open it in a new window first and then use the `Experiment` menu items to copy and paste it into your new study).

Solution Page 286

EXERCISE 3.2: ADD PRACTICE TRIALS

You might want to add a couple of practice trials before the main event. Burton et al. (2010) didn't do so, but you could try to, for the sake of practicing how to insert a Routine in multiple places on your Flow (and with two different conditions files).

Solution Page 286

4

TIMING AND BRIEF STIMULI: POSNER CUEING

> **Learning objectives:** This chapter will teach you some of the basic concerns about timing and how to optimize it for your task, especially for very brief stimulus presentations.

We'll create another experiment from scratch: a simple version of the Posner cueing task. By now the concepts of trials and conditions files will be understood by the reader so those can be handled quickly. Here we focus on monitor refresh rates and their limitations, the times when you should specify stimulus timing in frames, and the level of precision you might reasonably expect from an experiment on a computer (using a keyboard).

As well as reading this chapter, which gives a practical guide to building the experiment, we urge you to read Chapter 12, which will explain more about your computer and why these steps are necessary. The abbreviated version of that chapter is this: your stimuli must be presented for a whole number of frames, not arbitrary periods of time; image stimuli take time to load from disk, especially if they have many pixels; your monitor should be set to sync to the screen refresh (in your operating system's Control Panel); brief periods of time are ideally specified by number of frames; and keyboards have a latency.

4.1 PRESENTING BRIEF STIMULI PRECISELY

We'll discuss the theory and issues concerning monitors and timing in Chapter 13. Briefly, the issue is that your monitor operates at a fixed screen refresh rate (typically 60 Hz, so each 'frame' lasts for 1/60th of a second, or 16.667 ms). Stimuli can't be drawn for a duration that is not a whole number of frames; either they appear on that screen refresh or they do not. PsychoPy 'knows' when the screen refreshes occur, so the best way to present brief stimuli with very precise timing is to time their appearance in terms of the number of the *frame* on which they appear or disappear. For this to work you do need to know the refresh rate of your monitor and that the computer is set to synchronize with the monitor refresh. You can get more guidance on those issues in Section 12.2 but most computers will be synchronizing correctly by default and most standard monitors are running at a 60 Hz refresh rate. Assuming you have a 60 Hz monitor, you can calculate the number of frames needed for a particular duration with this equation:

$$N = t \times 60$$

 Info: Why would a study need brief stimuli?

In the Glasgow Face Matching Task the task is difficult enough that people struggle with it, even given unlimited time, and we can see how much they struggle simply by measuring their percentage correct. In the Stroop task it isn't so much that participants get the answer wrong, but that they are substantially slower to make a decision in incongruent conditions than congruent ones. In neither task was the duration of the stimuli very important; the effects could be seen when the stimulus was simply presented and left on screen indefinitely.

There are other tasks where that might not be true. At times we might want to test the absolute limits of how fast our perception is. Measuring how fast someone responds to the presence of an image doesn't really tell us how fast their visual perception is because their reaction time is the result of many processes (perception, decision making and responding). Reaction times, even when no decision has to be made, are on the order of 200–400 ms whereas participants are certainly able to detect the rough gist of a visual scene (e.g. was this a mountain or a forest?) in less time than that. To test the speed of perception, without including the time taken to respond, we might present an image stimulus for increasingly brief periods, quickly covered by a mask (to prevent participants using a retinal after-image to perform the task!), until the point participants fall to chance-level performance. So, in this instance, using brief stimuli is a way to measure the speed of perception without confounding that with your speed to react.

At other times, using a brief stimulus is a way simply to control difficulty. If your task is too easy you might find a *ceiling* effect: participants perform so well that you can't

(Continued)

detect any change in performance across conditions. Of course, if you make your stimulus presentation too brief (so that your participants can't see it) then you will almost certainly get a *floor* effect, where your participants are so *bad* in every condition that you also can't measure any differences.

A third reason for using very brief stimuli is that, at times, we want participants to use their peripheral vision rather than look directly at a stimulus (e.g. how good are you at detecting stimuli out of the corner of your eye?). If we present a stimulus not at fixation, how do we know that the participant won't simply move their eyes to the stimulus location? We need to find a way to stop them from 'cheating'. The easiest way to achieve this is to present the stimulus either on the left or on the right of the screen, so the participant won't know where to look in advance, and present it for a brief period. It takes roughly 200 ms for people to make a saccadic eye movement (Carpenter, 1988), so if we make our stimulus duration less than 200 ms then participants don't have time to 'fixate' on the stimulus.

where N is the number of frames and t is the time desired in seconds. Note that if N is not an integer value (i.e. if it has some decimal place value) then it isn't possible to present our stimulus for exactly that duration. For instance, to present a stimulus for exactly 20 ms would require 0.02 × 60 frames, which is 1.2 frames. Obviously that isn't possible; you can only have 1 frame (16.67 ms) or 2 frames (33.33 ms). Conversely, if you want to calculate the stimulus duration in seconds for a certain number of frames you can reverse the equation and use:

$$t = N/60$$

from which you can see that, for instance, 12 frames lasts 12/60 seconds, which is 0.2 s (or 200 ms).

 Warning: Check the log file

If brief stimuli are important in your study then you should check the log file after running the first participants to make sure that they are being presented for the durations you expect. The log file gives time-stamps for events as they occur, including the times when a visual stimulus starts and stops. For visual stimuli these time-stamps are typically extremely precise (with a precision on the order of 100 microseconds, but very much dependent on your computer). In the Posner task our stimulus was called probe, so we would look for entries of `probe: autoDraw = True` (indicating that the stimulus started drawing) and `probe: autoDraw = False` (the stimulus stopped drawing). The difference between these times tells us for how long the stimulus was visible.

4.2 POSNER CUEING

In this chapter we will measure the effects of covert attention, when you attend to a particular location on the screen without moving your eyes to it. To do this we use the Posner cueing task (Posner, 1980) in which participants must respond as quickly as possible to the presentation of a stimulus (we'll use a simple square) that appears on the left or the right of the screen. Before the target is presented we show a cue (a triangle) that points to the left or the right. Most of the time the cue will point to the correct location so your attention will naturally shift to that location, in expectation of seeing the target appear there. On occasional trials, however, the cue will point to the incorrect location; the target will appear on the wrong side and you won't benefit from the advantage of having your attention there. We can measure the effect of attention by looking at the speed of your response. Most people are much faster to respond when the target stimulus appears in the attended location. Posner tested the effects of this as a function of time and found that the effect of attention gradually increases until around 300 ms, at which point it remains stable. In order to replicate his findings by testing several 'stimulus onset asynchronies', all under 300 ms, we obviously need precise timing. Actually, to start with we will simply generate the basic effect but we will describe in the 'Extensions and Exercises' section (page 68) how to run the same task at multiple asynchronies.

The task is relatively straightforward to implement and there have been many variants on it since it was created. Some of the extensions highlight additional aspects of precision timing. You can extend the simple cueing task to study the Inhibition of Return (another finding of Posner's), which requires more precise timing, because the effect changes as a function of time. Or you could use an image as the cue (or target) which requires some special consideration of how to achieve precise timing with image stimuli being loaded from disk.

USING DEGREES OF VISUAL ANGLE

For this task we could specify the stimulus location in pixels as we have done before. Instead, let's use 'degrees of visual angle' (**deg**). For more information see Section 11.1 but, briefly, the advantage is that this takes care of the fact that the stimulus can be presented on different-size screens and at different distances from the participant. By using degrees of visual angle we ensure that the stimulus always has the same size/position (at the point of the participant's eye) despite different viewing conditions. It isn't essential here, but it's a useful thing to learn.

To use degrees as units there are two steps. First we must define the dimensions of our monitor in Monitor Center. To do that click on the ⬛ button to open Monitor Center. By default there is a monitor called **testMonitor** and we could use that, or you could create a new monitor name. For your monitor you then need to enter values for the 'Screen Distance (cm)', which is the distance that the participant will be from the screen. You also need to insert the 'Screen Width (cm)', which is the width of the monitor from the left most pixel to the right most pixel (i.e. just the part where stimuli are actually presented). Lastly you need to set the 'Size (pixels)', which is the number of pixels wide and high your screen is. With these three values PsychoPy can then work out how to convert stimuli from all different units. That means we can simply specify the size of our stimuli in degrees and let PsychoPy do all the calculations for us.

The second step is to go to your Experiment Settings ⬛ and select the tab labelled **Screen**, where you can set the monitor to be one that you just set up in Monitor Center, and you could also set the default unit of this experiment to be **deg** as in Figure 4.1.

FIGURE 4.1 Setting the Experiment Settings so that you have default stimulus units of 'degrees of visual angle'. To do this you need to set the name of the monitor to be one of those in Monitor Center and make sure that you have correctly set up the dimensions and distance for that monitor. Then you can set the units of the experiment to be any of PsychoPy's available options.

Once you've set up your experiment to use degrees as the default unit you can then use that for all your stimulus settings. In the other screenshots here we will also set the units for each stimulus but that isn't necessary if you've set the default units correctly.

 Pro Tip: Screen sizes in pixels

If you have a flat-panel (LCD/plasma) screen, or a projector, for your stimuli then you should try to set this to use its 'native resolution'. Although your screen can receive input from various sources and various different resolutions, the actual pixels of the screen are fixed and they cannot change. What the monitor does when it receives input that is not in its native resolution is interpolate the screen image to fit as best it can. This usually means that the images on the screen will be slightly blurry (this will be most obvious when you view fine lines or text) and possibly stretched if the aspect ratio of the screen is not exactly the same as the aspect ratio of the image being sent from the computer.

To set the resolution of the image that the computer is 'sending' to the screen you should see the relevant Control Panel (Microsoft Windows) or System Preferences (OS X) setting for the displays.

If you have a cathode ray tube (CRT) monitor (these are quite rare now) this does not apply. For a CRT you can set it to any resolution that the screen is capable of rendering and the actual pixels will change accordingly.

If you don't have a tape measure handy then the measurements will have to be approximate (and your units won't be exactly degrees). To give you some ideas of what the distances might be: if you could sit at arm's length from the monitor it will be roughly 50 cm away; if you have a standard laptop with a 13-inch screen (measured across the diagonal) then the visible part will be roughly 29 × 18 cm whereas if you have a large wide-screen monitor it might be more like 60 × 35 cm.

If you get an error message 'ValueError: Monitor testMonitors has no known size...' then see the explanation of error messages in Section 14.2.

SETTING UP THE CONDITIONS

As with the previous tasks we need to create a conditions file to tell PsychoPy what happens on each trial and what parameters will vary. In this particular task we will have the following:

- A *cue* that can point right or left. To achieve this we use a triangle that points to the right or to the left. Initially the triangle (a shape stimulus) points straight upwards but we can rotate this by 90 deg (clockwise) or −90 deg (anti-clockwise) in order to point to the right and left, respectively. So we create a variable cueOri to store the orientation of the cue on each trial. It's handy to keep track of what that orientation meant, so we also have a variable cueSide to say where the cue was pointing.
- A *target* that can appear on the right or left. To move this we will use a variable called targetX to specify the position in the horizontal dimension of the screen.
- A corrAns variable to help us identify trials where the participant was correct or incorrect.
- A valid variable will be useful during analysis just to sort our valid-cue trials from our trials with invalid cues.

The last thing we have to bear in mind when creating our conditions file is that we need to have 80% valid cues and 20% invalid cues. The easiest way to achieve this is simply to create 10 conditions where two of them are invalid cues and the rest are valid. We should balance the left and right directions for both cue and target, so we should end up with a table that looks like this:

cueSide	cueOri	targetX	corrAns	valid
right	90	7	right	1
right	90	7	right	1
right	90	7	right	1
right	90	7	right	1
left	−90	−7	left	1
left	−90	−7	left	1
left	−90	−7	left	1
left	−90	−7	left	1
left	−90	7	right	0
right	90	−7	left	0

You can see that just the bottom two conditions are invalid, the first four are valid to the right and the next four are valid to the left. It doesn't matter how we order the trials in our conditions file because they will be shuffled automatically by PsychoPy as the trials run.

Also note that the targetX value is going to be treated as degrees of visual angle because our target stimulus will be using those units (it will typically be 5–10 cm if the monitor is roughly 50 cm from the participant). If we want to use a different unit then we also need to use a different value here in the conditions file. That may sound obvious, but it's easy to forget that this value relates to the units of your stimulus.

VARIABLE INTER-TRIAL INTERVALS

In the tasks so far the trial has been defined entirely in a single `trial` Routine that contained a pause at the beginning (in which only the fixation point was visible) and constituted our inter-trial interval (ITI). In Posner's experiments there was a *variable* delay between each trial, which is useful in stopping participants from getting into a rhythm of responding; if participants start responding in such a way then they won't show any difference in reaction time between conditions. We could create a variable start time for our stimuli within a single Routine but this can be annoying because several Components will have to depend on the same variable start time. The easier solution on this occasion is to create two Routines, one for the ITI and another where we actually present the stimuli and collect the response (which we could carry on calling 'trial' as this is built into the default experiment).

Let's see how that works. Go to PsychoPy and create a new experiment, which you could save straightaway (save it in a new folder called **posner** so that you can put the other materials, like conditions files, in there as well). Now, in the Flow view insert a new Routine as in Figure 4.2.

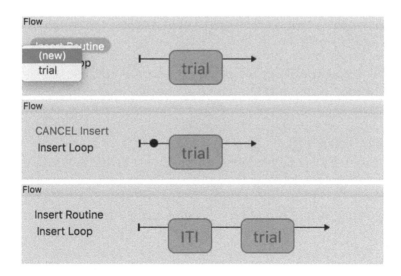

FIGURE 4.2 Adding a separate ITI Routine to the Flow of the Posner cueing experiment. Top panel: click on `Insert`, select `New`, and type in the name `ITI`. Middle panel: select where you want it to go (just before the `trial` Routine). Bottom panel: the finished product.

Info: What is a fixation point?

If you're new to behavioral science then it might not be clear what we mean by a *fixation point* or a *fixation period*. The idea of these is that we often need to control the location of our participants' gaze and the aim is to get them to hold their eyes steady, or 'fixate', on a particular point in space. Very often this is needed at the beginning of the trial so that we know how far away the stimulus was. Sometimes participants need to maintain fixation throughout a trial and only attend to objects in their peripheral vision.

Either way, if you need participants to maintain fixation then (a) you really need to give them something to fixate on and (b) you should really remind them in your instructions that this is important. While it might have become obvious to you what that little white cross was for, it probably isn't obvious to your participants unless they also do this sort of work!

Now click on the ITI Routine (either in the Flow or on its tab in the Routines panel) so that we can edit that Routine. To set the ITI we just need to create a single Component that has the duration we want for the ITI. When that single Component finishes, the experiment will progress immediately to the next Routine on the Flow, which will be the trial itself. So let's create a **fixation point** that lasts a variable duration. For the fixation we add a small cross by using a Polygon Component ⬧. Set the parameters as follows:

- `Name` = `fixationITI` or something similar (because sometimes a fixation stimulus appears in the ITI as well as during the trial itself).
- `Duration (s)` = `random()+1`. Also set the 'estimated duration (s)' to be, say, 1.5 s.
- `Shape` = `cross`
- `Size` = `(0.5, 0.5)`. Remember, we're using degrees. At a distance of 57 cm, 1 degree is 1 cm wide, so this will be roughly 0.5 cm wide on your screen.
- `Units` = `deg` if you like to be safe, but hopefully you did that above in the Experiment Settings so you could leave this to inherit the units from there.

So what does `random()+1` achieve? Well, `random()` gives a value between 0 and 1 and we have added 1 to our number so then it will be a number between 1 and 2 (seconds in this case) which is the same as the random ITI used by Posner.

As its value is variable, PsychoPy doesn't know how long the **fixation** will last, so for it to show up on the timeline for your Routine in the same way as previous stimuli have done, you need to set the **Expected duration** as suggested above. The **Expected duration** has no effect on the experiment when it runs; it merely helps you to visualize the study on the Builder timeline.

Now we need to set up the trial itself, so click on the **trial** Routine. First we need to create the cue. To do this add another Polygon Component with the following attributes. Note that the duration is set to be *12* and you need to remember to set that to be **duration (frames)** or it will last for 12 *seconds* by default. Your monitor is probably running at 60 Hz but PsychoPy cannot be certain of this (you might be running your experiment on a different computer to the one you created it on) so PsychoPy again won't show your **cue** object on the timeline unless you set the expected duration as well. So, altogether, the key attributes that need changing should look like this:

- Name = cue
- Stop duration (frames) = 12 (expected duration = 0.2)
- Shape = triangle
- Orientation = cueOri (and **set every repeat**)
- Size = (2,4) (again this is in degrees)

We also need a target stimulus. We suggest a different color for this just so it makes the instructions easier: 'Press as quickly as possible the key to indicate where the *green square* appeared (right or left)'; but the color isn't important for any other reason. Actually we could give the square slightly different fill colors and line colors, just for the hell of it! The really key parameter here is setting the position of the stimulus to vary in each trial according to the **targetX** variable in our conditions file:

- Name = target
- Start time (frames) = 12 (expected time = 0.2)
- Duration could be left at 1.0 s (this won't make any difference to the study)
- Shape = rectangle (the choice of what the target looks like is pretty irrelevant).
- Position = (targetX, 0) (and **set every repeat**)
- Size = (3, 3) (again this is in degrees)
- Fill color = SeaGreen (in the Advanced Parameters tab)
- Line color = MediumSeaGreen (in the Advanced Parameters tab)

Pro Tip: Set targetX variable not targetPos

It might be tempting to create a variable called `targetPos` and give it a pair of values like `[7,0]`, `[-7,0]`. We, however, created the single value variable `targetX` and typed `$(targetX, 0)` in the position field. The reason is that it's easier in the spreadsheet if values are numbers. In most spreadsheet packages you can 'autofill' numbers whereas you can't autofill a number that is in brackets. Also in PsychoPy it is more clear that this should be treated as a number, whereas the value `[-7,0]` might be confusing (it will be interpreted as being the string of characters `"[-7,0]"` rather than a pair of numbers). Although this may mean having to write more columns of variables (e.g. you might need `targetX` as well as `targetY`) it is a safer thing to do.

Also, note that we wouldn't write `($targetX, $targetY)` but `$(targetX, targetY)`. The `$` is a signal to PsychoPy that it should treat the entire entry box as code, not that specific values are variables. In fact, for Position, the `$` is expected anyway, so we can leave it out altogether.

The last thing we need is a way for participants to respond. For that we use a keyboard object in the same way as in previous tasks but this also needs to start at 12 frames (estimated as 0.2 s). This time we set a maximum time for the response by setting the keyboard to have a duration of 2.0 (seconds). This is often useful in a response-time task because it prevents people from spending a long time thinking about their response. It also means that responses where the participant had not obeyed your instruction to respond 'as quickly and accurately as they can' are not included in the analysis:

- Name = `resp`
- Start time (frames) = 12 (expected time = `0.2`)
- Duration = `2.0`
- Allowed keys = `'left'`, `'right'`
- Correct Answer = `$corrAns` (available after ticking 'Store correct')

At this point your `trial` Routine should look like Figure 4.3.

SETTING THE REPETITIONS AND CONDITIONS

As in previous tasks we need to create a loop that goes around our `trial` Routine and determines how the trials will repeat. On this occasion, however, we need the loop to include the ITI Routine because this is also being run on every repeat as part of the trial. Click the button on the Flow to 'Insert loop. . .' and set this to start just before the ITI and end just after the `trial`.

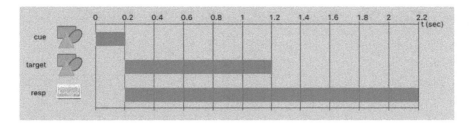

FIGURE 4.3 The Posner `trial` Routine, not including the ITI, which was defined by a separate Routine. Although the three Components in this Routine start and/or stop according to a certain number of 'frames', which don't have a predetermined time, we have given them estimated start/stop times so that they show up on the timeline.

When you have inserted the start and end points of the loop you can enter the parameters for it (Figure 4.4). In this case you can leave nearly all the parameters as their default values. Just add the conditions file by clicking on **Browse...** and check when you do so that the message correctly reports there being

FIGURE 4.4 The settings for the loop in the Posner task, which we've set to include two Routines (ITI separated from the stimulus presentation). Note that there are 10 'conditions' specified in order to generate 80% valid trials, so when we ask for 5 repeats here we will get a total of 50 random trials.

10 conditions with 5 parameters: cueOri, cueSide, targetX, corrAns, valid (don't worry if the order is different).

You could go ahead and make sure your trials run without any problems.

FINAL TOUCHES

Of course, as in the previous tasks, it really helps the participants if you have an instructions screen before the first trial to remind them what to do. In this case you need to tell them that they need to respond to the appearance of the green square (target), or they might be tempted to respond according to the presence of the triangle (cue).

Also, as always, it's a good idea to include a 'Thank you' screen telling the participants that they have finished. If the experiment ends abruptly then they might think the program crashed!

EXTENSIONS AND EXERCISES

There are many ways to use and extend this basic cueing paradigm. We present a few extra versions, and the different additional considerations they require, here.

EXERCISE 4.1: GAZE CUEING

Rather than cueing the location of the target with an arrow you could choose to use a graphic image (like a photo of a face looking to the left or the right). In the study we created above, the arrow directed attention partially by being *informative* about the target location (it was valid 80% of the time). Alternatively we could have made the cue uninformative about the actual location by making it invalid as often as valid. In theory some stimuli might have such a strong *inherent* ability to steer your attention that it wouldn't matter if the stimulus was actually uninformative. Gaze is potentially such a stimulus. A number of studies have suggested that we are so used to following the gaze of a person that we naturally do it even with a photographic stimulus, and even when we have been told that the gaze direction will not help us in the task. This is the phenomenon known as 'gaze cueing' (Frischen et al., 2007) and it has various potential uses in the study of clinical populations, such as people with autism spectrum disorder.

Solution: Page 286

EXERCISE 4.2: MEASURE THE EFFECT FOR DIFFERENT SOAS

Posner and his colleagues studied the attentional cueing effects for a variety of time differences between the cue and the probe (stimulus onset asynchronies or SOAs) and found some interesting characteristics. One of the surprising effects is that when the cue is *not* informative about the location of the probe we can measure both positive and negative effects of cueing (a speeding up or a slowing down or reaction times) according to what SOA was used. With very brief SOAs (say 100 ms) and an uninformative cue we often still find a faster reaction time when the probe is in the cued location. With longer SOAs (say 300 ms), however, we see the opposite effect, where participants are actually slower to detect the stimulus if it lands at the previous cued location. This is thought of as an 'Inhibition of Return' whereby inhibition prevents the attentional mechanism from revisiting the previously attended location, leading to an increase in reaction times at that location.

As a participant it takes some time to run the cueing experiment with multiple time-courses to map out this effect, but you might find it an interesting task to create the experiment with valid and invalid cues as in your Posner cueing task, but now with multiple SOAs built into your conditions.

Solution: Page 287

5

CREATING DYNAMIC STIMULI (REVEALING TEXT AND MOVING STIMULI)

Learning objectives: In PsychoPy you can change your stimulus properties continuously as a function of time. For example, you can make your stimulus 'throb' or bounce to engage younger participants, or you can make some appear gradually. Here we learn how to control stimuli as a function of time in a variety of ways.

In this chapter we will introduce the concept of stimulus attributes that can be updated on **every screen refresh** during the trial. With these dynamic attributes you can alter the size, orientation or position of your stimulus as a function of time. Unlike the previous chapters where we developed a single study, in this chapter we use several examples. We'll construct demos of effects that can reveal text gradually, rotate and expand some images, and make a throbbing heart!

A bit of high-school mathematics will be useful to make things change smoothly and nicely, so we've included a refresher in Appendix A.

We should also note that making stimuli dynamic isn't *necessary* for most tasks. Very often this might be considered something of a luxury – a bit of showing off – but once you know that things *can* be made to change on each frame it opens new possibilities as to the sort of study you could create. If the level of programming we introduce isn't for you then don't worry – you can present more 'standard' stimuli without it.

5.1 WHAT DOES *DYNAMIC* MEAN AND WHY IS IT USEFUL?

PsychoPy is unusual, compared with many similar packages, in that it makes time central to the structure of the experiment. The expectation is that objects naturally appear and disappear during a trial, together or independently. So in a PsychoPy Routine, the representation is like that of a track editor, as you might see in video or audio editing software. Consider the layout of a 'delayed match-to-sample' task. Here you would present a *sample* image followed, after a delay, by a pair of options, the *target* and the *foil*, where only the target is the same as the sample. Each trial would start with your fixation point, which should come on at 500 ms to alert participants and then remain visible for the rest of the trial. The *sample* might appear above that fixation point and then disappear shortly afterwards. After a further pause, a pair of stimuli should appear simultaneously and remain visible until the participant makes a decision. In PsychoPy the temporal layout of this trial would be very clear (see Figure 5.1).

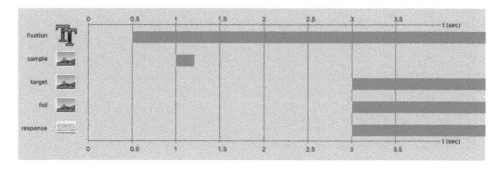

FIGURE 5.1   A demonstration of the delayed match to sample task Routine as it would be created in PsychoPy Builder.

The timeline view only depicts the temporal arrangement of the stimuli. For example, we can't tell from this view that, spatially, the target and foil will appear above the fixation point. To find out the spatial arrangement (and other appearance settings like color and orientation) we have to click on the stimulus icons to view their properties.

 Info: How do other packages do it?

In contrast to PsychoPy, many packages treat a trial more like a slide show rather than a video with tracks. That is, you'd see a series of images of what the screen would look like to the participant. In a study where things appear and disappear all at the same time, this is very convenient. In many studies, though, stimuli come and go at different

(Continued)

times, which means a stack of slides is needed to represent a trial. In the delayed match-to-sample, for instance, the trial might require one slide for the pre-fixation period, another for the period where the fixation point appears alone, another that shows the fixation point as well as the *sample* image, then back to one showing just the fixation point, and finally one with the fixation point combined with the target and foil stimuli. The advantage of the series-of-slides approach is that the spatial layout is easier to visualize within each slide, the downside being that the temporal organization is harder to determine.

Since PsychoPy treats time as central to experimental designs it also allows you to control stimuli *based on* time. You've already seen that we can set most Component parameters to 'update on every repeat'. For example, we can show an image that changes on every trial. But most stimulus parameters can also 'update on every frame' (every time the monitor physically updates), which means the image can also be smoothly animated (moved, for instance) *during* the trial. On each screen refresh the value of the parameter is checked and can be changed to a new value. Also, because PsychoPy uses hardware-accelerated graphics (i.e. the hard work is done by a dedicated processor on the graphics card), most of these changes are applied extremely quickly, so continuously manipulating stimuli during the experiment will generally not damage the timing fidelity of your study.

Now, one issue to deal with here is that, if these changes are typically occurring at 60 Hz (most monitors update 60 times every second), it means you have to supply an awful lot of values for it to do the updating, and typing those into a conditions file, as we have done in the previous chapters, would take a long time. We would need 60 rows of conditions file for each second of stimulus presentation on a typical monitor! Luckily, PsychoPy has a powerful alternative trick up its sleeve: you can specify parameters by using equations (or any raw Python code) as PsychoPy stimulus parameters. This allows you to control stimuli with a mathematical expression or by responding to events. For example, you can make an image's position dependent on the time elapsed since the beginning of the trial or make the tone of a feedback beep dependent on the number of times a button has been pressed.

5.2 INSERTING CODE INTO PARAMETERS

When you learned how to create a basic study in PsychoPy, you saw that inserting the $ symbol into one of your parameters told PsychoPy to understand what followed as a variable name instead of a literal piece of text. You were probably thinking of it as '$ tells PsychoPy that this is a variable name'. Actually, it's a bit more general than that. It tells PsychoPy that 'this box contains Python code', and as your variable name happens to be valid Python code, it is interpreted as such.

LET'S GET MOVING!

So, for example, let's make a stimulus change position. To do that we should make it update its position on the basis of the current time in the Routine. One of the most useful variables, which exists in all Builder experiments, is t. This provides the time in seconds since the current Routine started (whatever that Routine is). Let's create an experiment with a single Routine on the Flow and add a single Text Component to that Routine. Now we can set the position of that Text Component to be, say, (t,0) and set it to update **on every frame** using the drop-down menu to the right of the setting. The position of the stimulus is controlled with a pair of values in brackets that correspond to its x and y coordinates. So (t, 0) means that the horizontal position of the stimulus is set to be t, which varies in time, but the vertical position stays fixed at y=0 (which is the vertical midline). So, when the Routine starts, the stimulus will appear at the center of the screen (0, 0). After 1 second it will be at location (1, 0) which in normalized units is the right-hand edge of the screen, but still centered vertically. After 2 seconds the position will be (2, 0) but that position is off the screen in normalized units so it won't be visible (for further information about units see Chapter 11). Hopefully it's clear that the stimulus starts in the center and moves smoothly to the right-hand edge of the screen over the first second of the trial.

In this example you can increase or decrease the speed of your stimulus simply by multiplying the value of t. If you set the position to be (t*0.25, 0) then your stimulus will move at one-quarter of the speed, taking 4 seconds to reach the right-hand edge: (4*0.25, 0). You could also change the start position, simply by adding or subtracting a value. For example, the expression (-1+t*0.5, 0) would make the stimulus start at the left-hand edge of the screen (−1, 0) and move to the right at a rate of 0.5 units per second.

The speed of motion depends on the **units** setting of the stimulus. By default this is set for each stimulus to be *normalized* (actually, the default stimulus units are inherited from the Experiment Settings, which inherit the default of *normalized* from the PsychoPy preferences). You might find it more intuitive to set the units of your stimulus to be in *pixels* such that the speed (multiplied by t) is in *pixels per second*. So after 1 second, a stimulus with a position setting of (t, 0) and units of **pixels** will have moved just 1 pixel to the right of center, while the same stimulus with **normalized** units will have moved all the way to the right-hand edge of the screen. If you do change the units to use pixels don't forget also to change the size setting (or letter height, for a Text Component) to be a reasonable value in pixels as well. Otherwise you may find yourself not seeing the stimulus because you drew it smaller than a single pixel!

5.3 EXAMPLE 1: REVEALING TEXT GRADUALLY

Using the technique of making things move, it becomes very simple to create the effect of a sentence gradually being revealed to a participant. Maybe you want precise control over that rate at which a sentence is provided to the participant?

To do this we can draw our sentence first using a text object (and this can change on every trial, based on a conditions file, as in the previous examples) and then we simply draw a mask over the top of it, gradually moving away to reveal the text stimulus underneath.

Let's create an experiment with a single Routine and a Text Component with some sentence as its text, something long enough that we can see it gradually reveal, but short enough that it fits on one screen width. Something like 'When will participants get the meaning of this sentence?' should do. Now, by default text on the screen wraps with a width about half the screen (using normalized units) but we want our sentence to extend further across the screen. Go to the Advanced settings of the Text Component and set the wrap width to be 2, as in Figure 5.2.

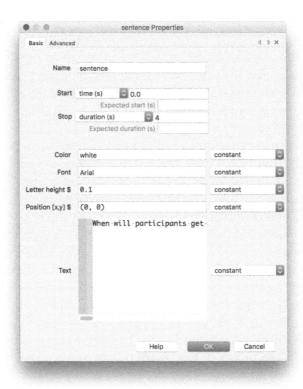

FIGURE 5.2 Properties of the sentence to be revealed. Basic settings are on the left tab, including the Duration. Advanced settings are on the right tab and include the new Wrap Width.

OK, so far so good. This is the new bit, where we create the mask. Note that objects in a Routine are drawn in sequence, from top to bottom. So 'lower' objects are drawn later and therefore obscure things that were drawn earlier (assuming they are opaque). So you need to make sure that the mask is *below* the Text Component on your timeline view. Your structure should look like Figure 5.3.

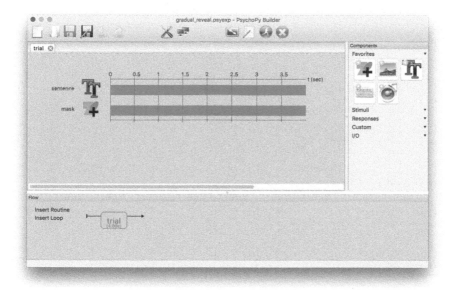

FIGURE 5.3   Structure of your Routine in which you have a text object that will be covered by a mask.

There are various ways we could create a mask. `Grating` and `Image Components` can be used as masks, for instance. On this occasion let's insert a rectangle by using the `Polygon Component`. This lets us create a *regular* polygon simply by specifying the number of vertices (3 for a triangle, 4 for rectangle, 5 for a pentagon, all the way up to an approximation of a circle). Then you specify the width and height of that regular polygon. In our case we need `vertices=4` and `size=(2,0.5)` as in Figures 5.4. By setting the size to 2 and forcing the units to be `normalized` we ensure that the mask initially covers the full width of the screen. We've set the height to be 0.5, but it could be any value bigger than the text we're aiming to obscure.

The key aspect for this task is to set the position dynamically so that it progressively reveals the text, with an expression like `(t*0.5,0)`. Again, you can make the mask move faster or slower by altering that 0.5 value. You could even replace it with a variable from your conditions file called `maskSpeed`, for instance, so that the speed of the mask varies from trial to trial.

You might find it helps conceptually if, to start with, you leave the mask in the default color (white) so that you can set how it moves against the default gray background. Once you understand what it's doing then you can set it to have the same color as the background of the screen. To do that, go to the `fillColor` and `lineColor` settings for the Polygon (see Figure 5.5) and set them to be **gray** (or whatever color your screen is, which you can control in Experiment Settings). When the mask is the same color as the background, it will give the impression of the text stimulus being progressively revealed, and the motion of the mask object itself will not be apparent.

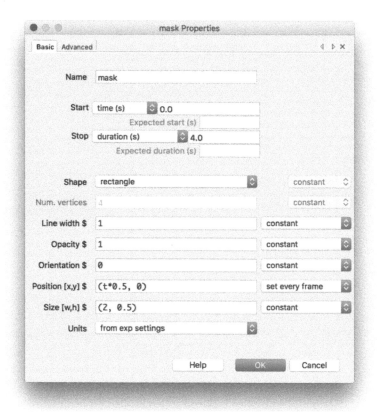

FIGURE 5.4   The 'Basic' properties of the mask that gradually reveals the underlying sentence. Here we need to set the position (as a function of time) and the size of the mask.

At this point you should have a sentence that is gradually revealed by the sliding mask.

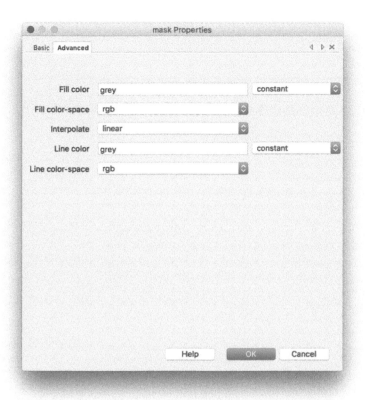

FIGURE 5.5   The 'Advanced' properties of the mask where we need to set the color. While you work on the study you might want to set it so you can see the mask, but in the end we want it to be the same as the background gray color.

 Pro Tip: What if I'm not good with equations?

If it is difficult for you to think of speed in terms of these equations of *position* across *time* then just keep asking yourself 'Where will my stimulus be at t=0 and at t=1?' In most cases, working out the position for those two time values will be enough for you to understand what the motion should look like.

5.4 EXAMPLE 2: SPINNING, EXPANDING IMAGES

It isn't just position that can vary in real time. Most other parameters have the same ability. Let's take some images of famous faces. We'll rotate them and make them grow from being tiny until they are visible. We could challenge participants to press a button as soon as they recognize the face.

 Info: Why would we make faces rotate and expand?

The scientific point of rotating, expanding faces isn't at all clear, but it was a popular challenge on TV quizzes in the 1980s and 1990s where contestants had to recognize famous people.

Download images of some famous faces. Put them into a folder called `faces` and give the images names like `face01.jpg`, `face02.jpg`, etc.

Then create a new experiment in Builder with a single Routine (there is one called `trial` by default) and insert a single Image Component into that Routine. Give it the following parameters (also shown in Figure 5.6):

FIGURE 5.6 Properties of an image which rotates and expands over time. Note that we didn't specify values for both the height and width of the image in the 'size' field. PsychoPy accepts a short-hand form where if we provide only one entry for either 'size' or 'position', it is used for both the horizontal and vertical values.

- start: `0.0`
- stop: `10.0`
- image: `$imageFile`
- size: `$t*40`
- orientation: `$t*180`
- units: `pix`

So, in this case the stimulus starts with a size of zero at `t=0` and grows at a rate of 40 pixels per second, while spinning at a rate of 180 degrees per second. That should be enough to confuse your participants a little!

5.5 EXAMPLE 3: CHANGE COLORS THROUGH THE RAINBOW

Changing colors continuously is also possible and might serve to keep participants interested. To do this using code we probably want to define colors numerically. PsychoPy offers a few color spaces to do this, described in detail in Section 11.2. Probably the nicest one for this task is the **HSV** color space. Here the first value of the color determines its hue (the color of the rainbow) and is usually thought of in terms of its angle around a circle (0–360 degrees). The second value determines its saturation (you can think of this as how strongly colorful it is) with a range of 0–1. The third and final value is simply called 'value' and loosely corresponds to the color's brightness (also 0–1). So, in order to make a stimulus change colors through the rainbow (see Figures 4.7 and 4.8), we could set our stimulus to have a color space of **HSV** (this is in the **Advanced** settings of the Text Component) and set its color to be `$(t*90, 1, 1)` which will result in an intense (because S=1) bright (because υ=1) color rotating through the rainbow (as h varies). As a full transit around the color spectrum is 360 degrees , using `t*90` would take 4 seconds to achieve this. You could try lowering the saturation by using `$(t*90, 0.5, 1)` to get a pastel version, or reducing the 'value' to get a darker version `$(t*90, 1, 0.5)`. To make the color change occur more rapidly, simply increase the value from `t*90` to, say, `t*180`.

 Pro Tip: HSV Colors

Colors are often specified using separate values for red, green and blue, which is what you might often see elsewhere in this book. They behave differently: rather than choosing a point on a color wheel (that doesn't have a natural start or end), it is like setting three sliders that each have definite minimum and maximum values. This is useful when we want independent control of those three color channels, but it isn't as easy to cycle through a rainbow as it is with the HSV color space.

You can perform similar changes with other objects, like Polygon or Grating Components, or anything else that supports color settings.

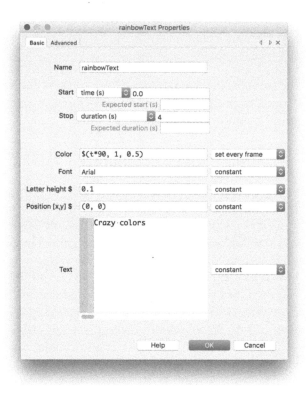

FIGURE 5.7 Setting the rainbow basic text properties. Note that the color is set to be `$(t*90, 1, 0.5)`. The other settings can be whatever you like.

5.6 EXAMPLE 4: MAKE A HEART THAT HAS A PULSE

So far the changes have been in a continuous direction, but what if we wanted position, orientation or size to change and then smoothly change back again? In this demonstration we'll make something change size but we want to do so in a way that after it grows smoothly for a period it then shrinks back, ready to start the cycle again. Making something move (e.g. bounce) or grow and shrink rhythmically is most easily done using a *sine* wave. You can read a reminder on what *sine* and *cosine* mean in Appendix A (page 281).

Creating a heart shape. For this demo you could use any image you like, but it will work best with a heart. Not a photograph – that would be gross! We mean a cartoon 'love' heart. Now you could get a simple image from the internet that

FIGURE 5.8 To create our rainbow text we need to set the ('Advanced') property `Color space` to be `hsv`.

contains a heart, or you can use the one included in the online materials, and make it into an Image Component (see Chapter 3). It's a good idea to find one where the outside of the heart is transparent in the image so that whatever color the background window is, it will show up correctly rather than having a square of white with a red heart in the middle, on a gray screen (ugh!).

 Pro Tip: Having an image that can also change color

If you want to be in control of the heart *color* then you could select one drawn as white on a black background and use it as a stimulus *mask*. That way the white part is visible and can have its color change, while the black part is invisible and shows the color of the background. See Section 16.3 for more information on using images as masks.

Changing the size. You may recall from your high-school mathematics that a sinusoidal wave goes up and down, varying smoothly between −1 and +1. So, we could use `sin(t)` to produce a wave of values that is dependent on time. We need to adjust that simple function, though, because its values would vary from −1 to +1 and it seems strange to have a size value of −1. If we specified a size of `4+sin(t)` then at the peak of the wave we would have a size of 5 (i.e. 4+1), and at the smallest point of the wave we would have a size of 3 (i.e. 4+(−1)), so that would give us something that varied smoothly but was always positive. If we use a unit of 'pixels', however, a size range from 3 to 5 would give us a pretty small heart. So, let's give it a bigger starting point (100 pixels) and then set the wave to have a larger amplitude of `50*sin(t)`. That would also pulse quite slowly, though, so we can multiply `t` by 3 before the sine function is applied, which speeds up the changes. Now the overall equation for the stimulus size is going to be `100+50*sin(t*3)`, which results in a size that varies smoothly from 50 to 150 pixels and back. Insert that into your image stimulus. You can see in Figure 5.9 how that should look. Give it a go; you should see a heart that grows and shrinks nicely.

FIGURE 5.9 Making an image throb, like a heart. Note the size is set to be $100 + 50*$ `(sin(t*3))` and must be **set every frame** and the units are set to be 'pixels'. If you accidentally leave them as 'norm' or inherited from the defaults (which are probably 'norm') then the heart will be bigger than the screen.

Making the pulse more like a pulse. Note that the sinusoidal wave doesn't really produce a very 'pulse-like' effect. It varies too smoothly and continuously, whereas a cartoon beating heart should be small for most of the time and then get bigger just for a relatively brief period. A slight tweak to our equation can make it look more like that. If we raise our sinusoid to a power then it will alter the shape of the curve, making it more pointy. Try using the equation $100+50{\times}\sin(t{\times}3)^4$ which we achieve in Python syntax by writing `100+50*sin(t*3)**4` (`**` is Python notation for raising a number to a power). If you're good at mathematics you might note that this has also frequency-doubled the pulse rate (the negative lobe of the sinusoid has become positive) but let's not worry about that – it works!

5.7 GOING FURTHER

As well as adding Python code to your Component parameters, which can obviously only be a single line long, you can add much more code into Code Components (you'll find the button in the 'Custom' category of the Component Panel). These components allow you to add unlimited lines of arbitrary Python code to different parts of your script. For more information see Chapter 6.

EXERCISES AND EXTENSIONS

EXERCISE 5.1: REVEAL AN IMAGE BY CHANGING OPACITY

Note that opacity is a parameter that varies from 0 (completely transparent, so invisible) to 1 (completely 'opaque', so fully visible). You could take an image and gradually reveal it using opacity in two ways. Either you could have an image that gradually *increased* its opacity, or you could draw a stimulus followed by some sort of mask that gradually *reduced* its opacity to reveal the stimulus behind. Try each of these and remember that when you set the opacity using an equation, it needs to **update every frame**.

Solution: Page 287

EXERCISE 5.2: ROTATING EYEBALLS

To make a pair of simple eyeballs you need four objects: two white eyes and two pupils. Position them on either side of the fixation and make the pupils

(Continued)

move in a sinusoidal pattern left and right. You'll need to play with scaling the amplitude of the motion (using multiplication) and with the center of the motion (addition and subtraction). Some handy tips for this exercise:

- Don't use normalized units for this because drawing the circular pupil is hard with them. Use 'height', 'pix' or 'cm' depending on what you feel most comfortable with.
- Make sure you draw the white elliptical part of the eye first and the pupil second (by having the component for the pupil *below* the component for the white of the eye in the Routine view).
- Start with just one eye while you get the settings right. When you've done that you can right-click the Component and then 'Copy' and 'Paste' it back in ('Paste Component' is in the **Experiment** menu of the Builder or `Ctrl-Alt-V`). That way, the settings for the second eye will all be done and the only thing that will need changing is the position.

Solution: Page 287

6

PROVIDING FEEDBACK: SIMPLE CODE COMPONENTS

Learning objectives: Here you'll learn how to add more flexible pieces of Python code to your experiment, with multi-line statements and the option to choose when they get executed.

The Builder interface is quite flexible in what it can achieve, but ultimately there's a limit to what can be done with such a graphical interface. When you want to go further, you can add custom Python code to almost any point in your study using 'Code Components'. With these, the options for your experiment become almost limitless. Most tasks need very little custom Python code but it's good to know the basics. The following examples all show you how to make use of such a Component.

As an example, we take the existing Stroop task from earlier and add a feedback option where the message can be customized according to the response of the participant. You might wonder why PsychoPy doesn't just provide some sort of feedback component so that you don't have to write code, but there are so many different ways you might want to customize the feedback you give that the dialog box to do this graphically would become as hard to use as writing the code! For instance, not only might you want to say 'correct' and 'incorrect', but you might want to tell people their reaction time (or not) or provide more complex criteria for what messages are given (if they get the answer right on this type of trial then do one thing, but if they get it right on another then do something else). The possibilities are limitless and this is where a code snippet can be so useful.

Pro Tip: If you ask the forum for help then send your code

If you contact the PsychoPy users forum, asking for help because some aspect of your experiment doesn't work, then think carefully about where the problem might conceivably stem from. Hand-generated code is obviously the place where many experiments can go wrong. If you have any Code Components in your study then you probably need to copy and paste them into the forum post so that others can see your actual code if it might conceivably be relevant.

6.1 PROVIDING FEEDBACK

One very common requirement is that we need to provide feedback to a participant. In this case we need an `if` statement so that `if` they are wrong the text of a feedback object says 'You were wrong' and gives them some positive message if they were correct. This can't easily be inserted into a Builder Component. What we can do in this case is insert a Code Component.

Open your Stroop experiment from Chapter 2. Now the first thing you need to do is add a new Routine called **feedback** and place it immediately after the **trial** Routine, but within the same loop. Click on the **Insert Routine** button in the Flow, as in Figure 6.1. Select the **(new)** option and give your Routine the name **feedback**.

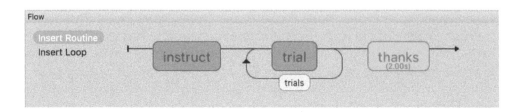

FIGURE 6.1 Inserting a new Routine into the Flow of our Stroop task.

When you've typed in the name you can select the place where the new Routine will be inserted. Put it after the **trial** Routine but before the end of the loop. Your flow should now look like Figure 6.2.

Now select the **feedback** Routine (either by clicking on it in the Flow or by selecting its tab in the Routines panel). It should be an empty Routine with no Components. We need to use two Components here, a Text Component to

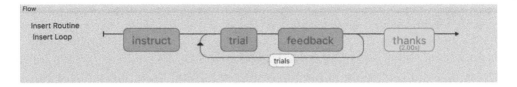

FIGURE 6.2 Flow of the Stroop task after adding the `feedback` Routine.

draw the actual feedback text and a Code Component to determine the contents of the feedback message. The order they appear in is important: the code within the Routine is always run in the order it appears, with the top item being run first. We need to make sure that the Code Component is executed before the Text Component or the contents of the Text Component will not be set as expected. We can reorder Components afterwards by right-clicking on them and moving up/down, but it's easier just to create them in the correct order (code first, in this case).

Create a Code Component and give it the name **setMsg** to remind yourself that this code is setting the contents of the feedback message. Now, a Code Component has several tabs to set code that will run at different points in the experiment. Think carefully about what your code needs to do and therefore at which locations it needs to run. For some things you may need to execute code in multiple parts of your study. For instance, with an eye tracker you

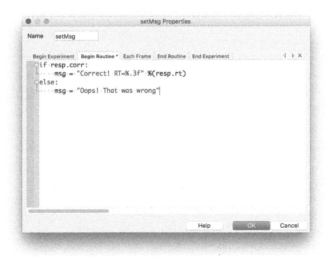

FIGURE 6.3 Setting the properties of the `setMsg` Code Component. All this is set to occur at the beginning of the Routine.

may need to initialize the hardware at the start of the experiment, then reset its clock and start sampling at the start of the Routine, check the eye position on each screen refresh and then disconnect the hardware at the end of the study. In our study all we need is some code that runs at the start of the Routine. Note that this is running immediately after the **trial** Routine and any variables created there will still be available to us in our new **feedback** Routine. Insert the code in Figure 6.3 into the tab called **Begin Routine**. Make sure you type it exactly. Note that two of the lines are indented (you can press **Tab** to get the indent).

Pro Tip: Choose good names for Components

It's a really good idea to give a little thought to the names of the Components that you add to your experiment. While you're adding your Component its purpose was probably (hopefully) obvious, but when you come back and look at the experiment later on (next year when you create a related study) the contents of each Component will not be obvious at all. It will then be really annoying if you have to click on each item to see what it was because the names they were given were simply 'text_1' or 'code_3'. Also, any components that are going to appear in the data file (e.g. keyboard items) need to be given good names so that in the data files you can see what they were: Was this the keyboard that merely advanced the experiment or was it the one where the participant gave their response?

Our Code Component creates the variable called **msg** at the beginning of the Routine and sets it to one of two values. The values are based on **resp.corr**. This only works because our Keyboard Component in the **trial** Routine was called **resp** and it always has an attribute called **corr**. Note that your data files also have a column called **resp.corr** if you've set them up in this way. The value of **resp.corr** is either **True** or **False** (or 1 or 0, which are equivalent to **True** or **False** in Python) and if **resp.corr** is **True** then we set **msg** to be the text 'Correct!'

So now all we need to do is create our Text Component to present our feedback message. The variable, **msg**, can be used just like the variables we were fetching earlier on from our conditions files, by inserting it into Components using the $ sign to indicate code. Go ahead and create a new Text Component and give it the values in Figure 6.4. Remember to set your message text to update **every repeat**.

FIGURE 6.4 Properties of the `feedbackText` Component. Note that '$msg' is going to be 'set every repeat' and that this needs to be done after the variable 'msg' has been created (in your Code Component).

📢 Warning: Order of Components in a Routine

Code for each Component of your Routine is executed in the order that the Components appear on the screen. For stimuli you can use this order to decide which stimulus appears 'in the front'. Lower stimuli in the Routine are executed later, so they will obscure stimuli that are higher in the Routine. In the case of a Code Component you usually want the code to come before the stimuli that it will affect (otherwise it will affect them on the *subsequent* frame or the *subsequent* routine not the current one).

6.2 UPDATING THE FEEDBACK COLOR

This already works (or, if not, go back and make sure your text matches exactly what was in Figure 6.4) but we could tweak it further. Let's set the text to be different colors as well. We could set it to be red if the participant was wrong and green if they were right. To do that we need to add a couple of extra lines into our if...else statement. As well as creating the variable msg we create msgColor and set it to either 'red' or 'green':

```
if resp.corr:
    msg = "Correct!"
    msgColor = "green"
else:
    msg = "Oops! That was wrong"
    msgColor = "red"
```

Now you need to go to the Text Component again and alter its properties so that the color is set to be $msgColor and the updates are set to every repeat for this as well.

6.3 REPORTING THE REACTION TIME

We could also set the feedback message to report the reaction time (let's just do this if the participant gets the answer correct). This is the most complex step of the current chapter so pay attention! The reaction time from a keyboard response is stored as an attribute rt and can be accessed using the variable resp.rt, where resp is the name of our Keyboard Component. So how do we insert the value of this reaction time (which is a number) into our string of text? In Python we can convert a number to a string using the function str() and we can add two strings together just using +, so the following would work:

```
msg = "Correct! RT=" + str(resp.rt)
```

Although this works, there are two problems. The first is that the reaction time is displayed to a ridiculous number of decimal places. Although the computer clock records the time with a precision of approximately nanoseconds, the reality is that your keyboard is not that precise. Let's reduce the number of decimal places to 3 (giving the reaction time effectively in milliseconds). For a standard USB keyboard this is still more precise than is warranted, but more reasonable. The second is that, if we wanted to add other text or other variables to this message, the method of *adding* strings quickly gets cumbersome. An alternative is to use Python string formatting. There are several different systems for doing this that end up being roughly equivalent, but we'll look at the newer one using "{}".format(value) which will be familiar to people used to programming in .NET. There is yet another, older method, using insertions like %i, %f that you may be more comfortable with if you know those methods from C or MATLAB (see https://pyformat.info/ for more detail about both methods) but we won't get into that method as well!

```
msg = "Correct! RT={:.3f}".format(resp.rt)
```

The way this works is that in the string there are some curly brackets {}, which indicate to Python that a variable needs to be inserted here. Then the characters :.3f indicate that it should be formatted as a floating point value with three digits after the decimal place. After the string finished it was 'formatted' by the function called format() to which we gave a variable to be inserted resp.rt (it could have been several variables but we only needed one). So we inserted resp.rt as a floating point value correct to 3 decimal places {:.3f} in our string.

We could easily have added further text after the insertion, or altered the value of the float or added other variables to the feedback as well. For instance, we could have:

```
msg = "{} was correct! RT={:.3f} ms".format(resp.keys, resp.rt*1000)
```

The code above inserts two variables, one of which is a string ({} fetches the value resp.keys) and one of which is an integer ({:i} with value resp.rt*1000). You can see there is further text after the final integer giving the units ('ms').

 Pro Tip: String formatting options

Here are some of the common ways of formatting inserted variables using string format() functions.

Code	Effect
{}	Auto-insert with default formatting
{:s}	Insert a string
{:.5s}	Insert first 5 characters
{:f}	Insert a float
{:.2f}	Insert a float with 2 decimal places
{:i}	Insert an integer
{:03i}	Insert an integer padded with zeros to be 3 characters long (001, 002, …)
{:3i}	Insert an integer padded with *spaces* to be 3 characters long
{:+i}	Insert an integer but force it to show its sign

The syntax above is based on a system in Microsoft's `.NET` Framework.

The website https://pyformat.info/ provides a fantastic reference for the myriad ways to format your strings using either syntax.

6.4 IDEAS FOR USEFUL CODE SNIPPETS

Table 6.1 should give you some ideas of pieces of code that you could add to your experiment, but there are infinitely (or at least a lot!) more options. How do you find them? How, for example, could you possibly have deduced that `t` was the value for the current time in the Routine, or that `random()` gives you a random number (rather than `rand()`, for example)? The best way to see what things are possible is to compile your experiment into a script and use that to go and investigate the code that will be in place. Any of the objects you see in that script you could also use yourself, in your Code Components or in the parameter boxes of your components.

TABLE 6.1 Some useful code ideas to insert into your Builder experiments.

Code	Effect
`random()`	Inserts a random number. Varies between 0 and 1
`t`	Time (in seconds) since start of Routine
`frameN`	Number of (completed) frames since start of Routine. Note that this is 0 on first frame and 1 on the second frame etc
`frameDur`	The (expected) duration of each frame. This is measured at the start of the experiment, if possible, and set to 1/60.0 if not
`if frameN % 5 == 0: .....`	Do something every 5 frames. Google for 'modulo' to find out about %. Don't insert the dots! These are just our way of saying 'put your code here'!
`globalClock.getTime()`	Time since start of study. Note that this is not the start of the first trial; it will include a period at the beginning where stimuli were loading and the dialog box was waiting for input
`continueRoutine=False`	Ends the *current* Routine. This cannot be applied to arbitrary Routines, unfortunately, only to the current one
`trials.finished=True`	Ends a loop (here we used the `trials` loop). This ends at the point when the loop goes to its next iteration, which may not be immediately
`expInfo['participant']`	Access values from the info dialog box (here we fetch the `participant`). This is a very useful way of controlling, for instance, which block someone is in, by creating a variable in the info dialog
`stim.status==FINISHED`	Tests whether the `stim` component has finished. Often used to sync two stimuli. Possible values for status are `FINISHED`, `STARTED` and `NOT_STARTED`. Note that a single '=' will usually give a syntax error here

Pro Tip: Finding out what attributes an object has

Table 6.1 gives you some idea of the sort of attributes that PsychoPy objects have, but to make it exhaustive would require a bigger book than this one! So how would you work out what attributes an object in a Python script has? Compiling the experiment to a script and seeing what is commonly used is one way, but most objects have more attributes that aren't used in every script, so how would you find those?

Python has a function called `dir()` that you can apply to anything to find out what attributes it might have. For instance, to find out what values exist in the `trials` loop you could do `print(dir(trials))`. You need to do this at some point after it has started. You could create a Code Component to execute it at the beginning of a Routine (choose one that's inside the loop so that the loop will have been created).

This will output many different items, including the following:

```
'nRemaining', 'nReps', 'nTotal', 'thisIndex', 'thisN',
'thisRepN'.
```

These indicate that items like `trials.nRemaining` and `trials.nReps` are variables that you could access within your scripts. This trick of using `dir()` works with almost anything.

6.5 REPORTING PERFORMANCE OVER THE LAST FIVE TRIALS

Often people want to keep track of the performance of participants, particularly as a criterion to exit a practice period (see Exercise 6.2). We'll measure performance over the *last five* trials and report it back to participants. Actually, we could use a larger period, like the last 10 trials, but the key is that we don't simply take the overall average; we want something that focuses more on recent performance rather than overall performance.

Save a new copy of the Extended Stroop demo but, instead of reporting the performance of the last trial to participants, take the average over the last five trials. To do this you'll need to adapt your current feedback code.

To track performance you *could* interrogate the Experiment Handler to fetch the data (which it stores for you as you go) but that requires more knowledge of the underlying objects. An easier solution is to keep your own list of whether or not participants were correct, and update and check this after each trial.

We can do this just by making a few changes to the Code Component called **message** in the **feedback** Routine that was already being used.

Open up that **message** Component and set the **Begin Experiment** tab to the following. The line creating the (empty) **msg** was probably there already. Thus:

```
msg = ''
corr = []
```

This just creates an empty Python 'list' object which allows us to store an arbitrary set of things and add to it along the way. What we need to add is, following each trial, whether or not the participant got the correct answer. From the existing code you should be able to spot that this is simply **resp.corr**. To add this to our list object called **corr** we need to use the **append** method, like this:

```
corr.append(resp.corr)
```

OK, so now we're keeping track of the sequence of correct/incorrect responses. Lastly, we need to use this list to calculate a performance. How would we do that in Python? If we keep adding entries to the list, one on each trial, then we want to extract the final five items in that list. In Python you can extract particular parts of a list (or letters in a string) by using square brackets. The general shape of those queries is **variableName[start:end]** (and since Python starts counting at 0) so:

- **corr[0:5]** would be the *first five* entries
- **corr[3:8]** would be five entries starting from the fourth (because we start counting at 0, number 3 is the fourth number!)

If you don't specify the start/end points (on either side of the :) then Python will take the entries from the *very start* or to the *very end*. Also, if you specify negative values as indices then it will represent the number backwards from the end of the list rather than the number forwards from the start. For example:

- **corr[:5]**, as before, gives the first five entries
- **corr[3:]** gives all the entries, starting from the fourth
- **corr[-5:]** gives the last five entries

Now we know how to extract the last five entries, we need to know how many correct answers there were. Given that we store these as 1 for 'correct' and 0 for 'incorrect' we can simply use the Python function **sum()** to calculate the total correct from a given list (or subset). Let's create a variable called **nCorr** that takes the sum of the last five.

We can keep adding this to the same place (the **Begin Routine** section of the **message** Code Component). This section should end up looking like this:

```
# create msg according to whether resp.corr is 1 or 0
if resp.corr: # stored on last run of routine
```

```
    msg = "Correct! RT={:.3f}".format(resp)
else:
    msg = "Oops! That was wrong"

# track (up to) the last 5 trials
corr.append(resp.corr)
nCorr = sum(corr[-5:])
nResps = len(corr[-5:])
msg += "({} out of {} correct)".format(nCorr, nResps)
```

The first lines of the code create the conditional `msg`, as before. Then we append the value `resp.corr` to our list of responses and calculate the number that were correct in the last five. We also want to know *how many* trials that is taken over; it would be strange to tell the participant '1 out of 5 correct' if they've only actually had two trials. The code `len(corr[-5:])` tells us the *length* of the list subset that we're using, just as `sum(corr[-5:])` tells us its sum.

The last step is to append this to the value `msg` that we've already created. You could use `msg = msg + ` .... but we used the special shortcut `+=` to do that for us. This is a common shorthand for 'add something to my variable' used in many programming languages.

 Pro Tips: Inserting good comments

Note that, even though our code block only has a few lines in it, we inserted several comments. That isn't just because this is a textbook, but something you should keep doing to remember how your code works. **Insert lots of comments for yourself.** You'd be amazed how, in the future, you won't remember what the lines of code were for. You can think of comments in your code as a love letter from current you to future you. Future you is probably very busy, so be nice!

6.6 EXERCISES AND EXTENSIONS

EXERCISE 6.1: ABORT PRACTICE WHEN PERFORMANCE REACHES 4/5 CORRECT

What happens when you want to abort your practice session based on a performance criterion? In Section 6.5 you learned how to track what the

(Continued)

performance was over the last five trials. Try and use the calculations in that code to abort your practice trials when participants reach 4/5 correct.

Solution: Page 288

EXERCISE 6.2: SHOW PROGRESS ON THE SCREEN WITH TRIAL NUMBER

Sometimes you want to be able to show progress through the experiment. Sometimes that's for the participant's morale in a long and boring study, and sometimes it helps you debug an experiment to see what's going on. There are also various ways to do it (e.g. in text or in a progress bar).

Insert a Text Component into your experiment, positioned in the lower right corner, that gives the number of completed trials in this loop and the total number of trials to be conducted, for example a simple string like '4/30'. This could be done for any of your experiments so far (e.g. just the basic Stroop task).

To do this you need to know how to identify the right numbers from the `trials` loop and combine them into a string.

Solution: Page 288

7

RATINGS: MEASURE THE 'BIG 5' PERSONALITY CONSTRUCTS

> **Learning objectives:** How to use rating scales and collect questionnaire data.

We've learnt a lot so far about experiments in cognitive psychology, studying reaction times to conflicting and consistent conditions, for example. Often in psychology we also want to collect 'ratings' from participants, and this chapter primarily focuses on how to collect those.

Ratings can be used for a wide range of different things, however. They may be ratings about a stimulus ('How attractive do you find this image?') or ratings about our confidence ('How certain are you about your last response?'). In fact, the same scale could even be used not for a rating at all but simply to provide a useful way of collecting responses along a continuum ('How long do you think that stimulus was presented for in seconds?').

The measurement of personality dimensions is, naturally, an area of substantial interest in the behavioral sciences. Even when a study isn't ostensibly about personality, it might be useful to consider whether variables of interest also correlate with personality dimensions. For example, when measuring participants' visual perception in a task, it might also be useful to know about that individual's 'Openness to experience'.

7.1 INSTRUMENTS FOR THE MEASUREMENT OF PERSONALITY

There are many personality measurement tools and lots of them are more precise and/or reliable than the one we use here. Some aim just to measure the 'Big 5' personality constructs (OCEAN: Openness to experience, Conscientiousness, Extraversion, Agreeableness, Neuroticism). Some of the tools aim to measure sub-dimensions within the Big 5 (often referred to as facets). To do that very well might take many questions, and some of them may require you to pay a fee. Here we'll use a relatively short instrument (that's what such a tool is called by people in the field) consisting of just 120 items, so that you won't take all day collecting a full data set on yourself! We've also chosen to use a public-domain package, meaning that we (and you) don't have to pay any license fees to use it legally.

The website http://ipip.ori.org/ has a range of further information about using these personality inventories and provides links to a number of public-domain versions, as well as information about their history. One of the tools listed on that site is the IPIP-NEO-120, developed by John A. Johnson (2014). This tool is designed to be used relatively quickly (so that it could be used alongside other measurements) but could also measure a number of facets for each. Johnson ended up measuring six facets for each of the Big 5 dimensions and each facet was measured using four items, leading to the grand total of 120 items on which participants have to rate themselves. As well as using the version that we create in this chapter you could corroborate what we find with the same items on Johnson's website (http://www.personal.psu.edu/~j5j/IPIP/ipipneo120.htm). Another strength of this inventory is that Johnson has also provided, on Open Science Framework (http://osf.io/tbmh5/), all the raw data from some very large samples (619,150 participants from this IPIP-NEO-120 instrument) so if you want to see some huge sets of normative data you can download the original data from that resource.

 Warning: Educational purposes only

It should be noted (as it is on Johnson's website) that this study and the associated materials are all provided for educational purposes. This is not a gold standard of personality. It should not be used by people without training in the caveats of personality measures, nor for clinical purposes. As with all the other studies in this book we are merely passing this on for educational purposes, for you to learn about collecting such data in a laboratory, but we expect you to have professional training and support (beyond the scope of this book) in how to use the tools wisely.

In Johnson's IPIP-NEO-120, as in most personality measures, the items (e.g. 'Leave my belongings around') are presented to the participants and they have to rate on a 5-point scale how accurately this describes them (1 = Very inaccurate, 5 = Very accurate). Some of the items are inverted in their logic. For instance, 'I love to read challenging material' and 'I avoid philosophical discussions' both relate to the same facet, but have opposite meanings in that facet. Therefore some items are then reverse scored (if the participant rates themselves as '5' this contributes 1 to the facet score and vice versa).

CREATING THE IPIP-NEO-120 IN PSYCHOPY

The first thing to do, as always, is to create a conditions spreadsheet that specifies what varies from one 'trial' to the next. In this instance we need a row for each of our items and in order to keep track of further information for analysis it's handy to have columns specifying not just the item itself, but information about it, like the name of the personality dimension and facet that it measures. We also need to know whether this item is positively or negatively scored.

To save typing in all 120 rows of information (all of which can be found at http://ipip.ori.org/) you can download the conditions file for this study from the companion website. You can see the first few rows in Figure 7.1.

	A	B	C	D	E	F
1	Number	Item	Scoring	Code	Facet	Factor
2		1 Worry about things.	+	N1	Anxiety	Neuroticism
3		2 Fear for the worst.	+	N1	Anxiety	Neuroticism
4		3 Am afraid of many things.	+	N1	Anxiety	Neuroticism
5		4 Get stressed out easily.	+	N1	Anxiety	Neuroticism
6		5 Get angry easily.	+	N2	Anger	Neuroticism
7		6 Get irritated easily.	+	N2	Anger	Neuroticism
8		7 Lose my temper.	+	N2	Anger	Neuroticism
9		8 Am not easily annoyed.	-	N2	Anger	Neuroticism
10		9 Often feel blue.	+	N3	Depression	Neuroticism
11		10 Dislike myself.	+	N3	Depression	Neuroticism
12		11 Am often down in the dumps.	+	N3	Depression	Neuroticism
13		12 Feel comfortable with myself.	-	N3	Depression	Neuroticism

FIGURE 7.1 The first few rows of the IPIP conditions file. For each item we store its text, whether it should be scored positively or negatively, and the personality dimension and facet that it describes. The codes are the standard IPIP codes for the different facets of personality (e.g. N1 is the first facet of the neuroticism dimension).

Then we need a Routine where we present some text (the sentence), and a Rating Scale Component with which to record the participant responses. The text should last indefinitely; we don't want to pressure participants to respond quickly on this occasion. The rating scale should also last indefinitely but, by default, participants can finalize their response by selecting a point on the scale slider and pressing the <return> key. So the last thing we should add is a note to point out that they need to press <return> to continue to the next item. We don't want participants to sit there looking at a static screen, wondering when the next trial will start. That would be awkward. By now you're probably up to speed on how to select the settings for the Text Components for the **item**. The key settings that need changing are below. Note that the name of the column in the conditions file that stores the item text is 'Item' so we'll give our object the name `item` so that it differs (in the capital first letter) from that column name:

- Name: `item`
- Text: `$Item`
- Start: `0`
- End:
- Pos: `(0, 0.5)`
- Units: `norm`

For the message you might use the following settings in another Text Component. We can put the message relatively low on the screen to keep it well out of the way of the main objects (the item and the response). We've also made the font size a little smaller (0.07 in normalized units) here than the main text of the item (0.1 in normalized units).

- Name: `msgContinue`
- Text: `Use the mouse to select a response and then press the <return> key`
- Start: `0`
- End:
- Size: `0.07`
- Pos: `(0, -0.8)`
- Units: `norm`

CREATING THE RATING SCALE

PsychoPy provides an input option called the Rating Scale (in the `inputs` category of the Component Panel). This provides a wide range of options for specifying rating scale responses, whether you want verbal category labels for responses, numeric values or a continuous linear scale. The rating responses for each item in the IPIP are on a 5-point Likert scale. The labels given to the end points are 'Very Accurate' and 'Very Inaccurate'.

The settings that we'll need can be seen in Figure 7.2 but as this is a somewhat complex Component in PsychoPy (it may be simplified in future versions) let's take a slightly more in-depth look at some of the options.

7.2 CATEGORIES, LIKERT OR CONTINUOUS RATINGS

There are several ways to control the types of scale and the labels that get added to the ratings.

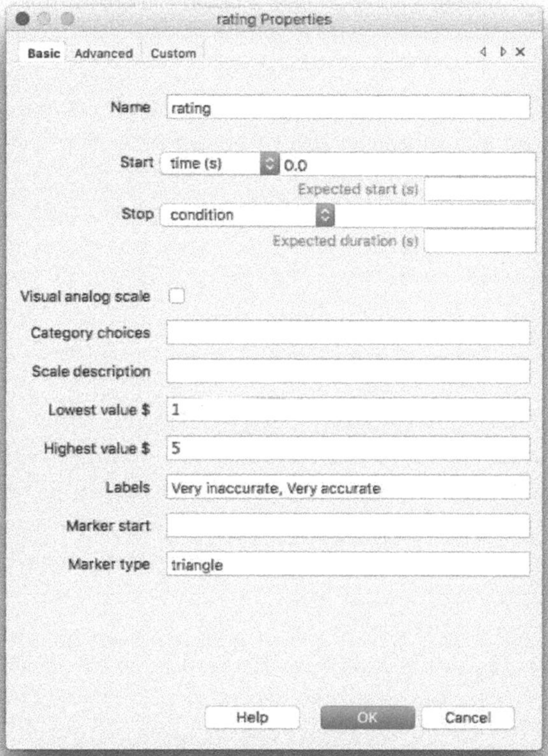

FIGURE 7.2   The settings for the Rating Scale in the IPIP personality measure. Note the way the `Labels` value has been specified with two comma-separated values to refer to the end points of the scale (don't use the `Categories` setting for an ordinal variable like the rating we need).

For **categorical scales** you set the value of the **Categories** parameter to the set of words that you would like to appear. These should be comma-separated values and the more commas you insert the more points you'll get on the scale. This makes most sense if you have categories that aren't ordered and each needs a label. For instance, you could ask participants to choose their favorite fruit and give categories of `Apple,Banana,Pear,Orange`. If you specify the `Categories` variable then the data will come back with text labels as the responses, which may be hard for you to analyze. For instance, in the current study it would be harder to analyze responses of 'Very accurate' and 'Very inaccurate' than to analyze numeric values where we could add/subtract them.

A Likert scale is a form of ordinal data in which participants can select one of several ordered values. Typically these are 5- or 7-point scales so participants would provide a value from 1 to 5 or 1 to 7, where the end points might be something like 'Not at all' to 'Very much'. To create a Likert scale in the PsychoPy Rating Scale Component you should **not** use the `Categories` setting; this is an ordinal scale and those are nominal (categorical) values. Instead you should set the `Lowest value` parameter and the `Highest value` parameter (e.g. set them to 1 and 7 for a 7-point scale) and then set the `Labels` parameter to indicate how these should be labelled on the scale. You can insert multiple labels, separated by commas, and these will be spread evenly across the scale. For instance, you could set a 7-point scale with labels `Sad, Neutral, Happy` and the 'Sad' label will appear for value 1 (the left most value), 'Neutral' will appear in the center, and 'Happy' will appear at value 7 (the right-hand value). In the data file the responses will be recorded as integers from 1 to 7.

For our personality test we need a 5-point rating scale with labels that go from 'Very inaccurate' to 'Very accurate'. In the original version every one of the response options was labelled. For instance, the middle value in Johnson's version is labelled 'Neither inaccurate nor accurate'. As well as being rather confusing this leads to an awful lot of distracting text on the screen. Therefore we have set (in Figure 7.2) a scale from 1 to 5 with labels that are simply `Very inaccurate, Very accurate.`

Continuous scales don't constrain the responses to be at particular integer values; participants can respond at any arbitrary position on the line. To get this behavior in PsychoPy tick the `Visual analog scale` option. When you use this option the values will always be returned as a decimal value between 0 and 1 and the scale labels do not show.

7.3 CONTROLLING WHEN THE RATING IS FINALIZED

The Rating Scale Component has a further page of `Advanced` settings. In the case of the current experiment some of these are also going to be useful. In particular, one of the settings says `Show accept,` which means that a button will be presented underneath the Rating Scale, which will show the current selected value and allow the user to finalize this decision by pressing the button. In our case that looks a little incongruous because the button will have a number on it (the numeric value of the current rating selected) which might confuse the participant. Let's hide the button altogether by unticking the `Show accept` box.

Participants will still need to accept their response as final, which they can do by pressing the `<return>` key, but this probably isn't obvious to them, so, in the absence of the 'Accept' button, we should probably provide a message to participants indicating that they need to press `<return>` in order to continue, hence the `msgContinue` Component that we created above.

Alternatively we could have ticked the **Single click** option. When that is turned on, the Rating Scale considers itself 'finished' as soon as any response has been made and the experiment will therefore advance to the next routine as soon as any rating is made. In our case that might be annoying; participants might want to adjust their self-rating after a moment of reflection, so we won't do that.

Another related option is the **Disappear** parameter. With this option enabled, users can set a particular rating to disappear as soon as the response is made. In our case that would not be noticeable because we advance to the next trial as soon as the response is made, but if your trial were to continue beyond the duration of the Rating Scale then it might be useful to hide the rating. For instance, you might have a photograph and ask people to rate the photo on three different scales ('Attractiveness', 'Brightness', 'Openness') and want each scale to disappear once a response is made for that scale.

MORE ADVANCED RATING SCALE SETTINGS

The Rating Scale Component is a complicated beast if you want it to be. There are lots of things you can control, like the shape of the icon that indicates your current decision, or how a trial should advance. For instance, by default, a button comes with your Rating Scale that says 'Key, click' to inform users how to respond. It then becomes the selected value once they've made a response, giving you the chance to confirm it. The surprise is that you can actually control the text presented on this button using a triplet of hidden settings, namely **acceptPreText** and **acceptText** and **showValue**, which is just one example of the level of customization here.

In fact, the Rating Scale ended up having so many settings that there were going to be too many to fit in a reasonable-sized dialog box! Jeremy Gray, who added this Component, decided to provide parameters in the dialog for the most commonly used settings and also a 'Customize everything' box (in the **Custom** tab) that receives text specifying all the possible arguments the Rating Scale understands.

If you choose to use the **Customize everything** option then note that none of the other settings are used except for the **Name** of the Component; once started you need to insert *all* your parameters into this **Customize everything** box. Here's an example of how the code might look in the box:

```
low=1, high=7,
precision=10,
labels=('No', 'OK', 'OMG Yes!'),
acceptPreText='Start rating!',
acceptText='Final answer?',
showValue=False,
```

The code will create a 7-point Likert-style scale, with three labels that will appear on the two ends and the center (if you give more labels then they will distribute evenly across the scale). Then we use `acceptPreText` and `acceptText` to control the text in the button before and after the participant makes any response. Note that the setting `showValue=False` is needed in order to allow the `accept-Text` setting to have an effect. With `showValue=True` (which is its default) the `acceptText` will be replaced by the currently selected value.

There are too many ways to customize the Rating Scale for us to go through here. One of the exercises at the end of the chapter is for you to work out how to find out about the others.

7.4 WHAT TO STORE

Also in the **Advanced** panel are settings to control what gets stored in your data file. You obviously want the final rating to be stored and typically you would store the response time as well (it might not be very informative, especially if your participant forgot they have to press the `<return>` key, but it isn't costly to save it). In some studies it might be useful to know the set of positions that the participant selected before finalizing their response. Beware if doing this, however, that it makes the data harder to analyze because the entries for each trial might now look like `[3, 4, 2]` if the participant pressed three keys, and this is harder to work with unless you're a whiz with your data package. It's much easier to analyze a single numeric value in a single cell.

The next step is not strictly necessary but can make your life easier in the analysis stage. In this study some of the items are scored negatively, whereas others are scored positively. For example, the item 'Find it difficult to approach others' in the Neuroticism factor is *positive*, because a high rating does indicate *higher* neuroticism. Conversely, 'Dislike changes' in the Openness factor is *negative* because a high rating here would indicate *lower* Openness. In the spreadsheet we can see which are which by their `Scoring` variable, which is '+' or '−'. For positive scoring the participant **response** (a number from 1 to 5) is simply the score for that item, and for negative scoring we have to invert that scale. The inverted scale just means the score is going to be `6-response`. This obviously means that a response of 1 becomes a score of 5 (6–1) and vice versa. We could perform this analysis after collecting our data, but doing so manually is the sort of thing that can lead to errors. Let's get PsychoPy to calculate the score automatically given the `scoring` variable and the participant's response, and save that as an extra column in our data file.

To do this we need a Code Component to perform the calculation on each trial. We can set it to run in the **trial** Routine, and we need to add the following to the **End Routine** section of the Code Component so that it gets executed after the participant has made their response each time:

```
if Scoring == '+':
    thisExp.addData('score', rating.getRating())
elif Scoring == '-':
    thisExp.addData('score', 6-rating.getRating())
else:
    print("Got an unexpected Scoring value: {}".format(Scoring))
```

To explain how this works, **Scoring** was a variable stored in the conditions file, and is being updated on each pass around the trials loop. The function **thisExp.addData(name, value)** can be used at any point to add data to the experiment. The value **name** (where we used the value 'score') determines the title of the column where the data will be shown, and the **value** is what will be inserted into the row for the current trial. Specifying a **name** that wasn't already listed will implicitly add a new column to your data file. If a trial passes and no 'score' value is added then that cell will just be empty for that trial. The last thing we do is insert the **value** for this trial which comes from the **rating** object (the name we gave the Rating Scale Component) and specifically it has a method called **getRating()** which we are calling (it also has a **getRT()** method). As we discussed above, we want either simply **rating.getRating()** or **6 - rating.getRating()** to invert the score.

One other thing we've done here is to include an **else** statement even though we never expect to get anything other than '+' or '−' as the value. This is often good practice to alert you to the fact that there's a problem. If we have an error, or a missing value, in our conditions file then the code in this block won't record any data (because the value of 'Scoring' is something other than the two values we prepared for). So what we're doing here is just a little bit of integrity checking on our own conditions file and warning ourselves if something unexpected happened.

OK, that's it. Your data file should now be spitting out correctly scored data according to the negative/positive keys for the items (Figure 7.3). Check it for a few trials and make sure it does as you expected.

7.5 FINISHING YOUR TASK AND SCORING THE DATA

As in previous experiments it is worth adding an instructions routine to come before the trials loop and another routine to say 'thanks' afterwards. You might also

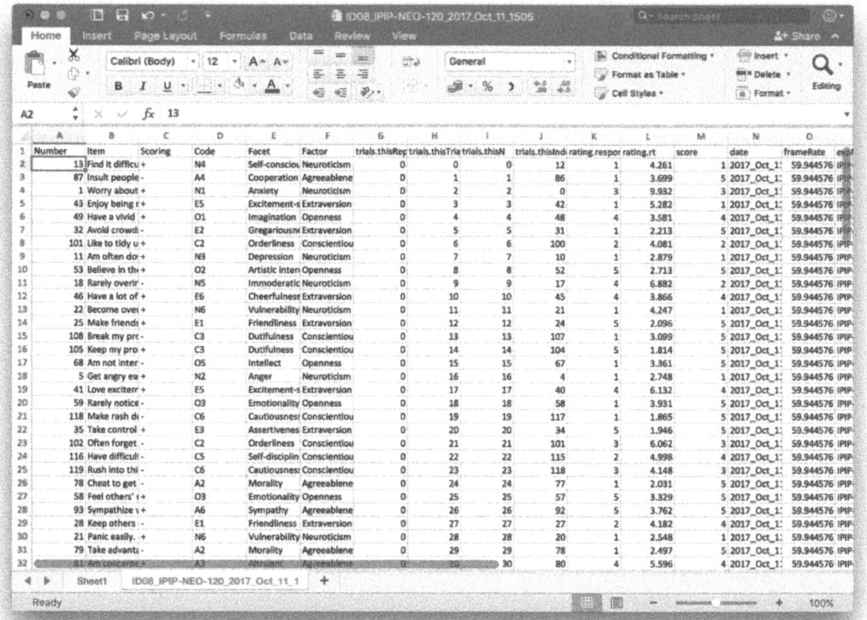

Number	Item	Scoring	Code	Facet	Factor	trials.thisRep	trials.thisTria	trials.thisN	trials.thisInd	rating.respor	rating.rt	score	date	frameRate	exp
13	Find it difficu	+	N4	Self-consciou	Neuroticism	0	0	0	12	1	4.261	1	2017_Oct_1	59.944576	IPIP-
87	Insult people	-	A4	Cooperation	Agreeablene	0	1	1	86	1	3.699	5	2017_Oct_1	59.944576	IPIP-
1	Worry about	+	N1	Anxiety	Neuroticism	0	2	2	0	3	9.932	3	2017_Oct_1	59.944576	IPIP-
43	Enjoy being r	+	E5	Excitement-s	Extraversion	0	3	3	42	1	5.282	1	2017_Oct_1	59.944576	IPIP-
49	Have a vivid	+	O1	Imagination	Openness	0	4	4	48	4	3.581	4	2017_Oct_1	59.944576	IPIP-
32	Avoid crowd:	-	E2	Gregariousn	Extraversion	0	5	5	31	1	2.213	5	2017_Oct_1	59.944576	IPIP-
101	Like to tidy u	+	C2	Orderliness	Conscientiou	0	6	6	100	2	4.081	2	2017_Oct_1	59.944576	IPIP-
11	Am often do	+	N3	Depression	Neuroticism	0	7	7	10	1	2.879	1	2017_Oct_1	59.944576	IPIP-
53	Believe in th	+	O2	Artistic inter	Openness	0	8	8	52	5	2.713	5	2017_Oct_1	59.944576	IPIP-
18	Rarely overir	-	N5	Immoderatic	Neuroticism	0	9	9	17	4	6.882	2	2017_Oct_1	59.944576	IPIP-
46	Have a lot of	+	E6	Cheerfulness	Extraversion	0	10	10	45	4	3.866	4	2017_Oct_1	59.944576	IPIP-
22	Become over	+	N6	Vulnerability	Neuroticism	0	11	11	21	1	4.247	1	2017_Oct_1	59.944576	IPIP-
25	Make friends	+	E1	Friendliness	Extraversion	0	12	12	24	5	2.096	5	2017_Oct_1	59.944576	IPIP-
108	Break my prc	-	C3	Dutifulness	Conscientiou	0	13	13	107	1	3.099	5	2017_Oct_1	59.944576	IPIP-
105	Keep my pro	+	C3	Dutifulness	Conscientiou	0	14	14	104	5	1.814	5	2017_Oct_1	59.944576	IPIP-
68	Am not inter	-	O5	Intellect	Openness	0	15	15	67	1	3.361	5	2017_Oct_1	59.944576	IPIP-
5	Get angry ea	+	N2	Anger	Neuroticism	0	16	16	4	1	2.748	1	2017_Oct_1	59.944576	IPIP-
41	Love exciterr	+	E5	Excitement-s	Extraversion	0	17	17	40	4	6.132	4	2017_Oct_1	59.944576	IPIP-
59	Rarely notice	-	O3	Emotionality	Openness	0	18	18	58	1	3.931	5	2017_Oct_1	59.944576	IPIP-
118	Make rash de	-	C6	Cautiousness	Conscientiou	0	19	19	117	1	1.865	5	2017_Oct_1	59.944576	IPIP-
35	Take control	+	E3	Assertivenes	Extraversion	0	20	20	34	5	1.946	5	2017_Oct_1	59.944576	IPIP-
102	Often forget	-	C2	Orderliness	Conscientiou	0	21	21	101	3	6.062	3	2017_Oct_1	59.944576	IPIP-
116	Have difficul	-	C5	Self-disciplin	Conscientiou	0	22	22	115	2	4.998	4	2017_Oct_1	59.944576	IPIP-
119	Rush into thi	-	C6	Cautiousness	Conscientiou	0	23	23	118	3	4.148	3	2017_Oct_1	59.944576	IPIP-
78	Cheat to get	-	A2	Morality	Agreeablene	0	24	24	77	1	2.031	5	2017_Oct_1	59.944576	IPIP-
58	Feel others'	+	O3	Emotionality	Openness	0	25	25	57	5	3.329	5	2017_Oct_1	59.944576	IPIP-
93	Sympathize v	+	A6	Sympathy	Agreeablene	0	26	26	92	5	3.762	5	2017_Oct_1	59.944576	IPIP-
28	Keep others	-	E1	Friendliness	Extraversion	0	27	27	27	2	4.182	4	2017_Oct_1	59.944576	IPIP-
21	Panic easily.	+	N6	Vulnerability	Neuroticism	0	28	28	20	1	2.548	1	2017_Oct_1	59.944576	IPIP-
79	Take advanta	-	A2	Morality	Agreeablene	0	29	29	78	1	2.497	5	2017_Oct_1	59.944576	IPIP-
81	Am concerne	+	A3	Altruism	Agreeablene	0	30	30	80	4	5.596	4	2017_Oct_1	59.944576	IPIP-

FIGURE 7.3 The raw data from a run of the IPIP-NEO-120. You end up with quite a lot of columns and rows of raw data but they can be summarized relatively easily using a 'Pivot Table' (see Figure 7.4).

want to add some further fields to the Experiment Info dialog (using the Experiment Settings menu). For instance, you might want to store the gender and age of the participant while measuring their personality characteristics.

You should now be able to run the task and collect data on how people rate themselves on these various items. The data are going to be saved in a csv file, as always. The resulting raw data files are quite large, with 120 rows of data and quite a number of columns. Analyzing them by hand would be a bit of a task. Luckily Excel has a trick up its sleeve to help us and, having done the scoring automatically in PsychoPy, is very easy. In fact, it presents an excellent chance to learn about 'Pivot Tables' in Excel (or most other spreadsheet packages). A Pivot Table is simply a way to summarize data from a larger table. In this case we can use it to find all the occurrences of the different codes (like E3, meaning the third facet of the Extraversion factor) and calculate the average score.

Select all your data (`Ctrl-A`), go to the `Data` menu and select `Summarize with PivotTable`. Microsoft likes to change the location and name of things on a regular basis, so we won't tell you exactly where those things are – it would spoil the fun! You may then get a dialog asking where you want to insert the Pivot Table.

FIGURE 7.4   Creating a 'Pivot Table' in Excel (or most other packages) makes it very easy to analyze your data for a participant. You need to use the fields (the column names in the raw data) called Code and Factor in the 'Rows box', and Score in the 'Values' box, to get this layout.

We think a new sheet seems reasonable, to keep the summary data separate from your raw data. Then a dialog box like the one in Figure 7.4 should appear. This shows various fields that you can use in your summary (the fields are the columns in your raw data) and different ways you can organize them (columns, rows, etc.). Drag the fields labelled **Code** and **Factor** into the 'Rows' box and drag the **Score** into the 'Values' box. Your summary of this participant's factor/facet scores should appear with all the averages calculated. You can play around with different configurations for these Pivot Tables while you work out what layout of values you like.

There you have it. A complete, abbreviated, five-factor personality test that you can run and analyze to your heart's content!

EXERCISES AND EXTENSIONS

EXERCISE 7.1: FIND OUT ABOUT RATING SCALE'S MANY ADVANCED SETTINGS

This task is very simple really (or at least it seems so). Just find out what other settings are available for the 'Customize Everything' box! What could be easier?

Solution: Page 289

EXERCISE 7.2: USE MULTIPLE RATINGS AT ONCE

Sometimes we want more than one rating scale on the screen at the same time. See if you can work out a combination of settings for the scales to make this possible and visually bearable. You probably don't want buttons that have to be pressed for both and you don't want them to end the Routine when complete either.

Note that you should be able to complete this task without needing the 'Customize everything' option; just using a combination of the dialog box parameters should work.

Solution: Page 290

8

RANDOMIZATION, BLOCKS AND COUNTERBALANCING: A BILINGUAL STROOP TASK

> **Learning objectives:** Many studies need trials to be presented in blocks and the blocks should be counterbalanced. Here, you'll learn how to create blocks of trials and how to control the order of those blocks, within and across subjects.

Many people ask us 'Can PsychoPy randomize my trials?', to which the answer is 'yes'. Note that the trials in all the experiments so far were randomly ordered, so it's clearly possible. It often turns out that what the person actually wants is to have trials organized by blocks and for these *blocks* to be presented randomly. This chapter will show you that creating blocks of trials to randomize is easy enough too, once you know how.

8.1 BLOCKING TRIALS

So far in our experiments, experimental conditions have varied from one trial to the next. We've seen how this can be controlled in a conditions file, which lists conditions in the format of one row per trial. Sometimes, however, we have conditions that we want to vary more slowly than trial to trial. That is, we want to group similar trials together into blocks. In effect, this means that while some variables may change from trial to trial, others change only when a new block of trials starts, and remain constant throughout that block of trials. Let's take an example from the famous 'Thatcher effect' (Thompson, 1980), which has been very influential in the field of face perception. To elicit this effect, the experimenter manipulates a photo of a face so that features like the mouth or eyes are inverted. This makes the face appear particularly grotesque. However, this striking impression occurs only when the face is presented upright; the otherwise striking manipulation is hardly noticeable if the entire face is shown upside-down. To investigate the generality of this effect, we could test if it also works with non-human faces (Dahl et al., 2010). This means making a design decision of whether to randomly intersperse human and monkey faces from trial to trial (e.g. `human human monkey human monkey monkey`), or to separate them into discrete blocks of all-human followed by all-animal trials (`human human human, monkey monkey monkey`).

The decision of whether to group trials into separate blocks, or to intersperse them, will be driven by a mix of practicality, previous literature and your hypotheses about underlying mechanisms or potential confounding factors. If you decide to group trials into blocks, then you also need to consider controlling the order of presentation of those blocks. Sometimes the ordering of blocks is straightforward: a block of practice trials must necessarily precede a block of actual experimental trials, for example. In other cases, we might be concerned about the transfer of learning across tasks. For example, we might carefully balance the order of blocks of human versus monkey face trials across subjects. Alternatively, we might be content to allow the order of blocks to vary completely randomly across subjects.

We'll illustrate how to run two blocks of trials by extending the Stroop task from Chapter 2, to present words from two languages rather than just English (Preston and Lambert, 1969). As well as controlling blocks of trials, we'll learn some general principles of using PsychoPy efficiently, such as reducing duplication of similar routines and loops.

8.2 THE BILINGUAL STROOP TASK

We've already encountered the Stroop task in Chapter 2. To recap, a key aspect of this phenomenon is that reading words in your native language is a very over-learned task, which is difficult to suppress. Hence when asked to report the color of some text, the semantic content of the text can interfere with what should be a simple color judgment. This interference is evidenced by the reporting of the color being slowed or incorrect. Because the effect is due to the automaticity of reading, it shouldn't occur when reporting the color of text written in a language that you aren't familiar with. For a fluent English speaker, it is easy to say that the word 'blue' is colored blue, but it is slower and more difficult to correctly report that the word 'blue' is colored red. By contrast, if that same English speaker is monolingual, saying the color of the word 'azul' poses no challenge, as there is no conflict between its printed color and its unknown semantic association with 'blue' in Spanish.

Info: Stroop for spy detection

Legend has it that the Stroop task was used in the Cold War to detect 'sleeper agents' (foreign-born spies posing long term as native-born citizens). If someone claiming to be born and raised in the United States nonetheless showed a Stroop effect for color words in Russian, that would be strong evidence that perhaps they were actually born and raised elsewhere. The Stroop effect is one of the few phenomena in psychology that might be robust enough to make individual judgments like this with some degree of confidence. And by its very nature, it is an effect that is hard to suppress voluntarily. Unfortunately, although it's a great story, we haven't seen any evidence that it was ever actually used in this way. If you find a reliable source, let us know!

So the magnitude of the Stroop interference effect should be stronger in a language in which one is fluent, rather than a language with which one only has some familiarity. It could therefore be used as an implicit test of how well a person has learned a language. We will create such an experiment, in which we will run the Stroop task in two languages. Here we will present the English words red, blue and green and contrast them to the corresponding Māori words, whero, kikorangi and kākāriki. The intention will be to compare a group of children in a Māori immersion schooling system (who should be bilingual in English and Māori) with a group whose education is primarily in English and who will have only some familiarity with Māori vocabulary. If the immersion schooling is effective in producing bilingualism, the Stroop interference effect should occur strongly in both languages for those pupils, while in the second group, interference should be marked only in English.

 Info: About the Māori language

Māori is the indigenous language of New Zealand. In the post-colonial period, its use in the education system was actively discouraged in favor of English. This resulted in a marked decline in the number of native speakers of the language. In the late twentieth century, a movement started to provide Māori language immersion education in some pre-schools, which eventually progressed to primary and secondary school level. This has gone some way to keeping the language vibrant and in use, although the number of fluent speakers remains small.

Pronunciation tips: The 'wh' consonant, as in *whero*, is generally pronounced as an 'f' sound (although in some regional dialects is it pronounced similarly to the 'wh' sound that some English speakers use in words like 'when'). Macrons indicate long-duration vowel sounds, so *kākāriki* is pronounced as *kaakaariki*.

8.3 BUILD A BLOCKED VERSION OF THE STROOP TASK

To create the blocked task, start with the basic Stroop experiment you created in Chapter 2. Its basic layout should look like the diagram in Figure 8.1: an introductory instruction routine; followed by the actual task routine, surrounded by a loop; and a concluding 'thank-you' routine. The loop controls the trials by being connected to a conditions file like the one in Figure 8.2, containing a column for each word to be presented (the **word** variable), its color value (**letterColor**), the arrow key corresponding to the correct answer (**corrAns**), and a column stating whether the word and its color are consistent (**congruent**).

If we wanted to randomly interleave the trials of Māori and English stimuli then we could simply add extra rows to our conditions file and allow PsychoPy's

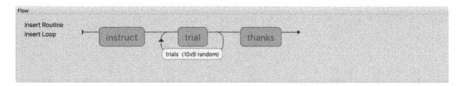

FIGURE 8.1 The layout of the simple one-block Stroop task from Chapter 2.

	A	B	C	D
1	word	letterColor	corrAns	congruent
2	red	red	left	1
3	red	green	down	0
4	red	blue	right	0
5	green	red	left	0
6	green	green	down	1
7	green	blue	right	0
8	blue	red	left	0
9	blue	green	down	0
10	blue	blue	right	1
11				

FIGURE 8.2 The conditions file for running the Stroop task in English. Note that the text coloring here is purely to make the organization of the file more visually apparent: PsychoPy doesn't know anything about the formatting we might apply to cells in a spreadsheet.

randomization to handle the mixing of the conditions across trials. For a blocked design, however, that isn't the correct approach. We want to split the variables for each block into separate conditions files (in this case, separate conditions files for the English and for the Māori language trials). The conditions file for running the task in Māori (see Figure 8.3) is identical to the English one (Figure 8.2), except for the words in the first column. Importantly, we should ensure that the variable names in the first row are identical across the two files.

So now we have the two conditions files, how should we structure the experiment? To run two blocks of trials, a common strategy for novice PsychoPy users is to create a separate routine for both blocks of trials, with each embedded in a loop connected to the appropriate conditions file for that block. Such an arrangement would look like the flow panel shown in Figure 8.4.

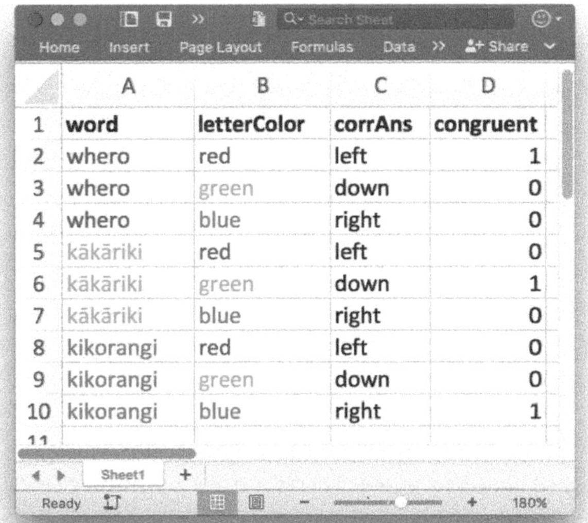

	A	B	C	D
1	**word**	**letterColor**	**corrAns**	**congruent**
2	whero	red	left	1
3	whero	green	down	0
4	whero	blue	right	0
5	kākāriki	red	left	0
6	kākāriki	green	down	1
7	kākāriki	blue	right	0
8	kikorangi	red	left	0
9	kikorangi	green	down	0
10	kikorangi	blue	right	1
11				

FIGURE 8.3 The conditions file for the Māori equivalent of the Stroop task.

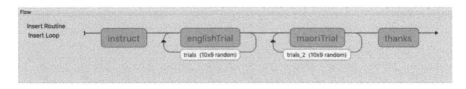

FIGURE 8.4 This might seem like the natural way to create a block of Māori and a block of English trials in the Stroop task, but this makes it hard to randomize the order of your blocks.

Although this arrangement looks logical, it isn't ideal for a number of reasons. For a start, it 'hard-wires' the order of the blocks, with English always being first and Māori second. This makes it challenging to control for order effects by running the blocks in the opposite sequence. With this arrangement, we'd need to create a second experiment, identical in every respect, except for having the order of blocks reversed. *We can't emphasize enough that you should strenuously resist the temptation to create multiple versions of an experiment.* Avoidable duplication is one of the cardinal sins of computer programming. And yes, even though you are using a graphical tool to produce your experiments, under the hood you are creating an actual Python computer program. The moment you create duplicated code, you also create a maintenance problem. For example, every time you make a tweak or improvement to the settings in one Builder file, you *must* remember to make *exactly* the same change in every other version. If any differences creep into the two versions, this could lead to an important confounding factor. Such a confound might mask a true experimental effect, or (just as bad) create an apparent effect that otherwise wouldn't exist.

The other sort of duplication in the arrangement above is that we have created two different routines to run each sort of trial. This is another common pitfall for novice PsychoPy users: failing to realize that it is often possible to 'recycle' routines under different conditions. In this case, there is no actual difference in the routines required to run the Stroop task in English versus Māori. In each case, we simply select a word, apply a color to it and then gather a response. The only difference is actually the conditions file that supplies the information required. The conditions file is specified in the loop, not the routine. So if the variable names in the two conditions files are identical, we can use exactly the same routine in each block.

In short, rather than an `englishTrial` and a `maoriTrial` we just need a single `trial` routine, and the language associated with that can change as needed.

NESTING LOOPS

The question then is how we attach our `trial` routine to two separate conditions files. The `trials` loop we used previously to control our conditions only allows for a single conditions file. How do we then control which block of trials is run? The trick is to encase the loop within *another* loop. We call this *nesting* the loops: the inner loop is nested within the outer loop. The inner loop controls the stimuli from trial to trial, as you saw in the experiments in earlier chapters. The outer loop controls which block of trials will run. To make their purposes clear, we could name the inner loop `trials` and the outer loop `blocks`. This arrangement is shown in Figure 8.5.

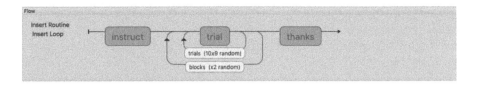

FIGURE 8.5 The ideal arrangement in Builder for presenting blocks of trials. The inner loop connects to a conditions file for information which changes from trial to trial (e.g. the words and colors of the Stroop task). The outer loop controls which conditions file the inner loop uses (either the English or Māori file).

How does the outer loop control which block of trials will run? The magic is in the way the two loops interact. In the inner loop, unlike in previous chapters, we don't insert a hard-wired, literal filename in the conditions file field (such as **English.xlsx** or **Maori.xlsx**). Instead, we insert a variable (or a Python expression) just as in other dialog boxes, which means that the conditions file-name is free to vary each time the loop starts. In this example, we're going to use this expression:

```
$language + '.xlsx'
```

As you've seen before, the **$** prefix tells Builder that this is a Python expression that needs to be evaluated, rather than a literal filename. The expression itself consists of a variable called **language**, which gets concatenated with the literal characters **.xlsx** (*concatenated* is programming jargon for 'joined together'). The clever bit is where the variable **language** comes from. We define it in a tiny conditions file that contains only three cells (see Figure 8.6).

 Pro Tip: Avoid non-ASCII characters in filenames

When computers were first created, they were limited in the sort of text they could process and display. From the 1960s through the 1980s, the dominant standard in the Western world was ASCII (American Standard Code for Information Interchange), which catered for up to 128 possible characters. This was (generally) enough to represent letters, numbers and punctuation in English. But it wasn't sufficient to represent other languages, some of which have thousands of characters. PsychoPy, however, generally

(Continued)

works pretty well with the modern Unicode standard for text encoding, which has mostly supplanted ASCII, meaning that it can read and display characters from most of the world's languages.

Unfortunately, some parts of computer operating systems hark back to the early days and are still prone to issues with non-ASCII characters. German users, for example, sometimes report that their experiment comes to a crashing halt simply because of an umlaut above a vowel in a filename. These issues are rare (and are generally caused by errors outside of PsychoPy itself). But they are common enough that we recommend users avoid non-ASCII characters in the filenames associated with their experiments. So in this case, we have dropped the macron in the word *Māori* to form the ASCII-friendly filename `Maori.xlsx`.

We name this file `blockOrder.xlsx`, and put that filename in the conditions file field of the outer `blocks` loop. What will happen is that the outer `blocks` loop will run twice, because this file has only two rows of conditions. On each iteration, it will get a value for the variable `language`, which will be either `English` or `Maori`. That value is then able to be used by the inner loop to control what conditions file it will use. For example, if the variable `language` from the outer loop contains the value `English`, then the inner loop dialog will evaluate the expression `language + '.xlsx'` to be `English.xlsx`. This is the conditions file that will be used to control the first block of trials.

In the flow panel diagram in Figure 8.5, you can see that we have selected an `nReps` value of 10 for the inner `trials` loop. The two Stroop conditions files each have nine rows, so the inner loop will run 90 trials in a random order. Once those 90 trials are complete, the second iteration of the outer loop will commence.

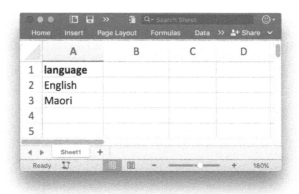

FIGURE 8.6 The conditions file for the outer (blocks) loop, which is used to set the name of the conditions file used by the inner (trials) loop.

All that loop does is switch to the next value of the **language** variable. Hence, when the inner **trials** loop starts again, to run another 90 trials, this time it will automatically use the information from the conditions file for the other language.

💡 Pro Tip: Using an expression to create the conditions filename

In our example we used the file **blockOrder.xlsx** to define a variable called **language** and then turned that into a filename by adding '.xslx' to it. Alternatively, we could simply have created a column in the blocks file that explicitly gave the full name instead. With a variable called **filename**, directly containing values like **Maori.xlsx** and **English.xlsx**, the step of adding '.xlsx' wouldn't have been necessary. We could then simply have set the conditions file field to contain the variable **$filename**.

On the other hand, this method gives you further practice in manipulating variables and shows you something that will be useful when you want to control block order according to what 'group' a participant is in. It also helps at the analysis stage, where there would be a simple 'Language' variable for you to use, which wouldn't need to have the **.xlsx** extension stripped out in your analyses and graphs.

OPTIONS FOR BLOCK ORDERING SCHEMES

The nested-loop arrangement allows us to switch efficiently from one block of trials to another, with the minimum of duplication. But how do we control the order of blocks? There are a few options, depending on the specifics of your experimental design.

Fixed order. Sometimes we simply want the blocks to be presented in a constant order. One of the most common examples of this is when there is a practice block of trials, which naturally needs to be presented before the block of experimental trials. In the context of this Stroop task, however, it might be that we decide that since all participants are fluent in English, we should always present the English block of trials first, as a constant 'baseline' condition. This is very easy to achieve: just set the **loopType** of the **blocks** loop to be **sequential**. Then for every participant, the block of trials specified in **English.xlsx** will always run first. Note that setting the **blocks** to be in a **sequential** order does not prevent you from having **random** trials within each block (or vice versa).

Random order. To vary the order of block presentation, the simplest option is just to select **random** as the **loopType** option in the loop dialog for the outer **blocks** loop. PsychoPy will then take care of randomly ordering the block order for each session. This might be entirely adequate, especially for large studies in which block order is just more of a nuisance variable than something that needs to be systematically managed. Furthermore, note that you can run each block more than once in a single study (using **nReps**) and the rules for randomizing these is just the same as earlier. Usually, however, if we are concerned with block ordering at all, we want to counterbalance it. Counterbalancing allows us to determine the number of participants that receive each of the possible orders.

Counterbalancing. In many experiments, we want to have the order of blocks vary across subjects, yet retain systematic control of that variation. For example, we might want to ensure that equal numbers of participants complete the English or Māori blocks first, and that this counterbalancing also occurs within each of the two groups (the bilingual and monolingual pupils). This generally requires a formal design matrix: a table with a row for each subject, specifying their group and the block order. Hence, we as the experimenter are taking responsibility for deciding the order of blocks for each subject, rather than letting PsychoPy choose randomly. We need to let Builder know what we have decided: you'll see how in the next section.

USING CUSTOM VARIABLES IN THE EXPERIMENT INFO DIALOG

Before a Builder experiment starts, you will have noticed the *Experiment info* dialog box that appears. By default, it contains two fields: one for a **session** code and one for a **participant** ID code. By clicking the *Experiment Settings* button on the toolbar, you can edit the field names and their default contents (see Figure 8.7). You can also disable the dialog from appearing at all by unchecking the *Show info dialog* checkbox. But crucially, you can also add custom variables as required for a particular experiment.

Custom variables don't *need* to be used anywhere in the experiment: they can be informational only. For example, you can add fields for the age and gender of your subject. Each of the variables in the info dialog automatically gets recorded in each row of the output data file. This ensures that you will have every observation tagged with the age and gender of your subject, which is very convenient at the analysis stage. In our case, however, we want to add a variable that *will* be used by Builder, to decide which order of blocks the outer loop of our experiment will use in each session.

Recall that we currently have a single conditions file for the outer **blocks** loop called **blockOrder.xlsx**, which contains this information:

```
Language
English
Maori
```

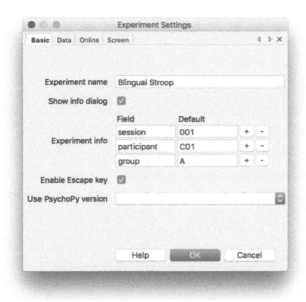

FIGURE 8.7 The Builder *Experiment Settings* dialog. By pushing the + button, we can add a new variable in addition to the standard `session` and `participant` information. Here, we create the `group` variable, to control which language block will be presented first (English for Group A, Māori for Group B).

To manually control the order of the blocks, what we need is to switch the `blocks` loop to use another file as required and that specifies the opposite order of blocks:

```
Language
Maori
English
```

Let's say our design has two groups: Group A will be presented with English trials first, and Group B will see Māori trials first. So let's rename the original `block-Order.xlsx` file to `GroupA.xlsx` and create a second file called `GroupB.xlsx` that contains the reversed order of languages. Now we need to tell the `blocks` loop which one to use in a given session. As shown in Figure 8.7, we do this by adding a new custom variable called `group` to the *Experiment info* dialog box. This variable specifies whether the subject is in Group A or B (let's give it a default value of **A**). To control the order in which the `blocks` loop will run, we use the **group** variable to construct the name of the relevant conditions file to use. We replace the contents of the `Conditions` field of the `blocks` loop with this expression:

```
$'Group' + group + '.xlsx'
```

Hence, by simply typing either **A** or **B** in the *Experiment info* dialog, we can control whether the **blocks** loop will run with the order contained in **GroupA.xlsx** or in **GroupB.xlsx**.

PAUSING BETWEEN BLOCKS

We are almost done. We've separated our trials into two blocks, while still being able to randomize trials within those blocks. We've also seen how to control the order in which those blocks run. One issue remains though: the current flow panel (Figure 8.5) shows that as soon as the first block is complete, the next will start immediately. There would be no warning or transition between the trials of one language and the next. This could confuse the subjects for a period while they adjust. We may also want to give them the opportunity for a rest between the blocks.

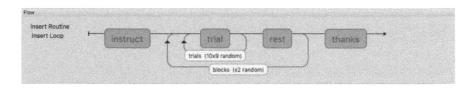

FIGURE 8.8 A blocked version of the Stroop task, incorporating a rest routine between block repetitions.

An obvious way to achieve this would be to add a new routine like the one labelled **rest** in Figure 8.8. As this new routine is not embedded with the inner trials loop, it will only be presented after the inner loop has completed. Hence, it will act to provide a rest between the first and second runs of the **trials** loop. This is a bit messy, though, because it will also run after the second block, so the subjects will get the opportunity to pause for a second time, even though the experiment is effectively complete at that stage (except for passing through the **thanks** routine). Additionally, rather than just being a pause routine, we may also want to take the opportunity to present some instructions prior to the next block. We certainly don't want to present these again if the experiment is about to end.

Instead, let's do something a bit clever and shift the instruction routine inside the outer loop, as in Figure 8.9. This means that it will run before each block rather than just once, at the beginning of the experiment. If the instructions are the same in each block, that's all we need to do: this instruction routine doesn't end until the subject pushes a key to continue, so this routine also acts as a de facto pause routine.

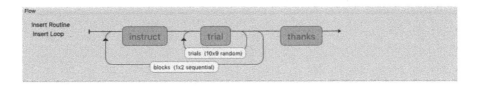

FIGURE 8.9   The final version of our bilingual Stroop task. The instructions routine has been shifted inside the outer loop, so it runs before each of the blocks. This means that it can also do double duty as a 'rest' routine between blocks.

But what if we do want to present different instructions before each block? This is achievable by simply adding an **instructions** variable to our block-level conditions files (as in Figure 8.10).

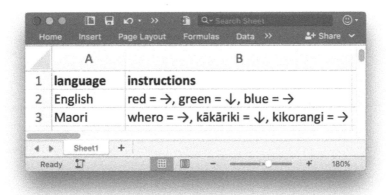

FIGURE 8.10   We can easily allow our instructions to vary across blocks, by including them as a variable in the conditions file for the block loop.

The **instructions** variable can then be used to control the text presented to the subjects. That is, in a **Text** component, insert the variable name **$instructions** rather than using fixed, literal text. This allows us to automatically present instructions that are tailored to the block about to run.

EXERCISES AND EXTENSIONS

EXERCISE 8.1: CREATE A BLOCK DESIGN WITH FACES AND HOUSES

To practice creating block-design experiments, try to create a study where participants are presented with images that are either faces or houses, arranged in blocks of trials. Don't worry about creating a task to do; just try to present the images (for 1 second each).

Aim for a design where each block is chosen *randomly* from either houses or faces, with three blocks of each.

Solution: Page 291

EXERCISE 8.2: COUNTERBALANCE YOUR FACE/HOUSE ORDER

Create a counterbalanced version of the above task, such that you can control the order of alternation (faces first or houses first) using an entry in the info dialog box.

Solution: Page 291

9

USING THE MOUSE FOR INPUT: CREATING A VISUAL SEARCH TASK

Learning objectives: How to use the mouse to get spatial responses and how to specify a pseudo-random stimulus position using code.

In this chapter we will create a visual search task, in which the participant has to find and click on a target stimulus among distractors. We're not holding back anymore – this experiment has quite a few proverbial bells and whistles, but we'll take you through all the steps gradually and you can of course always download the finished version to inspect from the companion website.

We will use a Mouse Component simply to allow the participant to click to end one routine and go on to the next. In the visual search task itself, though, rather than just knowing that the mouse has been clicked, we also need to know *what it was pointing at*. Builder's Mouse Component allows us to specify visual stimuli that are valid targets for clicking. It also allows us to record data about the stimulus that was clicked. Additionally, we'll use code to give some extra capabilities to our script. First, we'll provide the participant with a 'rest' routine that runs only periodically. Second, we'll use code to control the pseudo-random positions of our stimuli. Lastly, code will allow our stimuli to respond dynamically to the mouse.

9.1 GETTING SPATIAL RESPONSES

The experiments so far have relied entirely on the keyboard to get responses from our participants. To provide a spatial response, we generally need to use input systems like a touchscreen, an eye tracker or the humble mouse.

In this chapter we create a visual search task where the participant must click on a target stimulus to show that they have found it among a cloud of distractors. We'll also build on our Code Component skills. We show how simple it is to insert a 'pause' routine that is only presented periodically. We also use some code to randomize the positions of our stimuli. In this experiment, that would be very clumsy to do with a conditions file, which would become very large and complicated. Instead, we'll keep the conditions file quite simple, controlling only the number of stimuli and their colors. In code, we'll control the spatial randomization.

9.2 VISUAL SEARCH

Searching for a needle in a haystack is difficult because the target (the needle) appears very similar to the background of distractors (the hay). Searching for a haystack itself, however, is much easier, as it stands out (literally) from the flat background of the surrounding field. We'll build a task that shows the difference between these two sorts of search.

Our search target will be a small hexagonal stimulus. On any given trial, we'll display anywhere from zero to eight similarly-sized pentagons. These subtly different stimuli act as competing distractors in our search for the target. The distractors will always be colored black. On half of the trials, the target will also be black, and on the other half, bright red. Let's jump ahead and see the results such a search task generates. Figure 9.1 shows some example data gathered from the experiment that we build in this chapter. The graph shows that if the target is black and it is presented in isolation (i.e. with zero distractors), it takes this particular subject just over a second to find and click on it. When distractors are added, the time taken to search for the target rises linearly with the number of distractors. That is, the search time increases progressively by roughly 200 ms for each additional distractor. This implies that the search progresses serially, with stimuli needing to be inspected individually in turn until the target is found. When the target is red and presented in isolation, it also takes just over a second to be clicked on. But as the number of distractors increases, the search time for a red target remains constant. That is, the bright red target seems to 'pop out' relative to the black distractors, and so it gets detected immediately. That is, regardless of the number of distractors, a serial search pattern isn't required. Because the salient color difference can be detected in peripheral vision, the eyes can jump straight to the target, rather than requiring a detailed fixation on each stimulus to discriminate whether it has five or six sides.

9.3 IMPLEMENTING THE TASK

Our task will consist of three routines (see Figure 9.2). The first routine will provide instructions and lasts until the participant presses a mouse button to proceed.

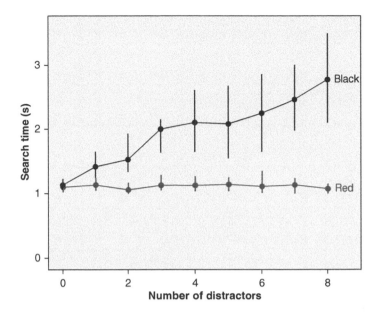

FIGURE 9.1 The time taken to search for and select a hexagon stimulus, as a function of the number of competing pentagon distractor stimuli. When the hexagon is black, the time taken to search for it increases linearly with the number of same-colored distractors. When it is red, however, it 'pops out' and the time taken to find it is constant, regardless of the number of distractors. (This data set consists of 720 trials from a single individual. Points indicate median search times and the bars indicate interquartile ranges.)

The second routine will display a fixation stimulus for a fixed duration, providing an inter-trial interval. The final routine, containing the actual search task, will show the hexagonal target (in red on this particular trial) and the pentagonal distractors (if any), in pseudo-randomized locations. It lasts until the participant clicks successfully on the target. On every 18th trial, the instruction routine is shown again. This allows the participant to rest periodically during the long run of trials.

9.4 INTRODUCING THE MOUSE COMPONENT

Parts of implementing the experiment should be well drilled for you by now. The experiment starts by presenting some instructions to the participants. So insert a new routine called `instruct`. Add a Text Component, set to show indefinitely, containing text such as this: *'Click the hexagon as quickly as possible. Press the mouse button to start.'*

The participant will click a mouse button to end the routine. Using a mouse click for this purpose is very similar to responding to a keypress. We simply want

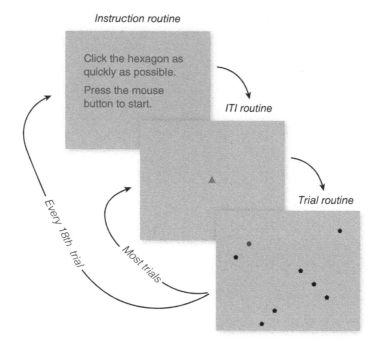

Instruction routine

Click the hexagon as quickly as possible.

Press the mouse button to start.

ITI routine

Trial routine

Every 18th trial

Most trials

FIGURE 9.2   The overall procedure for the visual search task.

to detect that a click has occurred: no recording of spatial information or reaction time is required. So we insert a Mouse Component, as in Figure 9.3. Previously, with a Keyboard Component, we allowed our indefinite-duration Routines to be terminated by selecting **Force end of Routine**. The equivalent for the Mouse Component requires checking the **End Routine on press** setting. Because we aren't interested in where or when this mouse click occurs, or even what button was pressed, just select the **any click** option for the **End Routine on press** setting, and **never** for Save mouse state.

 Pro Tip: Variable naming conventions

Note that we've given the component a specific name (`instruct_mouse`) so that it won't conflict with the name `mouse`, which we're reserving for use within the trial routine itself. Also note that, in previous chapters, variable names have used a different convention for separating the words. So far we have used capitals at word boundaries, which is often known as `CamelCase`. In this chapter we're using `snake_case`, where underscores are used to separate words. The difference is a matter of style and preference. Some languages tend to use one, and some tend to use the other. Most Python libraries now use `snake_case`, which is also recommended in the official Python style guide (a document called PEP8). Unfortunately, PsychoPy was written before PEP8 was widely used, and was based on existing libraries that used CamelCase. PsychoPy generally still uses CamelCase, and the style guide itself also says don't change just to fit the style guide! The point is that it's up to you what you use in your own code, but make sure you adopt a consistent rule. Otherwise will you end up making mistakes because you can't remember whether you called your variable `wordColor`, `WordColor` or `word_color`. For this chapter we will consistently use snake_case, so that you can make your choice after experiencing both.

Because we are just using the mouse click to end the routine, we aren't interested in recording information in the data file about the mouse (such as its location or what button was pressed). So in this case, under **Save mouse state**, we select **never**. In other situations, you might be relying on a Mouse Component to provide important data from the subject. So other options for saving the mouse state include **final** (stores the mouse location as at the last moment in the routine), **on click** (stores the location at the time the button was clicked, which is not

FIGURE 9.3 The Mouse Component dialog for the instruction routine.

necessarily at the end of the routine), and **every frame** (allowing a continuous recording of the mouse trajectory).

You can ignore most of the other settings in this dialog, but do tick the **New clicks only** checkbox. What this means is that the Mouse Component will only respond to clicks made while it is active. Like keypresses, mouse clicks go into a storage buffer in case they can't be handled immediately. This is a feature of most computer operating systems. You might have noticed how sometimes you can be typing away in a document but nothing happens, as the computer somehow seems to be busy with something else. Then, when it gets freed up, a stream of your previously typed letters suddenly gets regurgitated into your document in one hit. So although those keypresses were being detected, they had to be stored in a queue until they were able to be processed. The same thing happens with PsychoPy. If the participant presses a mouse button during a routine where there is no Mouse Component, that button press still gets stored in the event buffer. When our Mouse Component does become active, it checks the buffer for any button presses. If it finds one, it will react to it as if it has just occurred, even though it may have been sitting unnoticed in the buffer for many seconds. To stop that happening, the **New clicks only** setting 'flushes' the buffer, emptying it of any pre-existing mouse events. That way, any responses will only be detected if they occur after the Mouse Component started. The equivalent setting in the Keyboard Component is labelled **Discard previous**. If you ever find that a routine just flashes up briefly and ends without any response being made, a good guess is that the event buffer hasn't been flushed.

 Warning: Analysing data with multiple values per cell

PsychoPy normally saves data in neat `.csv` files, with one value per column in each row of the file, where one row corresponds to a trial. This neat tabular format makes it very easy to import into pretty much any analysis software. The Mouse Component, however, makes it possible to save multiple values per trial for the mouse state. Breaking the 'one value per cell' convention can make it challenging to import: some pre-processing of the data may be required. Make sure you try out your analysis pipeline on some test data before running the experiment for real. Of course, this is something you should be doing for all experiments anyway.

Now push the green **Run** button: it's never too soon to check that the experiment is correctly specified and will run correctly. It can be easier to squash individual errors as they arise, rather than deal with a dozen of them when the experiment is 'complete'. As this experiment is relatively complex, we won't be going straight to the finished product as shown in Figure 9.2. Instead, we'll build it up iteratively, progressively adding new features while aiming to keep it 'runnable' as much as possible as we develop it. This cycle of frequent testing is a good habit to get into. It is relatively easy to find and fix a single bug if it has been introduced by the last incremental change since the previous successful run. But if you try to create an entire experiment before running it for the first time, there's a good chance that you'll get swamped in a sea of multiple errors.

 Pro Tip: Using a laptop?

The PsychoPy Mouse Component doesn't distinguish between input from a trackpad and a mouse. The pointer only has one location, and it doesn't matter which hardware you are using to control it. Similarly, a click on the trackpad is registered just like the equivalent mouse button. In fact, if you have a touchscreen laptop, there's a good chance that will be treated just the same as well!

9.5 CONTROL STIMULUS VISIBILITY FROM A CONDITIONS FILE

Next, insert a new routine called `trial` after the `instruct` routine. We won't add any stimuli to it yet: first we need to connect to our conditions file to access the variables needed to control the appearance of those stimuli. So insert a loop that surrounds the `trial` routine and point it to a conditions file that looks like the one in Figure 9.4.

The conditions file handles a lot of the design of this task. The first column (`target_color`) specifies whether the search target will stand out from the distractors (red) or blend in with them (black). We will define eight distractor stimuli and control their visibility individually using the eight opacity variables (`opacity_1` to `opacity_8`). For example, on rows where all of the opacity values are 1, all eight distractors will be visible. On rows where all of the opacities are 0, all of the distractors will be invisible and so the target will appear alone on screen.

 Pro Tip: Adding useful variables to data files

The last column in the conditions file (`n_distract`) is just a count of the number of visible distractors on a given trial. We won't actually use this value explicitly when running the experiment but, like all conditions file variables, it will nonetheless get

(Continued)

stored in the data file. Having the levels of this factor explicitly specified in the data will be very useful at the analysis stage (e.g. it was used to label the *x* axis in Figure 9.2). Before gathering data, think about what 'information only' variables should be in the conditions file, even if they aren't needed by PsychoPy to actually run the experiment.

	1	2	3	4	5	6	7	8	9	10
1	target_color	opacity_1	opacity_2	opacity_3	opacity_4	opacity_5	opacity_6	opacity_7	opacity_8	n_distract
2	black	1	1	1	1	1	1	1	1	8
3	black	1	1	1	1	1	1	1	0	7
4	black	1	1	1	1	1	1	0	0	6
5	black	1	1	1	1	1	0	0	0	5
6	black	1	1	1	1	0	0	0	0	4
7	black	1	1	1	0	0	0	0	0	3
8	black	1	1	0	0	0	0	0	0	2
9	black	1	0	0	0	0	0	0	0	1
10	black	0	0	0	0	0	0	0	0	0
11	red	1	1	1	1	1	1	1	1	8
12	red	1	1	1	1	1	1	1	0	7
13	red	1	1	1	1	1	1	0	0	6
14	red	1	1	1	1	1	0	0	0	5
15	red	1	1	1	1	0	0	0	0	4
16	red	1	1	1	0	0	0	0	0	3
17	red	1	1	0	0	0	0	0	0	2
18	red	1	0	0	0	0	0	0	0	1
19	red	0	0	0	0	0	0	0	0	0

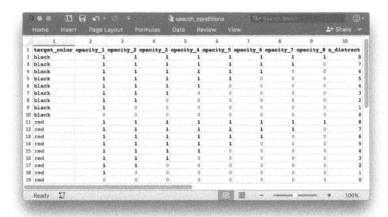

FIGURE 9.4 The conditions file for the task. We often recommend using the simple text-based `.csv` format, but Excel (`.xlsx` or `.xls`) files have the advantage of allowing formatting, which can make the design more visually apparent. PsychoPy can only read the text and numerical content of the cells, but judicious use of colors and font weights can help make it more readable to a human.

So in summary, the experimental design has two factors: target color (two levels: red or black) and number of distractors (nine levels: 0 to 8). Insert a loop around the `trial` routine and connect it to the conditions file, setting the `loopType` to yield a `random` selection of rows (Figure 9.5). We've selected 20 repetitions,

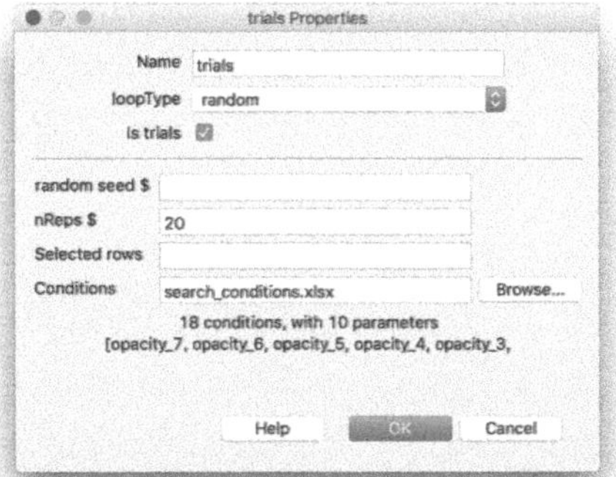

FIGURE 9.5 Loop dialog for the visual search task.

yielding a total of 360 trials (2 × 9 × 20), but you'll probably want to use a lower number of repetitions while you are still testing the experiment.

9.6 CONTROL STIMULUS POSITIONS USING CODE

The initial structure of our experiment should look like the flow panel in Figure 9.6. At this stage, though, it is just a skeleton and still needs to be filled out with actual stimuli. Before we do that, we need to decide how to control where the stimuli will appear during the search task. With lots of trials, it would be quite unwieldy to specify the target locations in the conditions file. Instead, we stick to our 18-line conditions file to control stimulus color and visibility, and use code to randomly sprinkle the stimuli across the screen on every trial.

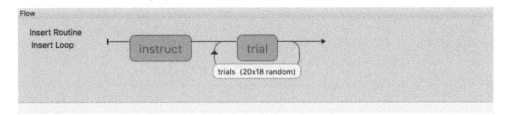

FIGURE 9.6   The initial flow panel for the visual search task (this will change as we develop the experiment).

Start by inserting a Code Component in the **trial** routine. In its **Begin Experiment** tab, put the code below. This creates lists of nine possible **x** and **y** coordinates, spread evenly across the screen (we're going to use pixels as the units throughout this experiment):

```
# define possible coordinates for the target and the distractors:
x_pos = [-400, -300, -200, -100, 0, 100, 200, 300, 400]
y_pos = [-400, -300, -200, -100, 0, 100, 200, 300, 400]
```

On each trial, we'll randomly shuffle these two lists. The first stimulus will get the first shuffled coordinates from each list, the next will get the second coordinates, and so on. Because the two lists are shuffled independently, this produces 81 possible combinations of [x, y] coordinates for the stimuli to occupy.

Pro Tip: Random locations, or shuffle a grid?

In Chapter 10, we'll cover the distinction between random and quasi-random design factors. Here we've chosen to use quasi-random target locations (effectively sampling without replacement from a finite set of 81 possible locations). An alternative would be truly random selection, in which stimulus coordinates are sampled with replacement from all possible pixel coordinates. That is, they could appear anywhere on the screen, with their positions independent of each other (so there would be nothing to prevent them from overlapping). In this case, the use of quasi-randomization is slightly more complicated to code (we have to create and shuffle lists of possible coordinates rather than just make repeated calls to a `random()` function). But this approach gives us some practical advantages. With truly random stimulus locations, it would be quite possible for stimuli to coincide spatially on occasion: if stimuli overlap, it becomes hard to know which one the participant is trying to click. Instead, by randomly assigning positions from a fixed list of possible values (effectively forming an invisible 9 × 9 grid), we ensure that no stimuli can overlap (indeed, a minimum distance of 100 pixels between nearest neighbors will always apply).

In the `Begin Routine` tab, put the code below, so that at the beginning of each trial, the stimulus positions are randomly refreshed:

```
# randomize the stimulus positions at the start of each trial:
shuffle(x_pos)
shuffle(y_pos)
```

We're now finally ready to begin creating our stimuli. Let's start by inserting a Polygon Component to serve as the `target` stimulus (Figure 9.7).

For timing, we set the target to be visible from the very beginning of the trial but don't specify a stop time (as it needs to stay on indefinitely, until the participant gives a correct response). Appearance-wise, to make it a regular hexagon, we specify that it should have six vertices. We also slightly tweak its default orientation by 30 degrees so that the bottom side is horizontal (this just helps make it appear more similar to the default orientation of the pentagonal distractors, which have a horizontal base). The opacity is set at a constant 1.0, as the target needs to be visible on every trial. We set the line width to be zero (so we can control its color using just the `Fill color` attribute on the `Advanced` tab). The size is set to be 20 × 20, in units of pixels.

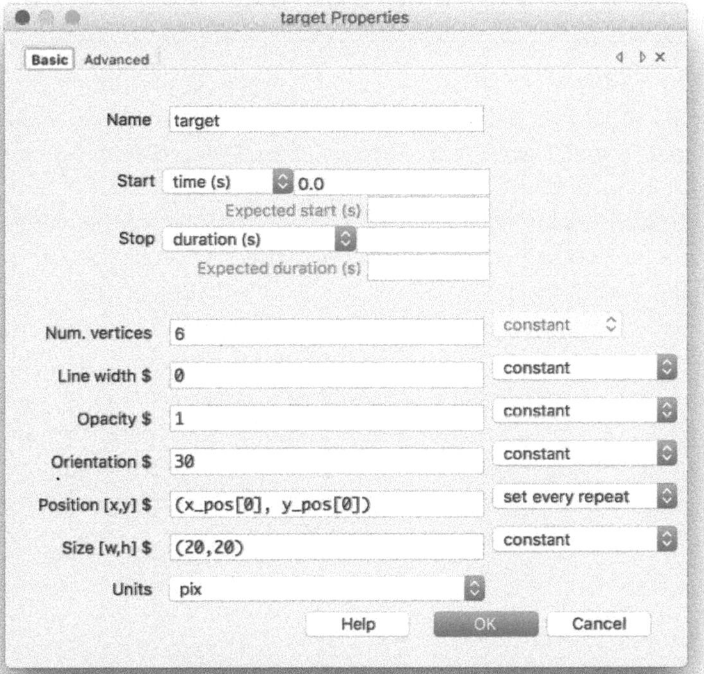

FIGURE 9.7 The basic tab of the Polygon Component for the target stimulus. The Position field contains the first (or, strictly, the 'zeroth') pair of coordinates from our freshly randomized lists.

The clever bit is where we specify the position of the stimulus, updated on every repeat. We simply take the first entry of both the **x_pos** and **y_pos** lists. (Remember that Python counts from zero, so the initial item in a list is strictly the 'zeroth' item.) Because these lists will get shuffled on every trial, the target will jump about, seemingly at random.

Note that for the random positioning to work properly, the Code Component needs to be *above* the Polygon Component in the Builder window. That means the list will get shuffled on every trial *before* the Polygon components get to refer to it. If the stimulus components were above the Code Component, then on the first trial the stimuli would be using the still-unshuffled list, because the shuffling code wouldn't have been run. Thus on the first trial, the stimuli would all appear on a diagonal line across the screen, as the **x** and **y** coordinates would still be paired, in order. On subsequent trials, the stimuli would be displayed using the coordinates from the trial before, meaning that the stimuli actually presented on each trial and the positions recorded in the data would not correspond. If you ever find issues with stimuli or recorded data appearing to be off by one trial, the vertical ordering of components is very likely to be the cause.

Lastly, on the **Advanced** tab of the target Polygon Component (Figure 9.8), we connect the **Fill color** field to the `target_color` variable from the conditions file, updating every repeat, so that the target can switch between red and black across trials as required.

We can now insert another Polygon Component, to represent the first of the distractor stimuli. This will be similar to the settings of the target stimulus but the number of vertices should be set to five, so that it will appear as a regular pentagon. Unlike the target, we put a variable name (`opacity_1`) in the **Opacity** field (Figure 9.9), as this setting is how we will control the number of visible distractors (remember to set this to update every repeat). That is, for each distractor, if its opacity value is 1, it will appear, but if it is 0, it will be invisible. On the **Advanced** tab, set the color to be a constant value of **black**: unlike the target, the distractors are always this color. Lastly, in the position field, we specify the next entry in each of the coordinate lists: (`x_pos[1]`, `y_pos[1]`).

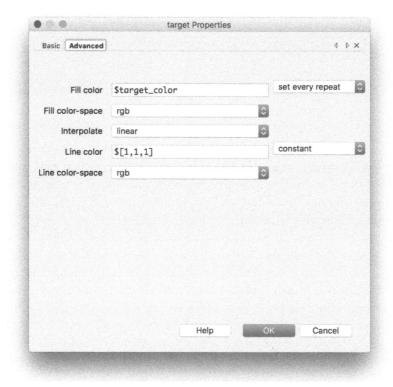

FIGURE 9.8 The `Advanced` tab of the target stimulus. This is where we control how it switches from red to black between trials.

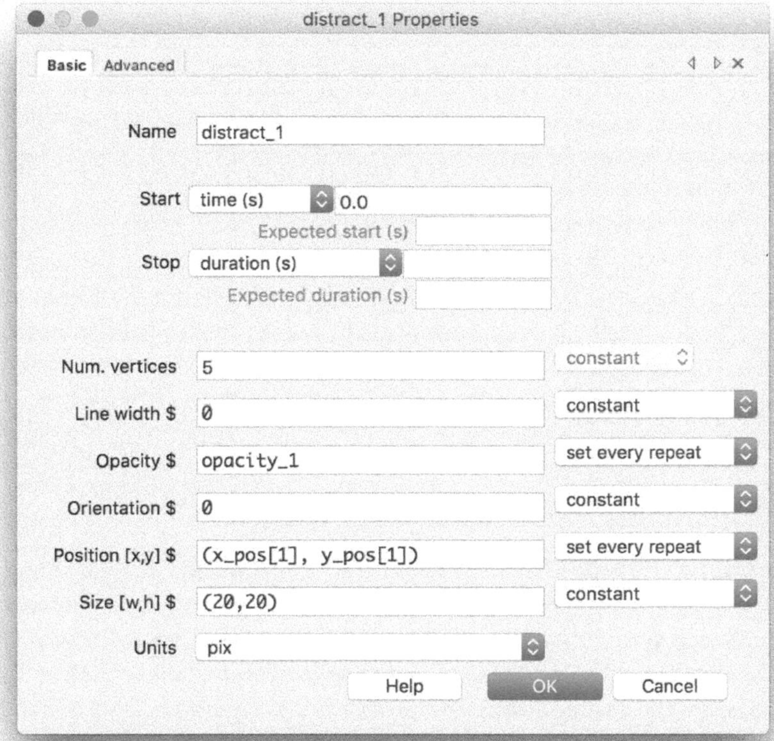

FIGURE 9.9 The Basic tab of the first distractor's Polygon stimulus component dialog. Unlike the target, the opacity of the distractors changes from trial to trial, allowing us to control how many of them will appear.

Your heart might start to sink now, when you realize that we still need to define seven more distractors. That could mean inserting lots of Polygon Components and repetitive typing to set their properties. Fortunately, Builder gives us a shortcut to reduce some of this drudgery. As the distractor stimuli will all be very similar, we can just right-click on the icon for the first distractor component and select copy from the contextual menu that appears. Then we go to the Experiment menu and select Paste Component. This will insert a duplicate of the first distractor component (but make sure that it gets a distinct name, such as distract_2). Now all we need to do for each of the copied components is change the values that need to be specific to that particular instance of the distractor. For example, distractor_2 should have an Opacity value of opacity_2 and a Position value of (x_pos[2], y_pos[2]), and so on, incrementing as required up to the component named distract_8.

Pro Tip: Learning to code to save time

This copy and paste approach reduces some work, but it is not hard to see that creating many stimuli could soon become impractically laborious. For example, a visual search task could easily have, say, a 30 × 30 grid of distractors. Creating 900 stimulus components in a graphical interface like Builder would not be feasible. Requirements like that are really much more suited to being implemented in code rather than via a graphical interface. That is, in code, it is as easy to create 9 stimuli as it is to create 900. If you find yourself creating experiments in Builder that contain an uncomfortable amount of duplication, it is likely time to consider learning how to implement at least that aspect of the experiment in code.

9.7 RESPONDING TO MOUSE CLICKS SPATIALLY

If everything is set up correctly, when the trial routine runs we should see a red or black hexagonal target and a quasi-random number of black pentagonal distractors, scattered across the screen. Don't press **Run** yet, as we still haven't provided a way to end the trial. We need to respond to mouse clicks and, if the target is clicked, store the reaction time and proceed to the next trial. So unlike the Mouse Component we inserted in the instruction routine, here we will need to evaluate the location of the mouse pointer at the time the button was pressed.

Insert a Mouse Component in the `trial` routine, simply named `mouse`. Figure 9.10 shows the settings we will use. Once again, we give it a `Start` time of zero and an indefinite `duration`, because the trial will last until a correct mouse click is performed. In the instruction routine, for the `End routine on press` option we selected `any click`. In the `trial` routine, however, we instead select `valid click`: we want the routine to end only if the target stimulus has been clicked. How do we specify what a valid click actually is? This is quite easy: as shown in Figure 9.10, simply type the name `target` in the `Clickable stimuli` field. This means that only a click on the stimulus named `target` will be registered as valid: clicks anywhere else will be ignored. Note that you aren't restricted to a single stimulus: you could enter a list of valid stimulus names here, separated by commas.

Lastly, note the `Store params for clicked` field shown in Figure 9.10. This is asking us what information we want to store in the data file about the stimulus that was clicked. We've typed two stimulus parameters here: `name` and `pos`. The `name` parameter here is redundant in this particular experiment: we've only allowed one valid stimulus, so the `name` parameter will always have a value of `target`. But hopefully you can see that it would be useful to record the name in other circumstances (e.g. you might want to record which of a number of photos

FIGURE 9.10   The Mouse Component used in the `trial` routine.

a person selected in a face recognition task). We've also selected the **pos** attribute of the stimulus. This might also seem a bit redundant, as the position of the mouse pointer will itself automatically be recorded in the data file. The mouse location is recorded very precisely (down to the pixel) and, oddly enough, it can sometimes be useful to get a less precise measure. That is, in this case we will be recording the centre of the image stimulus, which will usually vary a bit from the precise location of the mouse pointer. Such stimulus-related rather than mouse-related measures can be useful for some analyses, so we record it here just in case.

Figure 9.11 shows all the components we should now have in the **trial** routine.

9.8 SELECTIVELY SKIPPING A ROUTINE

Now try running the experiment. You should find that nothing happens if the mouse is clicked anywhere other than within the target. When the target is clicked, the trial routine ends and we immediately go on to the next trial. As we are planning to run 360 trials per participant, it would be a good idea to provide occasional breaks between the trials. But having a pause between every trial is a bit excessive for this task. A reasonable compromise would be to have a pause between, say, every complete iteration through the conditions file. In this case, that would be every 18 trials (although this is an arbitrary value; we could choose any other number so that pauses occur either more or less often). Using periodic pauses

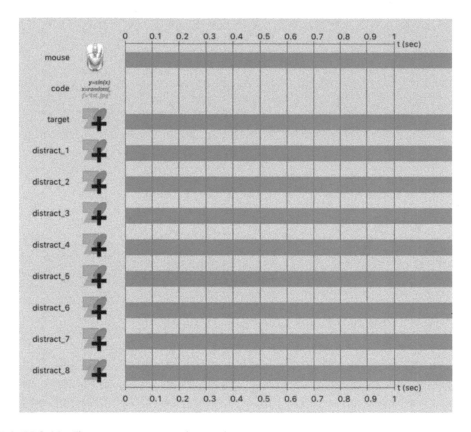

FIGURE 9.11 The components required to run the `trial` routine.

allows the participant to quickly whip through the trials but not get worried about losing concentration, as the next break is never too far away.

We could be lazy and shift the existing instruction routine inside the loop: those instructions remain valid throughout the experiment, and hence this routine already provides a convenient way to pause between trials. This new layout is shown in the flow panel in Figure 9.12. How can we limit the instruction routine so that it won't appear on every iteration of the loop? This can be done with a snippet of code in the **Begin Routine** tab of a Code Component inserted in the instruction routine. We will check whether the current trial number is a multiple of 18. If it isn't, we set `continueRoutine` to `False`. If this variable is `False` at the beginning of the routine, the effect is that the routine doesn't even start. It is immediately terminated, before any stimuli are displayed, and PsychoPy immediately moves on to the next routine in the flow panel.

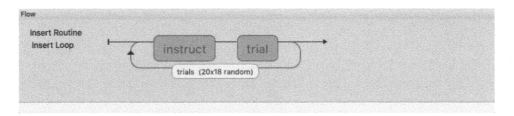

FIGURE 9.12   The revised flow panel for the visual search task, with the instruction routine shifted within the trial loop so that it can function as a periodic pause routine.

Effectively, what we want to do is only show the instruction routine if the trial number is a multiple of 18. We can find out if one number is a multiple of another using the very useful Python 'modulo' operator, %. At first glance this may appear a little confusing, but the % operator in Python has nothing to do with calculating percentages. Instead, it gives us the remainder when we divide one number by another. For example, if we want to know if a number is even, we check to see if its remainder modulo 2 is zero. For example, 10 % 2 evaluates to 0, as there is no remainder when dividing 10 by 2. Meanwhile, 9 % 2 evaluates to 1: being an odd number, 9 leaves a remainder of 1 when divided by 2.

In our case, we test whether the current trial number is a multiple of 18, and only proceed with the instruction routine if it is. Note that the first trial is number 0, which is a multiple of 18, so the experiment will begin with instructions. Here is the code to put in the **Begin Routine** tab:

```
# only pause for a rest on every 18th trial:
if trials.thisN % 18 != 0: # this isn't trial 0, 18, 36, ...
    continueRoutine = False # so don't run the pause routine this time.
```

 Pro Tip: The modulo operator % is very useful

For example, with the ability to tell odd from even numbers means we can easily produce a flickering stimulus. We can do this by only showing it on alternating (say, even-numbered) frames. Builder maintains a counter variable called frameN that increments with every screen refresh. This variable comes in handy when we want to flicker a stimulus on and off, or alternate between different stimuli.

9.9 MAKING SMOOTH TRIAL TRANSITIONS

Now we have most of the experiment functioning. But currently, the moment the correct stimulus is clicked, the next trial begins immediately, with a new set of stimuli being displayed. This can be quite jarring, as the target appears to jump across the screen the moment it is clicked. In such situations, it can be useful to provide a brief pause before displaying the next set of stimuli.

We could go back into the **trial** routine and edit all of the stimuli so that they don't appear until after a 0.5 s portion of the trial has elapsed, and insert a single central fixation stimulus to occupy that period. This would be quite laborious, however, involving the same editing of many stimulus components. To avoid this, instead we can insert a whole new routine immediately before the **trial** routine. This will just contain a single central fixation stimulus, set to last for a fixed duration of 0.5 s. The effect of this is that the stimuli in the **trial** routine will all appear at the 0.5 s mark on each trial, without our needing to edit them all individually.

The final version of the flow panel for this experiment is shown in Figure 9.13, showing the arrangement of all three routines within the loop. Note that the **instruct** and **trial** routines are colored red, to indicate that they don't have a fixed duration (because completing each of them is contingent on a mouse click). The ITI routine, however, is green to indicate that it has a specified duration (0.5 s).

The visual search task is now complete. Try running it and examining the resulting data. The serial search vs pop-out effect is sufficiently strong that you should see the effects shown in Figure 9.1 within any given individual. Happy hexagon hunting!

9.10 POINTING RATHER THAN CLICKING

In the search task above, we wanted to take an action when the participant explicitly clicked on the **target** stimulus. The Mouse Component allowed us to do that simply by specifying one or more stimuli to be 'clickable'. Sometimes, though, we want to take some action just because of where the mouse is pointing, without requiring a button click. For example, we might want to highlight a stimulus in some way when the mouse pointer is hovering over it. Builder's Mouse Component doesn't cater for this directly, so we need to roll up our sleeves and write a little code to provide this capability.

Let's say we want the target stimulus in the search task to be magnified when the mouse pointer hovers over it. What we need to do is have some code that runs on every screen refresh, checking if the mouse coordinates are within the target stimulus, and, if so, change its size. Fortunately, PsychoPy's visual stimuli have a

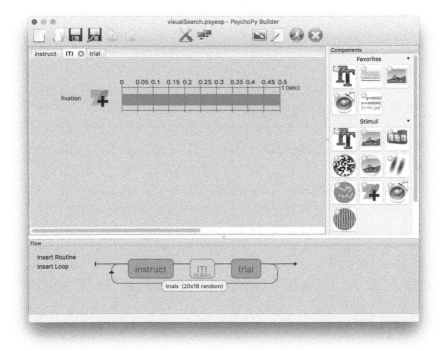

FIGURE 9.13 Inserting a new inter-trial interval (ITI) routine to reduce the visual disruption between the end of one trial and the start of the next. This is the only routine with a fixed duration. Hence it appears in green in the flow panel, which now shows the final structure of the experiment.

`.contains()` function that allows us to check if the mouse pointer coordinates are within its bounds. So in the **Each frame** tab of the Code Component on the **trial** routine, insert this code:

```
# check if the mouse pointer coordinates lie
# within the boundaries of the target stimulus:
if target.contains(mouse):
    target.size = (40,40) # highlight by expanding the target
else:
    target.size = (20,20) # go back to the default size
```

The effect of this code is that the stimulus grows when the mouse pointer is hovering over it, and shrinks back to normal when it moves away. This visual effect isn't really needed in our search task (and might even impair the ability to hit the target) but hopefully you can see how this technique might be useful in other situations. For example, it could be used to make a border appear around a stimulus to act as a highlight, perhaps as a visual indicator that the stimulus can be clicked.

EXERCISES AND EXTENSIONS

EXERCISE 9.1: CHANGE AN IMAGE'S CONTRAST BY HOVERING THE MOUSE OVER IT

Say you have a pair of images displayed. How would you change the contrast of whichever image you happen to be hovering the mouse over?

Solution: Page 291

EXERCISE 9.2: USE THE MOUSE TO MOVE A STIMULUS AROUND THE DISPLAY

How could you let the participant click a stimulus and then drag it with the mouse to a new position?

Solution: Page 292

PART II
FOR THE
PROFESSIONAL

This second part of the book is more of a reference, going into implementation details for a number of the topics that have been covered early in the book. If you have (or want) a career in the scientific study of behavior then understanding the following details is probably rather useful.

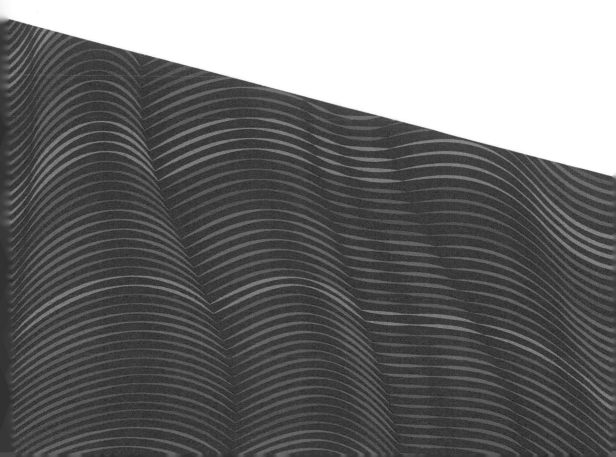

10

IMPLEMENTING RESEARCH DESIGNS WITH RANDOMIZATION

Learning objectives: Learn how various randomization schemes can be implemented using Builder.

Randomization can occur at multiple levels of research designs, whether at the level of randomly selecting participants from a population, assigning them to conditions, controlling the order of presentation of blocks of trials, or specifying the location and timing of individual stimuli within trials. Randomization is one of the key techniques that allows us to achieve experimental control in behavioral research. Even in an observational, questionnaire-based study, we may need to randomize the order of presentation of question items. Not everything can be randomized: sometimes we will need to cluster similar trials together in blocks. We must often then pay attention to the order of presentation of the blocks themselves. Here we discuss how such things can be implemented in PsychoPy. Unlike preceding chapters, instead of getting stuck into creating a specific experiment, we'll be giving generic advice on implementing these techniques with PsychoPy.

Randomization is one of the most useful tools available to a behavioral scientist. We begin with one of the most important topics (randomly assigning study participants to conditions). Then we move on to more granular randomization, such as at the level of individual stimuli, which is where PsychoPy is particularly useful. For a given study, there may be a priori reasons to precisely balance particularly relevant factors, such as ensuring equal numbers of men and women, or young and old people, within each condition. For many other factors, though, we should let the power of randomization take effect.

10.1 HOW CAN WE ASSIGN SUBJECTS TO CONDITIONS OR GROUPS?

One way to assign participants to groups is to make a truly random and independent decision for each subject. Such simple random assignment could, for example, involve tossing a coin for each person, with 'heads' meaning assignment to the experimental manipulation and 'tails' sending a person to the control group. This 'pure' approach to randomization is not, however, always optimal in achieving a specified research design. For example, we can't guarantee that equal numbers will be assigned to each group. It also limits our ability to systematically balance groups across other factors (such as wanting equal numbers of men and women in each condition). We might also end up with occasional long runs of testing people in one group or, conversely, alternations, such that one group has more people tested in the morning than in the afternoon. So simple random assignment can be incompatible with competing design goals like systematically balancing confounding factors across conditions.

 Pro Tip: Randomization can't do magic

We need a reasonably large number of subjects to be confident that randomization will smooth out differences between groups. With small numbers of participants, random assignment can still easily skew one group to be clearly different from another on some important confounding variable.

In many research designs, we need to apply random assignment within some systematic constraints, such as there being equal numbers of subjects in each group, comparable proportions of males and females across groups, and so on. Fortunately, this can often be done very easily, using nothing more complicated than a spreadsheet.

Say we want to randomly assign equal numbers of participants to consume tea, coffee or water before completing a psychomotor vigilance task. Across these three conditions, we also want to assign equal numbers of men and women, and have equal numbers of testing sessions in the morning and afternoon. We'll represent all combinations of these conditions in a table, so that participants can be assigned to the set of conditions specified by each row in that table.

These sorts of tables are well suited to being created in code, but as this is a book on the graphical Builder approach, we'll use a spreadsheet instead. Let's create a balanced design so that each level within the three factors (gender, session time and stimulant) will be presented in combination with every other level. Spreadsheets make this easy. Here we use the ubiquitous Microsoft Excel, but the principles are the same for most other spreadsheet software. Start by putting a label for each column in the top row (say, `gender`, `session` and `stimulant`). There are three levels of the `stimulant` variable (tea, coffee and water), two for `session` (morning and afternoon) and two for `gender` (male and female). That means we need 12 combinations to balance all the factors ($3 \times 2 \times 2$). Figure 10.1 shows how we could fill in those 12 rows of the table.

FIGURE 10.1 A conditions file showing the balancing of three factors, the first two having two levels (male vs female, and morning vs afternoon), and the third having three levels (tea vs coffee vs water). Judicious use of Excel's drag-to-fill operation lets us easily create such tables without having to manually type values in each cell.

Underneath the `gender` heading (in cell `A1`), type `male` (i.e. in cell `A2`). Click on that cell to select it and move the mouse pointer to the bottom right-hand corner of the cell border. You should see the cursor change (in Excel, it switches from a white cross to a black one). If you now click and drag across the cells below (down to `A7`), the `male` entry will fill in all of the cells you drag over. Then type `female` in the next cell (`A8`), and repeat the drag-and-fill operation down to cell `A13`. This drag-and-fill technique saves time and, by copying the content, prevents manual typos.

The drag-and-fill function is quite clever, and not restricted to just copying a single value. For example, in the `session` column, drag `morning` to fill cells `B2` through B4, and **afternoon** in cells B5 through B7. Select all six cells, and again move the cursor to hover over the bottom right corner until it changes to a black cross. When you drag down now, Excel will realize that you want to continue a pattern, and it will fill the empty cells with consecutive triples of **morning** and **afternoon**. Do this all the way down to B13. Lastly, do a similar thing in the final **stimulant** column, with cells repeating the values **tea**, **coffee** and **water**.

When we look at the table, we see that each row changes to a different value of **stimulant**, while **session** cycles from morning to afternoon only every three rows, and **gender** changes only once, after six rows. This allows us to easily make a visual check that the factors are balanced within each other. (The actual order might be arbitrary: we could instead have **gender** alternate on every row, for example, with **session** cycling though its values more slowly.) This arrangement shows us several things. First, the minimum number of subjects to achieve a balanced design would be 12. Second, we will very likely need more subjects than that to achieve a sufficiently powerful study, and there needs to be more than one person experiencing each combination of factors to allow us to statistically test the highest level interactions between them. So the total number of participants must be some multiple of 12 (24, 36, 48, 60, and so on). To produce the full table of conditions, simply copy and paste the first 12 rows as many times as necessary to produce a table with enough rows for each planned participant.

So now we have a balanced list of experimental conditions, of a length sufficient for the number of participants that we plan to recruit. How do we handle the allocation of each subject to a row in this table? Allocating subjects to conditions sequentially is a bad idea (e.g. recruiting all the males before the females), as this can lead to systematic biases due to changing influences over the duration of the project. One simple technique is to randomly shuffle the rows in the table. We can then just assign subjects to sequential rows in the table from beginning to end, as the shuffling will have broken up its ordered progression of rows. Each subject assignment can then be a simple sequential progression down the now-randomized rows of the table.

How do we randomly shuffle a table? This can be achieved by adding another column to the table that contains random numbers, and then sorting the table on the values in that column. Do this by adding a fourth column heading (say, **order**), and in cell D4 enter the formula = **RAND()**. The = symbol tells Excel that the contents of this cell are a formula to be calculated, and not just some literal letters and symbols. Excel will evaluate that formula and put a random value, between 0.0 and 1.0, in that cell. Drag this cell down so that all cells in that column get the same random-number-generating formula. Then click on any cell in the table and choose **Sort** from the **Data** ribbon (or, on a Mac, from the **Data** menu). Choose to sort by the **order** column (as these are random numbers, it doesn't matter whether we sort in ascending or descending order).

This approach (sorting a table by a column of random numbers, and then sequentially assigning participants to rows in the table) solves a number of problems. It allows us to keep a balanced design while still randomly allocating subjects to conditions. And it means that the randomization happens only once: we don't have to implement a randomization process (such as tossing a coin) individually for every subject.

 Warning: Dangers of sorting

The simple act of sorting poses one of the biggest risks in storing and manipulating data in a spreadsheet. The danger is that not all columns get sorted together. For example, let's say you have a master demographics table for your experiment, which links the anonymous subject IDs to the personal details for each participant. The list is currently sorted by age but you want to return it to being sorted by the ID code. You select the ID code column and sort it in ascending order. To your horror, you see that although that column got sorted, the rest of the table stayed in place. Hopefully, you quickly select Undo or close the file without saving. If not, unfortunately you have now uncoupled the ID codes from their owners: a major problem (of course, you have a backup of the file, right?).

The issue here is selecting just a sub-region of the table. Excel will sort whatever is highlighted. If you select just a single cell, it will attempt to extend that selection to cover the entire table. But if you explicitly select just a subset of columns, Excel assumes that you know what you are doing and will apply the sort only to that set of columns while leaving the others in place. Get into the habit of *always* pausing before sorting a table, to check that the whole table is selected.

This issue is just one of the reasons why it is increasingly recommended to analyze and manipulate data in code, rather than directly manipulating it in a spreadsheet. In the coding approach, we generally leave the original data untouched, and so errors can be rectified by revising the code and running it again, knowing that the data file itself isn't being altered.

Note that each time you make any changes in the spreadsheet, or simply close and re-open it, all of the random values get recalculated. Those cells contain formulae and so should be viewed as dynamic, 'live' contents, rather than static values. This means that sorting the table by that column a second time would give a different result. If this is an issue, and you would like to store a snapshot of the original random numbers, then select the values and then paste them using the **Paste special** command or equivalent. This allows you to paste the fixed, literal values of the cells, rather than the underlying formulae.

Pro Tip: Random seed

No computer software can produce truly random numbers. In fact, for a given algorithm, for the same starting value, known as the 'seed', it will always produce the same sequence of random values. By default Python uses the clock to generate the seed, so you get a different pseudo-random sequence every time.

There are times when we don't want this to happen. For example, sometimes we want a 'random' sequence which is the *same* for everyone. For instance, in the Balloon Analogue Risk Task, if the balloon pops at a very small size in the first few trials, participants will tend to be wary of blowing subsequent ones bigger. Meanwhile, participants who randomly encounter only big balloons at the start of the task will be encouraged to be more risky. In a task where the aim is to measure individual differences, we might not want there to be any individual differences in the experimental sequence.

It might also be for reproducibility that you want to fix the sequence: if you're concerned that the sequence is influential enough that your experiment might fail to replicate with a different one, then you might want to specify a seed that can be used in future replications.

Either way, if you want to set the random seed to get the same random trial sequence every time, PsychoPy allows you to do this in the loop dialog, where you can set a value for the seed (say, an arbitrary value like 839216).

LET BUILDER KNOW THE RESULTS OF THE ASSIGNMENT

Variables that are entered into the info dialog box that appears at the start of an experiment are automatically stored in the data output file. You'll already be familiar with entering the unique subject ID for each session: this is crucial, as it ensures that each observation in the data file is tagged with the ID of the person who generated it.

We also should add a field for any group names or condition levels to which the participant has been assigned. This is obviously true for any variables that Builder needs to use to control aspects of the task, such as stimulus attributes. But it is also the case even if the variable doesn't need to be used within the experiment itself. For example, let's continue the example of comparing the effects of drinking coffee or tea vs water on alertness in a psychomotor vigilance task. The assignment to the beverage condition happens outside of PsychoPy, as does the manipulation (actually drinking the beverage). That is, the experimental procedure itself will be identical for everyone, and is not contingent on which beverage group people are in. We should, however, still enter a value for each person's beverage condition at the start of the experiment. This is done by adding a field to the information dialog that by default appears at the start of each experimental session in Builder. This ensures that the condition name will be saved in each row of the data output file. This will simplify our subsequent data analysis immensely, as all observations will be automatically tagged with the correct condition name.

As described above, the randomization scheme will generally be expressed in a table, with one row per participant. With a bit of code, PsychoPy could certainly cycle through such a table, keeping track across sessions of which row is next and mechanically assigning conditions to each subject as required. Running an experiment does not always go to schedule, however. One participant might only make it halfway through a session, for example, meaning that their data need to be discarded. You might decide to re-assign the next subject to the same set of experimental conditions to keep everything balanced. Or a male participant misses his appointment. The next participant is female and so you need to skip over one row in the assignment table, and then go back to fill in the missing cell later, with the next male participant. Sometimes you need to have the flexibility to depart from the strict order of the assignments (while still avoiding any biases). The complications of trying to implement this sort of flexibility in software can outweigh the simplicity of manually allocating subjects to conditions from a spreadsheet table.

10.2 UNDERSTANDING LOOP ORDERING OPTIONS

We've discussed how to randomly assign subjects across groups or conditions, but a lot of important randomization occurs *within* the experiment, such as randomizing the order of presentation of stimuli. This is usually achieved through the Builder loop dialog, which controls the order of presentation of the rows in a conditions file. You've already used this feature in preceding chapters. Our intention here is to describe more formally each of the options available through that dialog, and map them to the sorts of research designs you might want to implement.

PsychoPy uses 'sampling without replacement' from the rows in a conditions file. Imagine putting a set of chess pieces in a box and shaking it vigorously to shuffle them. One by one, you take pieces from the box and line them up on your desk. Because of the shaking, they will come out in a random order. As we are sampling without replacement, pieces don't go back into the box, and so they can't be chosen more than once. So, although we are getting a random order of pieces, the no-replacement rule does provide some certainty and structure. We know, for example, that once we have drawn out the black queen, she will not be selected again. Like the chess pieces, in PsychoPy terms each row from a conditions file will be selected once, and only once, on each repetition of the loop. This means that you can rely on any balancing of factor levels that you have specified in the file being maintained.

There are a number of ways in which we can control the order of the rows being selected. These are depicted graphically in Figure 10.2 and explained in detail below. In that figure, we use vertical bars to represent the value of some variable, taken from each of the 10 rows in the conditions file. Think of the height as representing some arbitrary quantity, like the duration or intensity of a stimulus, or the difficulty of an arithmetic problem. In the experiment depicted in the diagram, the loop will run five times, giving us five repetitions of the 10 conditions in the file, for a total of 50 trials. The four horizontal panels in the figure correspond to the different randomization schemes discussed below.

SEQUENTIAL

To cycle through the rows of the conditions file in order, select **sequential** *as the* **loopType** *option in the loop dialog.*

In some tasks we want to have an ordered progression of conditions. This arrangement is depicted graphically in the first row of panels in Figure 10.2: this shows a variable that increases in value systematically from the first row of the conditions file to the last. The height of each bar represents the value of some variable from each row of the conditions file. For example, you might want to present sentences or mathematical problems of increasing complexity, so that participants can benefit from progressive learning across trials. An example from the field of neuropsychological assessment is the *backwards digit span task*. On each trial of this task, the participant hears a sequence of digits and is asked to read them back, but in the reverse order. This task needs to be sequential, starting with just two digits and progressing until the subject can no longer perform the task. In the first row of Figure 10.2, such a task is represented by the steady increase in the height of the bars across trials.

In Figure 10.2, we depict designs in which the conditions file is repeated five times (i.e. the **nReps** value of the loop dialog is set to 5). So in the example in the first row, the task difficulty increases progressively within each block, but then resets to the easiest value at the start of the next one. This sort of design provides an assessment of how performance changes with practice. In the case of the digit span task, we might expect to see a slight improvement over the course of several blocks of trials, as participants learn strategies to optimize their span of recall.

Note that, with sequential presentation, we never get consecutive repetition of any row in the conditions file. This is something to be aware of, because consecutive repetition of the same value can cause issues in some tasks. For example, let's say we are stepping a target across the screen from trial to trial. If the coordinates on successive trials remain the same, the target would appear to 'stick', staying still for longer than normal. With sequential loop presentation, although we can't get

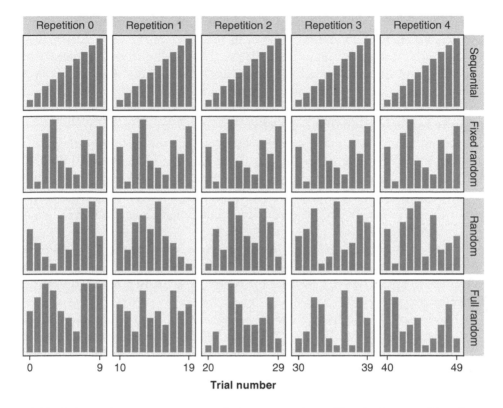

FIGURE 10.2 A schematic representation of values in a conditions file with 10 rows, and how their order of presentation varies, depending on the loop dialog settings. Each bar represents the value of some arbitrary variable, in each of the 10 rows of a conditions file (e.g. the volume of an auditory stimulus or the difficulty of a question item). The loop has an nReps value of 5, so it will cycle through the 10-row file five times, to run a total of 50 trials. See the text for a description of how to implement the various ordering schemes.

the same row selected on successive trials, there is nothing preventing us from putting the same *values* in those rows, however, which means that successive presentation of values is always something to be aware of. We'll revisit the possibility of this issue for each of the randomization options below.

FIXED RANDOM

Sometimes we want an order of conditions that appears to be random to the participant, but is in fact constant: every participant will experience the same pseudo-random order. We term this a 'fixed random' order.

This doesn't actually have a separate option in the loopType popup menu, and there are two ways to implement it. One method is to again select sequential as the `loopType` option, but using a manually crafted conditions file, with its random-like order of conditions built in to the order of the rows. Alternatively, you can select a `random` option, but specify a seed value to the randomization algorithm (explained further below). This means that although PsychoPy will do the randomizing for you, it will always produce the same order.

Having a 'fixed random' sequence might seem like an oxymoron, but there are many reasons to want the order of conditions to appear random to the participant, yet be constant across different experimental sessions. From the participant's point of view, the stimuli appear to be random: the participant does not know that everyone else will experience the same 'random' sequence. Such an arrangement is often termed 'pseudo-random': the experimenter has imposed one or more constraints on the order of presentation, which is not able to vary in a truly random fashion.

'Fixed randomness' is depicted in the second row of Figure 10.2. Here we see what looks like a random sequence of values but, because in this case the loop is set to repeat, we can see that the sequence actually reoccurs identically all five times.

A good example of a fixed random sequence, again from neuropsychology, is the California Verbal Learning Test (Elwood, 1995). In this widely used assessment task, a person is asked to recall a list of nouns from four categories (tools, fruits, clothing, and herbs and spices). The same list is presented and recalled several times within a session, with a consistent order of presentation each time. In part because of this consistency between trials, the number of correctly recalled items should increase across the session. To the participant, there is no simple discernible order within the list, but some constraints are nonetheless applied (such as never presenting consecutive items from the same category). If test results are to be standardized across subjects, it is important for the items to be in the same order, not only within the session, but across subjects. If the order varied, then we wouldn't know if recall performance truly reflected a given person's learning and memory ability, or was at least partly due to some orderings of the list being easier to learn than others. In PsychoPy, we would implement a task like this by crafting the order we want and putting those values in successive rows of the conditions file. We would then need to select `sequential` as the `loopType` option, because we have handled the pseudo-randomization ourselves, and just want PsychoPy to adhere to it.

Another example comes from motor-sequence learning tasks. For example, participants might have to click on targets as soon as they appear, at seemingly random times and locations. Over time, however, as the random sequence is repeated, implicitly or explicitly the participant begins to learn the underlying pattern. Also over time, we should observe that reaction times decrease, perhaps to below what should be possible in response to a truly random and unpredictable target.

PsychoPy users also sometimes create fixed pseudo-random sequences because they want to apply constraints beyond the simple randomization options that Builder's loop dialog provides. For example, we might want to ensure that stimuli of a certain type are never presented consecutively more than a certain number of times. So we might start with a randomly generated list, and then manually edit it by shifting rows around to hand-craft such constraints into it. Be wary of this approach, though. Let's say we have trials where a peripheral target can appear randomly to the left or right of a central fixation stimulus. You might be worried about what would happen to reaction times if the participant gets into a rhythm because the target has appeared for a prolonged streak of trials on one side. Hence, you might edit the conditions file so that the stimulus never appears more than three times consecutively to the left or right. Our participants are quite shrewd, however, and in a long enough session might learn this rule, consciously or unconsciously. They then know with certainty where the fourth target in a certain sequence will appear, as it will have to be in the opposite direction to the three preceding ones. This non-random constraint may itself have a larger effect on biasing reaction times than actual truly random streaks and clusters being presented.

To review, there are two ways to run fixed random sequences using Builder:

- We can hard-wire the sequence into the order of the rows in a specially crafted conditions file itself, rather than having PsychoPy apply its own dynamic randomization. This pseudo-random sequence is then simply stepped through sequentially (i.e. using the **sequential** loop type). This is the approach to take if you want to ensure some constraints are applied to the seemingly random order of presentation, such as limiting the consecutive appearance of certain values.
- Alternatively, we can create a conditions file as normal, and select the **random** loop type (see below), but with a specified value in the **random seed** field. Having a constant value as the 'seed' for the loop's random number generator means that the same random sequence will be generated every time the experiment runs. Use this in the case where you aren't too concerned about exactly what properties the random sequence has (so you're happy for PsychoPy to create it for you), but you want to ensure that the same sequence is experienced by every participant, each time the loop runs.

As with the sequential ordering described in the section above, it isn't possible for the same row of the conditions file to be presented on successive trials. That is, by definition, the row number presented on each trial must be different from the previous one.

RANDOM

You want the order of rows to be randomized within each cycle through the conditions file. Select random *as the* loopType *option in the loop dialog.*

This is the simplest and most common way to randomly order conditions. With this option, PsychoPy randomly shuffles the order of presentation of the rows within the conditions file. If the loop has an **nReps** greater than 1, then it will be re-shuffled on each repetition of the loop, as shown in the third row of Figure 10.2. This provides a constraint on the randomization. For example, if the height of each bar represents item difficulty, then the most difficult item is presented just once within each block of 10 trials. That is, its five occurrences must be spread throughout the blocks of the session: they can't all be clustered together in adjoining trials. For example, a given row from the file can be presented on any trial within each block, but it can only occur once within each block. This characteristic is why this option is the popular work horse for PsychoPy loops. It provides a compromise by giving us variation from trial to trial, yet still imposing a constraint, so that a given row from the conditions file can't appear in truly random clusters of successive occurrences.

Repetition of the same row in consecutive trials *can* occur, but only if that row happens to be randomly selected to be both the last trial in one repetition of the loop and the first trial of the next. For example, in the third row of panels in Figure 10.2, the last trial of repetition 1 and the first trial of repetition 2 have the same value. The maximum length of such a repetition would be two consecutive trials, however, as each row can be selected only once per block.

FULL RANDOMIZATION

You want full-on randomization: rows from the conditions file can be selected on any trial within the whole session, with no constraints. Select fullRandom *as the* loopType *option in the loop dialog.*

The **fullRandom** option only really makes a difference when you have more than one repetition of the loop. If the **nReps** value is 1 (i.e. you have a single repetition of the loop controlling all of the trials), then there is actually no difference between the **random** and **fullRandom** options. In either case, the conditions file order is simply shuffled randomly. The **fullRandom** option only makes a difference when the conditions file is repeated (**nReps** times). In that case, the order is shuffled across *all* of the total number of trials, without regard to the loop repetition number. It is as if the rows in a conditions file have been duplicated **nReps** times, and the shuffling applied to the whole lot at once.

This is shown in the example in Figure 10.2, where the shuffling has been applied as if there was a single conditions file of 50 rows, rather than being applied separately five times to the original file of ten rows. Let's say that the heights of the bars in that figure represent stimulus size. Then in the third row of panels in the figure, we see that when the **random** loop type is applied, the largest stimulus (represented by the highest bar) occurs once, and only once, within each repetition of the loop. Compare this with the **fullRandom** panels in the bottom row: four of the five maximum height values happen to be randomly clustered within the first repetition.

As **fullRandom** randomization is applied across the total number of trials, there are no constraints upon the number of successive identical items. This reduces participants' ability to predict upcoming stimuli. For example, the subject might become aware that a particular target has not occurred in the current block of trials and hence predict its occurrence with certainty on the last trial. This can be an issue for a number of tasks. For example, Builder comes bundled with a demo of the Balloon Analogue Risk Task, or BART (Lejuez et al., 2002). This is like a gambling task: the subject pushes a key repeatedly to inflate a balloon on screen; the bigger it gets, the more reward they can earn. At a random size on each trial, however, the balloon will burst. The participant only earns the reward if they end the trial before the balloon bursts. We want this to be a test of risk taking rather than pattern recognition, though. So we don't want any constraints on the randomization, or else the participant could benefit by 'card counting'. For example, if we use the **random** loop type, participants might soon learn that the smallest balloon size doesn't usually appear on successive trials. Thus if they encounter the smallest size on one trial, they know that they can inflate the balloon at least one level higher on the next. We can avoid this (potentially unconscious) learning by applying full randomization. Those occasional messy random clusters of successive identical values are exactly what we need in a gambling-like task, to avoid predictability.

Conversely, a truly random order can come at the cost of possible bias randomly appearing in the distribution of values. As we mentioned above, in the bottom row of Figure 10.2, four of the five highest values occur in the first repetition. Such randomly occurring streaks might themselves lead to some degree of anticipation or prediction by the participant. You will need to carefully consider the relative merits of full randomization versus the options of randomization constrained within blocks, or specified by a manually crafted fixed random order.

PRESENTING ONLY A SUBSET OF CONDITIONS

Specify a subset of row numbers in the Selected rows *field of the loop dialog.*

In some studies, there may be many more combinations of conditions than can be feasibly presented to any given subject, yet you still want coverage of the full set of conditions. Say you have a conditions file that has 200 rows, but in a session of reasonable duration, only 50 trials can be completed. This could be done by entering the Python expression 0:50 in the **Selected rows** field. Although Python is zero based, this expression results does result in 50 rather than 51 trials. A quirk of the language means that for this sort of expression, the last number is not itself included. That is, the range 0:50 will actually selects rows numbered 0 to 49, for a total count of 50 rows.

If the **loopType** option is **sequential**, then you will get the first 50 rows of the conditions file, presented in order. If the **loopType** option is **random**, then you still get the same 50 rows, but shuffled into random order. Effectively, we get a fixed selection of row numbers, but we can randomize the order within that selection. This means that we have to specify a different set of rows for each participant. What if you would rather get a random sample of any 50 rows, selected from throughout the entire set of 200 rows? This is possible if, rather than specifying a literal range of row numbers, we insert a Python function to generate a random sample of row indices. This code does exactly that:

```
np.random.choice(200, size = 50, replace = False)
```

At the start of each experiment, Builder imports a Python library called **numpy** (and, for convenience, abbreviates it as **np**). The **numpy** library contains all sorts of useful numeric functions (hence its name), including some randomization functions that are more flexible than the ones provided in the core Python language. In the code snippet above, we are using **numpy**'s **random.choice()** function to select a set of 50 numbers, from a range of 200 numbers (ranging from 0, the default start value, up to 199). We also specify that the sampling is without replacement, so that no row indices will be selected more than once. The **numpy.random** library provides many flexible randomization and sampling options: look online for its documentation to see how they might fit any more specific needs that you might have.

ADAPTIVE DESIGNS

All of the loop control options above are based on the fundamental idea that we specify the values of our stimulus parameters in advance of running the experiment, and hence can list them systematically in a conditions file. In the realm of psychophysics, designs where the researcher sets the stimulus values in advance are termed 'the method of constants'. In contrast, there are families of designs where it is the participant, rather than the experimenter, who controls the stimulus values from trial to trial. These are known as *adaptive designs*. They were pioneered in psychophysics, and their implementation and analysis remain most sophisticated in that field. For example, if we want to find a person's perceptual threshold for detecting a particular phenomenon, it is not efficient to present many trials that are either well above or well below threshold, as the participant will almost always detect, or fail to detect, them respectively. Those trials that are far from threshold therefore will contribute little information. What we want is to concentrate our trials in the region close to the threshold value, in order to get an accurate estimation of it. But as there are individual differences in threshold levels, we can't specify in advance what stimulus values will let us concentrate around the critical level. Instead we use adaptive staircase techniques, which are algorithms that alter the stimulus value from trial to trial, depending on the participant's responses on previous trials.

Adaptive staircase algorithms can be invoked by selecting the **staircase** or **interleaved staircases** options for the **loopType**. We won't deal with these specialized loop options any further in this chapter. For further details on these methods see Section 16.6.

10.3 SUMMARY

Hopefully you can now identify relevant features and techniques of Builder that enable different randomization schemes. In this chapter, and in earlier ones like Chapter 8 on blocking, you will have seen how the content and structure of conditions files, and the settings of the loop dialog, are particularly important for expressing and implementing your research design.

11

COORDINATES AND COLOR SPACES

Learning objectives: One of PsychoPy's features is that you can specify locations, sizes and colors in a range of coordinates (units), but that also provides you with something to learn!

Have you ever been frustrated by having to convert the size of your stimulus (which you created in 'pixels') into 'degrees of visual angle' so that you can write your paper? Did you have to create some complex code to switch this to a different size in order to present it on another screen? Or do you want a stimulus that automatically changes size and shape to fit the screen?

PsychoPy can help you with your woes. It was created with a range of different units to control both the spatial characteristics of your stimuli (size, position, etc.) and their colors.

11.1 COORDINATE SYSTEMS

One of PsychoPy's traditional strengths is that you can specify the location, size, etc., of your stimulus in a variety of 'units' such as degrees of visual angle or pixels. Although these different systems of units are very flexible and useful, they can be a little surprising on first encounter. Each has its own advantages and disadvantages.

One thing in particular is that PsychoPy doesn't follow some of the conventions that you may have seen elsewhere. For instance, **the origin** (0,0) in all of the coordinate systems described below is not the top left (nor bottom left) corner of the screen as a computer scientist might expect. For PsychoPy the (0,0) point is always the center of the screen and negative numbers always indicate a distance moved to the left or downwards, whereas positive values indicate displacements to the right and up.

Also, note that when setting the units for a stimulus, those units are applied to *all* the relevant settings for that stimulus. At the time of writing this book, you cannot specify the size of the stimulus in `cm` and the position of the stimulus in `norm`.

 Warning: Errors in units

Beware that changing units (or relying on the default units, which can change) is one way to create some confusing experiment bugs where your stimulus disappears; a position of [20,0] with units of `pix` would correctly put your stimulus 20 pixels to the right of center but the same position with units of `norm` would attempt to draw your stimulus 10 *screen widths* off the right which would not be visible! Similarly, if you set the size to be [0.5, 0.5] with `norm` units your stimulus will take up one-quarter of the height and width of the screen (read up on the `norm` units if it isn't clear why) but the same size with units of `pix` will (fail to) draw your stimulus with size smaller than 1 pixel!

In particular, beware of relying on the default units set in the PsychoPy preferences because, when you go to a different computer, you might find a different default there! When you create a new experiment it's a good idea to set the default units for that experiment (in the Experiment Settings dialog) at the start.

Basically, there are many ways to cause your stimulus to disappear and one of PsychoPy's flaws, at the time of writing this, is that it does not warn you that the stimulus you requested doesn't really make sense!

PIXELS (pix)

Pixels (`pix`) are probably the simplest units to use. Most people have a rough sense of what they represent (the number of dots on the screen making up your stimuli) and there are no surprises to come and bite you with pixels. Then again, it's much more annoying to calculate, from pixels, what the 'real-world' units are, and reporting the size of your stimulus just in pixels might not be sufficient to allow someone to replicate your study (because pixels differ from one computer to another).

CENTIMETERS (cm)

Obviously the notion of centimeters as a unit is quite natural to most people. You can of course simply draw your stimulus in pixels and then measure it on the screen using a ruler, but it's more convenient to have PsychoPy do the necessary conversion from cm to pixels (the native unit of a monitor). The one slight caveat with this is that you need to give PsychoPy a little more information about your monitor.

Although PsychoPy is capable of determining the size of your screen in pixels, computer operating systems don't report the width and height of the visible screen in cm and therefore PsychoPy isn't able to determine how many pixels there are per cm. To do this, go to Monitor Center and provide the spatial information (size in cm and size in pixels) as described in Section 13.4.

NORMALIZED (norm)

For normalized units it might be helpful to visualize the system using the diagram in Figure 11.1.

Here, the center of the screen is at (0,0), as with all units, and the left and bottom edges are represented by −1 while the right and top edges are +1. This is great for specifying a position that will be the same fraction of the screen on all screens. For instance, the position (0, −0.9) in normalized units will be centered horizontally, and 90% of the distance from the center of the screen to the bottom, whatever the screen size. Neat, right?!

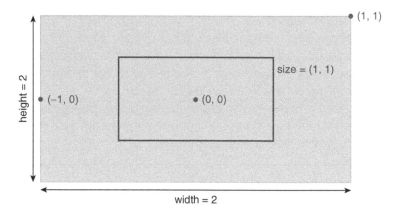

FIGURE 11.1 An illustration of **normalized** (norm) **units** assuming a wide-screen aspect ratio monitor (e.g. 1920 x 1080). Note that positioning seems quite intuitive (some points are shown in blue). The size is, initially, surprising in two ways, however. First, when the size is set to be (1,1) (as shown by the red square) you might well expect to see a square, but in fact you see a rectangle with the same aspect ratio as the screen. This is because the units here are effectively fractions of the screen and that screen size obviously differs in the width and height. The second surprise is that, to make a stimulus the full size of the screen, it should be given a size of (2, 2) rather than (1, 1) because the width and height of the screen are both actually 2 in this coordinate space.

The more confusing aspect when using **norm** units is thinking about sizes. The first thing is that the size of the entire screen is 2 (whereas you might think it should be 1). If you think it through, the left of the screen has a position of −1 and the right of the screen has a position of +1, so it does make some sense that the width of the entire screen must be 2 because the distance between −1 and +1 is obviously 2! Let's use that to reason through the height of some letters. If we set the letter height to be 0.1 with **norm** units, how big is that? Well, if we know the screen has an overall height of 2 in **norm** units then that means this letter is 1/20th the height of the screen (whatever that happens to be).

The second issue that can surprise people when using **norm** units is that specifying a seemingly equal width and height (e.g. (1,1)) does not result in a square stimulus but a rectangle! It results in a stimulus that has the same aspect ratio as the screen, which is nearly always wider than it is tall.

So **norm** units are great for laying things out at particular *locations* and for generating images that are full screen on all monitors (just set the size to be (2,2) and it will be the full width and height of the screen always!) but they're difficult for making things square.

HEIGHT (height)

With **height** units (shown diagrammatically in Figure 11.2) the issue of size is much more straightforward. A value of 1, in either direction, is the same as the height of the screen. Therefore, if you set the size to be (1,1) then you will get a square stimulus that is the biggest square to be fully visible on the screen.

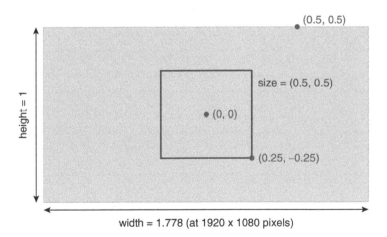

FIGURE 11.2   An illustration of **height units** assuming a wide-screen aspect ratio monitor (e.g. 1920 × 1080). The intuitive thing in this coordinate system is that the size of objects seems very sensible: when you ask for a size of *(0.5,0.5)* you get a square object whose width and height is half the height of the screen. What is less intuitive is that to know how wide the screen is you need to know its aspect ratio, and it doesn't seem quite as intuitive that placing an object on the top edge of the screen (for instance) is achieved by giving it a *y* position of *0.5* (because this is a half-screen distance up from the center of the screen).

The confusing part about `height` units, conversely to `norm` units, is that the position needs a little more thought. The top and bottom of the screen now fall at positions +0.5 and −0.5 (because this results in a full height of the screen equal to 1). The *width* of the screen depends on the aspect ratio of the monitor. For a standard HD screen (which has a resolution of 1920×1080) the left and right edges are at ±0.888889 (this is 1920/1080/2).

DEGREES OF VISUAL ANGLE

In an experiment where the size of a stimulus is important to the study it will often be reported in terms of the size the stimulus appeared *to the participant*, rather than its physical size on the screen. Obviously, the apparent size to the participant depends not just on that size, but on the distance they are sitting from the screen. To report the size of the stimulus in a common system that accounts for how big the stimulus was to the participant, we typically report the size/position of the stimulus in *degrees of visual angle*.

As with `cm` units, you could calculate this yourself, with knowledge of trigonometry, but you could also provide PsychoPy with the necessary information to have it done for you (it's so much easier to request your stimulus to be 2 degrees than to have to work out how many pixels that would require). To perform those calculations PsychoPy again needs some information about your screen; this time it needs to know the width in centimeters, the width in pixels but also the distance from the screen. Critically, bear in mind that if you move your screen, or your participant, to a different place in the room you may need to alter the distance that PsychoPy thinks your screen is to the participant! Now, to complicate things a little further, there are several ways that PsychoPy can calculate degrees of visual angle for you, depending on how precise you want to be.

The most common way to calculate degrees is to determine the width (in pixels) of 1 degree at the center of the screen and assume that this is the same all across the screen. This is convenient for two reasons: it makes calculations much easier if we assume a degree is the same number of pixels at all parts of the screen; and it makes stimuli 'look right'. The assumption isn't quite correct because your screen is probably flat, which means the corners are slightly further from your eyeball than the center of the screen (making another assumption that you are sitting directly in front of the screen rather than off to one side). Therefore 1 degree of visual angle contains more pixels at the corner than at the center, because degrees of visual angle depend on distance as well as physical size. How bad is error and do you need to worry? The effect is only noticeable in the periphery: if your stimuli are 3 degrees from the center then the location will be incorrect by 0.2%; but by 10 degrees eccentricity the error reaches 2%, and obviously increases the further you go. Unless you need very precise positional measurements and typically use stimuli in peripheral vision you can probably get by with this commonly used approximation. This is provided by PsychoPy if you use the units called `deg`.

💡 Pro Tip: Why are experiments often run at 57 cm from the screen?

You may or may not have noticed, but a surprisingly large number of studies report that the viewing distance of the screen from the participants was 57 cm. Not 56, not 58, but exactly 57 cm. This is essentially a trick that many people use to make it easier to calculate stimulus size in degrees (if they don't have PsychoPy to do the calculations for them). At 57 cm from the screen, a 1 cm stimulus located at the center of the screen subtends exactly 1 degree of visual angle. Conveniently, this scales linearly with distance, so at a distance of 114 cm, a 1 cm stimulus is now exactly 0.5 deg. So if you see 57 or 114 cm screen distances numbers cropping up in a journal article it's to make life easier with the maths. Of course, the edge of the screen, assuming a flat one, is now more than 57 cm from the eye, so this system does not correct for flat screens (it has the same precision as PsychoPy's `deg` units).

PsychoPy also provides two further coordinate systems to correct for the flat-screen geometry: `degFlatPos` and `degFlat`. With `degFlatPos` units the position of each stimulus is correctly specified but the size of the stimulus is not. This is convenient in that the sizes do not then look different at different parts of the screen. Square objects remain square and the sizes (in cm) are constant but the distances between them (in cm) increase as you get further from the center of the screen. This unit is useful for people studying eye tracking who might want a small stimulus (and don't care especially about the precision of its size) but want to know, very precisely, its location even at eccentric positions.

Lastly, the units `degFlat` are the most precise, correcting for a flat screen in the positioning of every vertex, such that stimuli that have the same size and spacing in degrees now have greater spacing and greater size (in cm) when in the corners of the screen. The differences will be small unless you have a very large screen (again the errors caused by the approximation are relatively small) but might be important if the spatial calibration needs to be exactly right.

Of course, these corrections all assume a flat screen with a participant directly in front of it. If your screen is not flat then you need to apply a warp to the stimulus rendering (PsychoPy can do that too but it requires a little Python code and is beyond the scope of this book). If your participant does not sit directly in front of the screen then we leave it to you to work out your stimulus size and shape!

11.2 COLOR SPACES

There are many ways to specify colors in PsychoPy: for example, using the name, a hexadecimal string (like #00FFCC) or a triplet of values. If you use a triplet of values you also need to specify the color space that those values correspond to so that PsychoPy knows how to interpret them. The details of each of these color systems are as follows.

BY NAME

You can simply write the name of the color as we did above. Any of the names of the 'X11 Colors' are recognized (see https://en.wikipedia.org/wiki/X11_color_names for the full list). The names should be written in lower case, and for names with multiple words (e.g. salmon pink) you use lower case and exclude the spaces (e.g. salmonpink).

RGB COLOR SPACE (PSYCHOPY STYLE)

A natural way to specify colors is to use a triplet of values for red, green and blue.

In PsychoPy's default color space these are specified in a rather unique way in that they range from −1 to 1 (conventionally the range is 0–255 or 0–1). In PsychoPy, the values range from −1 to +1 so that a value of [1, 1, 1] would be white, [−1, −1, −1] would be black, [+1, −1, −1] would be maximum red alone and [0, 0, 0] represents the middle gray. See the topic 'PsychoPy Signed Colors' to understand why this is used.

 Info: PsychoPy's 'signed' colors

PsychoPy's default color scaling, with values ranging from −1 to +1 rather than 0 to 1 (or 0 to 255), may seem confusing at first, but it was based on a good reason and turns out to have some useful features. It stems from the fact that PsychoPy was originally written to run experiments in vision science and, in those studies, the norm is for the screen to be mid-gray (which corresponds to zero in this space) and 'black' is the biggest luminance decrement from that mid-gray whereas 'white' is the biggest luminance increment.

One of the key advantages of this scale is that it makes calculations based on colors much easier. In particular the values of the space become synonymous with *contrast*. For example, if you have an image with RGB values in PsychoPy's color space you can halve the stimulus contrast by dividing the color values by 2, and when a color is 0, the stimulus has a contrast of 0! Also, if you want to invert the colors of the image (turn the blues to be yellow, turn the whites to be black, etc.) you simply give your color a negative sign and you get the inverse! In traditional RGB space you need to subtract your color value from 255 to get its color inverse. Yuck!

We should also note that the value of +1 in this space is not *quite* the maximum value that can be output from the monitor; it actually relates to the value 254 in the traditional color space. This is not something you will typically notice or care about unless your study really needs the stimulus luminance to be absolutely maximal. The advantage it brings is that it results in an odd number of luminance levels. Why is that useful? If you have an even number of light levels then there is no middle value. If your values are 0–255 then the mean luminance will need to be 127.5, but a standard monitor can't produce that luminance level, only 127 or 128 (see page 188 for an explanation of monitor output levels and 'bits'). So, by default, PsychoPy uses a gray screen with a luminance level of 127 and then a maximum level of 254 so that the mean luminance is exactly halfway between the minimum and maximum. Note that in the alternative, rgb255 color space that PsychoPy provides, you can request the maximum value 255, but that the middle gray will not then be perfectly centered.

RGB TRADITIONAL COLOR SPACE (RGB255)

You can choose to use the more common 0–255 range for the RGB values by selecting 'rgb255' as the color space. In this color space black is represented as (0,0,0) and white comes from (255,255,255).

HEXADECIMAL COLORS

Hexadecimal color specifications are also fairly common for those of you that have done web programming. They look like #00FFCC and PsychoPy recognizes them as strings that begin with #. Other than that, these hexadecimal values operate in exactly the way you've seen elsewhere: the three pairs of hexadecimal digits specify the respective intensities of the red, green and blue respectively (in the example #00FFCC red is set to 0, green is set to 255 which, in hexadecimal, is FF and blue is set to CC which is 204). If this seems foreign and confusing to you, don't worry about it; just use one of the other spaces.

HUE, SEPARATION, VALUE COLORS

HSV color space allows you to specify the Hue, Saturation and Value of a color as the triplet as well. The Hue in this color space is given in degrees around the full circle (so 0 to 360), the Saturation ranges 0–1 as does the Value.

Now, `Value` is a difficult color term to try and describe (which is presumably why the creators just called it 'Value'!) but, when the `Value` is 0 the resulting color is always black (irrespective of the H, S settings) and when V is set to 1 you get no black at all. So `Value` is a bit like 'brightness'. Fully saturated bright colors have S and V both set to 1. To create pastel-style colors you could set V to be 1 and set the saturation (S) to be low (e.g. 0.2). With S=0 (and V=1 still) you end up with pure white, and the color `Hue` has no effect. You can play around with HSV space in most applications that have a color picker (e.g. any drawing package).

DERRINGTON, KRAUSKOPF AND LENNIE COLORS (DKL)

All of the color spaces discussed so far are 'device-dependent'. The RGB or HSV value on one device does not generally correspond to the same color on another, because the exact color of the red, green and blue channels differs from one monitor to the next. To use a color space in which colors are the same across different devices, you need to have access to a calibration device that can measure the outputs of your monitor (see Section 13.6 for further details). Without performing the full color calibration (which requires an expensive 'spectroradiometer') you cannot use this color space.

The DKL color space was made popular by Derrington, Krauskopf and Lennie (1984), based on a chromaticity diagram by MacLeod and Boynton (1979). The space is typically represented as being spherical. It has an *isoluminant* plane, for which all colors have the same luminance, and colors are then specified with reference to this isoluminant plane. We can consider the *azimuth* of colors moving around the isoluminant plane as indicating the hue. Colors above the isoluminant plane are brighter, and below it darker, and this is usually also specified as an angle (the *elevation* from the isoluminant plane). The distance from the center of the circle indicates the saturation or contrast (as with PsychoPy's RGB color space this was designed by vision scientists and centers on gray). The radius is normalized, with a value of 1 being the maximum that a monitor can output in the white direction (confusingly, not all angles in the space are able to achieve the full radius of 1 due to limitations in 'gamut', or range of colors, that monitors can produce).

So, in this space we specify colors in terms of their azimuth (deg), elevation (deg) and contrast (−1 to 1, where −1 is effectively a contrast reversal).

11.3 PHASE OF TEXTURES

The final system of units that needs a mention is the phase of textures, but this only relates to grating-based stimuli. If you don't use such things then feel free to move along.

In most mathematical or engineering systems phase is defined in terms of an angle and therefore has units of either degrees or radians. It is a circular quantity, repeating at 2π radians (360 degrees). This makes sense in terms of phase typically being used to refer to progression around a circle or along a sinusoidal wave. For most of us, however, it makes calculations rather annoying. In PsychoPy we took the (further) unconventional step of giving phase a unit of 'cycles'. So phase in PsychoPy naturally ranges from 0 to 1 and then wraps in both directions around that. Since we nearly always want this to specify fractions of a cycle we can now just provide those directly without having to multiply repeatedly by 2π or 360. In particular, if we want a grating stimulus to 'drift' at a particular rate (let's say 2.5 cycles per second) we simply give it the phase of $t \times rate$ (e.g. t*2.5). How easy is that?

Ultimately, the issue is that PsychoPy units break with convention in a number of ways but they have been chosen deliberately because the conventions were actually not very convenient! We hope that, once you get your head around these coordinate systems, you'll find it a lot nicer than the conventional ones. Next we just have to go and convince the rest of the world that luminance does *not* need to vary over 0–255 and phase does *not* need to be measured in radians.

12

UNDERSTANDING YOUR COMPUTER TIMING ISSUES

Learning objectives: Understanding the physical limits of computers for reaction time studies (e.g. refresh rates and keyboard latencies).

Do your best to read this chapter fully. Although it may seem technical and boring, understanding the capabilities of your computer is really important if precise timing matters to your studies. You should not assume that the software is taking care of everything for you even (or especially) if the software manufacturer tells you that sub-millisecond precision is guaranteed.[1] The take-home messages are that you should test the performance of your system yourself. Luckily PsychoPy gives you the tools you need for some of these things (whereas some aspects of timing need hardware to test them properly).

If you don't manage to read the rest of the chapter then do at least take away the following messages:

- your stimuli must be presented for a whole number of frames, not arbitrary periods of time
- image stimuli take time to load from disk

---

1 No software manufacturer can guarantee sub-millisecond precision so when it claims to we suggest you be wary. It's a great headline but, as you'll see in this chapter, the reality is that your keyboard has a variable latency of around 30 ms, the top of your screen displays 10 ms before the bottom, and the ability to update depends on the complexity of the stimulus. What the manufacturer means is that the *clock* has this level of precision (irrelevant if the rest of the hardware doesn't) and that some things, like the presentation of simple visual stimuli, can be that precise if you have a decent computer.

- your monitor should be set to sync to the screen refresh
- brief periods of time are ideally timed by number of frames
- keyboards have a latency

12.1 UNDERSTANDING SCREEN REFRESH RATES

One aspect of 'understanding your computer' is that the screen updates at a fixed refresh rate. If you have a standard flat-panel display (most likely an LCD screen) then the chances are that your screen is updating at 60 Hz. OK, you probably knew that on some level, but an awful lot of people don't think about the consequences for their experiment. If we told you that you can't change your visual stimulus except on a screen refresh, this would probably seem obvious, but the fact that your stimulus can't be presented for exactly 220 ms might still come as a surprise.

If your screen updates at 60 Hz then the period between refreshes is 16.666667 ms. Your stimulus can be presented for an *integer* number of screen refreshes (we call them 'frames') like one of the options below. You can use the following equation to calculate the number of frames, N, required for a given duration in seconds, t and assuming a frame rate of 60 Hz:

$$N = t \times 60$$

Conversely, of course, you can calculate the duration (again, t) that a certain number of frames (N) will last, again assuming a 60 Hz rate:

$$t = N/60$$

So why can't you have your stimulus on screen for exactly 220 ms? If we multiply 220 ms (0.22 s) by the frame rate we would need 13.2 frames ($0.22 \times 60 = 13.2$), but we can't present a stimulus for 13.2 frames. We can present it for 13 or 14 frames (which would be $\frac{13}{60} = 216.667$ or $\frac{14}{60} = 233.333$ ms) but nothing in between. Luckily the 60 Hz frame rate does divide fairly well into many durations (e.g. 50 ms = 3 frames, so all multiples of 50 ms will be safe).

CAN I CHOOSE NOT TO SYNC TO THE FRAME?

It might be that the system settings on your computer (the Control Panel if you use Windows) has a setting to turn off/on synchronizing to the screen refresh (sometimes referred to as '*vsync*' or 'sync to *vblank*' because it is the point when the old cathode ray would be moving 'vertically' back to the top line). You might think it wise to turn this off and then your stimulus won't be restricted to those times. Sadly that isn't true. Although the computer will now probably attempt to update the screen (by changing its output signals) at a higher rate, like 300 times per second, the screen itself will still only be updating at that very fixed rate.

When *vblank* is turned off you might see 'tearing', where the computer 'frame' is physically displayed while the screen refresh was half finished, so the top half of the screen received one frame and the bottom half received the next one. This will be most noticeable if things are moving fast.

In addition to the potential for tearing you won't know when your stimulus is actually visible to the participant. One of the nice things about our stimulus being tied to the screen vertical refresh is that we get to know when that occurred (usually to a precision of less than a millisecond), whereas if we aren't detecting screen refresh times, because everything is out of sync, then we don't know how long after our command to draw our stimulus (up to 16.667 ms) the stimulus was *actually* able to appear.

DROPPING FRAMES

The next potential problem with the timing on a computer system is that, although it can calculate things really fast, calculations do take time; you can't expect everything to be achieved instantaneously. There are some operations that take a particularly long time, like loading images from a disk. Alternatively, your experiment might not be very challenging but your computer may be doing other things in the background (like downloading updates, checking your email and synchronizing with Dropbox), all of which also take some time. If you use a very powerful computer then those things might have little impact, but on a standard laptop they might slow down the running of your experiment considerably.

So what happens if we take more than the 16.667 ms between our screen updates, or if our computer suddenly gets distracted by its desire to update its anti-virus software? If PsychoPy can't get all the necessary code to run within the 16.667 ms time window then you will 'drop a frame'. When this happens the contents of the PsychoPy window in which your stimuli are presented will simply remain the same for another frame period and the next chance to update will be exactly one frame later than you had intended. It will be as if this frame simply lasted double the time (33.333 ms). The frame-dropping issue is depicted graphically in Figure 12.1.

In some cases a frame being dropped will be inconsequential. It might cause your movie to look a little jerky or your stimulus to last 16.667 ms too long. In other cases (e.g. if you study motion perception and need a smooth continuous motion, or if you study the high-speed perception of single-frame presentations) it could be disastrous and you need to take steps to check for frames being dropped during the study.

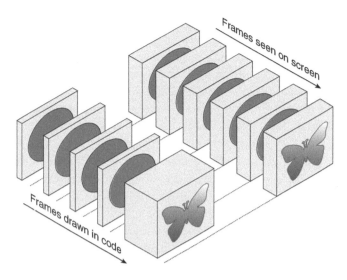

FIGURE 12.1   A graphical representation of how we get dropped frames. The top series of gray slabs represent the images physically appearing on the monitor on every screen refresh. They appear like clockwork, at reliably precise intervals (say, every 16.667 ms for a 60 Hz display). The dotted lines represent the time of onset of each image. The lower series of slabs represent the time taken to run the code to draw each image. On each frame, the code must finish running before the dotted line if it is to send the completed image to the graphics card in time to be drawn to the screen on the next refresh. That is, images are refreshed on screen at a constant rate of 60 Hz and the task of our code is to keep up with that inexorable hardware cycle. In the first four frame intervals, the code alternates between drawing pre-defined red or green circle stimuli, a simple task that can easily be completed within one frame interval. For the fifth interval, however, the experimenter attempts to draw a new picture, which requires reading from a large image file stored on a slow hard drive. This process takes too long to be completed within one screen refresh interval, and so a frame is 'dropped'. That is, as the code can't send the new image to the graphics card in time, the existing image (of the red circle) simply gets drawn again. This has the effect that, on its second appearance, the red circle stays on screen for 33.333 ms rather than the intended 16.667 ms, and when the butterfly image finally appears, it is 16.667 ms later than scheduled.

FURTHER ISSUES WITH MONITOR TIMING

As well as the fact that your monitor updates at a fixed frequency, you should also be aware of two other issues with monitor updates of a stimulus. The first is that the monitor updates pixel by pixel, generally from the top line of the screen towards the bottom. You may not be surprised by that but, again, you may not have thought about the consequences. The process of scanning down from the top takes up the majority of the refresh period, so if your frame is updating every 16.67 ms then roughly 12 ms of that might be taken up by the gradual sweep downwards from the top. What this means is that stimuli towards the top of your screen are presented several milliseconds before the stimuli at the bottom. So, before you make any claims about stimuli being recognized faster when they are presented 'above the fixation point', make sure that it isn't simply an artifact of your screen refresh.

One other issue that is increasingly a problem is that screens sometimes have a delay on the presentation they add *after* the computer has finished its processing. This is caused by 'post-processing' where the monitor adjusts the color and brightness of pixels to make your images look nicer. It's most common in flat-panel TVs and these shouldn't be used for scientific studies if you care about stimulus precision. There are two problems with this post-processing. The first is that you might have spent a great deal of time calibrating your stimuli (especially if you study visual perception) to make sure that the overall luminance or contrast is constant across stimuli, but the monitor then adjusts the image afterwards, potentially undoing all your good work. The second problem is that this post-processing can take time and this is *not* something that PsychoPy (or any software) can take into account because the monitor doesn't feed that information back to the computer. Essentially, it means that the screen refresh is not occurring when the computer receives the synchronization signal. The only way to detect this problem or to know when a stimulus actually occurred is by physically measuring it with dedicated hardware such as a photodiode and/or timing device, although as a first step check in your monitor settings to see if you can turn off any scene enhancements like 'movie mode', 'game mode', etc. Some monitors have a display setting called 'Direct Drive' that indicates post-processing is turned off.

12.2 TESTING YOUR STIMULUS TIMING

There are a few things to check if precise timing of visual stimuli is important to you. The first is to test what actual refresh period you have on your computer. Rather than relying on what the system preferences (Control Panel) tell you, it will be more accurate to go to PsychoPy and get it to measure the intervals that it detects between frames while rendering a stimulus. There are a number of advantages to this. It can tell you the exact refresh rate (recall that the refresh rate is often actually very slightly off the nominal 60 Hz) and it can tell if the screen is not synchronizing properly or if the timing is erratic.

There is also information to be gained from checking the log files in the data folder after you run your study, as these can tell you the durations of your stimuli after presentation. The precision of the timing information in these log files is dependent on the event that is being timed. For visual stimuli it is precise to the level of variability you see in the test of timing below, typically in the region of 200 microseconds (0.2 ms). If you do drop a frame, because something prevented the stimulus being generated in time for the screen refresh, then that will be reflected correctly in the log timing, and the true time that the stimulus actually appeared will be shown. For auditory stimuli and for keyboard responses, however, the limitations in timing are not things that PsychoPy can detect or measure, so the times being presented here are simply best estimates not accounting for keyboard or audio card latencies.

RUNNING A TIMING TEST ON YOUR MONITOR

The reality is that all computers differ and we can't tell you what yours will be like. In general fast computers will perform well with PsychoPy (especially those with high-performance graphics cards) but we have also seen good performance from some quite modest machines. We really don't recommend you use a cheap laptop (a 'netbook') for any serious computing. Ultimately, whatever device you intend to use, if you care about the timing of stimuli then you should investigate the timing for that specific machine.

Running this timing test is one of the rare times in this book that we'll ask you to use the other main view in PsychoPy, the Coder view. You can get this from the >View menu or by pressing Ctrl-L (or Cmd-L on a Mac).

In the Coder view go to the menu item >Demos>timing and select timeByFrames. This will open a Python script that you can then run to test your screen timing under simple conditions (just updating a couple of visual

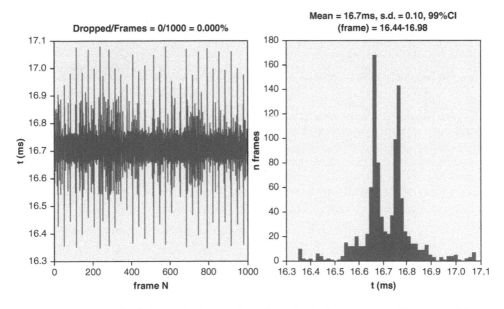

FIGURE 12.2 Example of screen refresh interval graphs under ideal circumstances. The timing of the system is being measured accurately to well under 1 ms precision (around 200 microseconds in most cases). Not bad for an ultralight laptop!

stimuli and testing what the refresh intervals were). We'll look at a few output graphs from that script. All the following were generated on a two-core Macbook Air laptop (i.e. not a high-spec computer but not a very poor machine either). We tested the performance for 1000 screen refreshes.

In Figure 12.2 we see the performance in ideal conditions. As many applications as possible were shut down and the stimulus window was in 'full-screen' mode. We see that the mean refresh interval is 16.71 ms (slightly more than the notional 16.667 of the screen) and all the refresh intervals are in the range 16.7±0.4 ms. That is, the timing of the system is being measured accurately to well under 1 ms precision (around 200 microseconds for the vast majority of the refreshes).

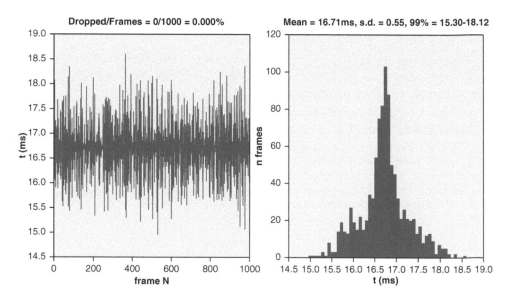

FIGURE 12.3 Example of screen refresh intervals with less precise timing. Frames are not dropped but the measured refresh times are more variable.

In the second example (Figure 12.3) the screen was set to run in windowed mode instead of 'full-screen', which tends to impair timing. No other significant processing was occurring when the test was run and, on this laptop, the timing was less precise (reported frame periods had a precision of just over 1 ms). Note that the actual occurrence of the screen refresh was still extremely precise; the variability here is in the detection of that refresh by the script.

Although, on this particular computer, the poorer timing did not actually result in any dropped frames — the stimulus was still presented with excellent temporal precision — this might not be true on your own computer. This is something you would need to test if you want to avoid using full-screen mode for some reason.

Info: Full-screen mode

A lot of users are puzzled by 'full-screen' mode and how it differs from the window just being the size of the screen. It differs in that, when your window is simply made the size of the screen, the other windows are still being processed; the operating system is still checking the state of those windows and working out which windows need to know about events like mouse clicks. It needs to check, for instance, whether your mouse is about to click on another window to drag it across the screen. In full-screen mode this no longer occurs. A window that is set to be full-screen takes priority over everything else and no other windows are visible. That means the operating system can focus all its processing on your experiment but it does have the downside that you can't now present another window (e.g. a dialog box) on top of your stimuli. If you really need to present other windows then you need to come out of full-screen mode and accept a slightly poorer timing precision.

Another problem with full-screen mode is that, if the experiment does freeze (e.g. due to an error in your experiment code), then it can be hard to escape the full-screen experiment. It is often wise while debugging your experiment to use windowed mode (in the Experiment Settings dialog you can turn off full-screen) and then just switch to full-screen again before collecting your real data.

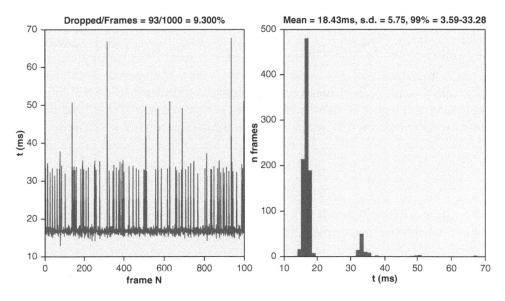

FIGURE 12.4 Example of screen refresh intervals with substantial timing problems. The laptop was running other processes in this run of the script and has dropped a large number of frames as a result.

In the third example (Figure 12.4) we have turned off full-screen mode but also turned *on* other background applications and, specifically, we have caused Dropbox to do some processing by adding a new folder to it. This additional processing of Dropbox and the other applications has caused the timing to get a great deal worse. Note that the axes on the graphs have changed scale and the frame intervals are now much longer and more variable. The majority of the frames are still around 16.67 ms: as in the second example, they would still have been exactly the same but the measurement of this is slightly more variable. Now, however, we also see a cluster of intervals of roughly 33 ms between refreshes, indicative of dropped frames. We can also see a number of occasions where multiple frames were dropped, resulting in 50 ms or even 66 ms intervals.

This last example shows how catastrophic it can be for your stimulus timing when the system is not running well. It was caused not by using a different software package for your experiment or an upgraded computer, but a simple change to one of the settings (full-screen) and a failure to turn off other running applications. Again, note that your own computer may differ. You may you have a laboratory computer of such high performance that these other events don't derail your timing. Alternatively you may have a machine that can't keep up with stimulus presentation even with everything optimally configured. You may have more demanding stimuli than those in this basic timing test (e.g. high-resolution movie files) so that timing gets worse during your actual study.

There is one more problem, only relevant on a Windows computer, that this timing test can identify, which is that you might see an average frame period of less than 10 ms. This might sound like a good thing in that your screen is updating extremely quickly but, unless you know that you have a very unusual monitor, this probably indicates a problem instead. Most likely it means that your monitor is not set to synchronize with the computer on its vertical blank interval (the refresh). Although PsychoPy (and the computer) updated the memory representation of the screen at a high rate (maybe 300 frames per second) the screen itself did not run any faster than its designated 60 fps, so what happened was that most of the changes being made by the graphics card in memory were simply ignored. The downside of this is that we really don't know what state our intended screen was in when the physical refresh of the monitor occurred. Even worse, the rendering might have changed *during* a refresh period (while the lines on the screen are in the process of being updated) and, if you have fast-moving stimuli, then this might result in visible 'tearing' artifacts.

The time intervals that PsychoPy reports back to you in this form of timing test are very precise. If your timing test reports that your screen refreshes were taking 16.7±0.4 ms then you can rest assured that this really is the timing of the system and that the timing of your visual stimuli really is being precisely timed to the frame and reported with a high (sub-millisecond) precision.

TESTING WITH A HIGH-SPEED CAMERA

These days one great way to test whether you are actually getting the sort of performance you expect from your stimulus presentation software is to record it using a high-speed camera capable of taking slow-motion movies. While high-speed cameras used to be very expensive, they are now readily available and a useful addition to the modern laboratory. To be useful for this purpose, your camera needs to be able to capture video at a higher frame rate than the screen is refreshing. The Canon Powershot G16, for example, is a compact camera capable of recording movies at 240 fps (albeit at a reduced resolution). This camera can also take close-up (macro) images of the pixels in your screen so you can also see exactly how your image is being portrayed by the pixels (e.g. to see how smoothing is working on your text). Note that we earn nothing from Canon camera sales and we are sure that other companies are also making great consumer-level cameras! If you want a suitable camera then search for references to 'consumer compact slow-motion video', in your favorite search engine and then look for something supporting at least 240 fps.

Sometimes with very brief or fast-moving stimuli our visual system itself can cause a stimulus to look 'wrong' even when it is being rendered correctly by the computer; visual illusions, such as adaptation effects, can occur. One of the useful things about testing your stimuli with a high-speed camera is that you can work out whether a particular artifact is a result of failures in stimulus presentation (PsychoPy or the monitor failing to produce the stimulus properly) or a result of your visual system (your eye failing to see the stimulus properly).

12.3 TIMING BY SCREEN REFRESH

PsychoPy is unusual in providing multiple ways to time the onset and duration of your stimuli and these have different advantages and disadvantages. In particular it is possible in PsychoPy to time your stimulus in terms of the number of 'frames' (screen refreshes). For brief stimuli this is generally recommended for two reasons.

The first is that it simply helps *you*, as an experimenter, to remember that you can't have stimuli presented for any arbitrary period. Although many people are aware on some level that their monitor is changing the image at a fixed rate it's very easy to forget that a stimulus of 220 ms is impossible (on a 60 Hz monitor). If you have to think about how many frame intervals you want the stimulus to be presented for, then it requires you to think about the duration of a frame and what that entails.

The second reason is that it helps PsychoPy to know how to carry out the timing. There will be times when PsychoPy will find itself some fraction of a frame from the target duration in seconds. What should the software do if it finds that the time is currently at 89 ms and the experimenter has requested a 100 ms stimulus? The frame is expected to last 16 ms, so should we try to squeeze in another one? If you tell PsychoPy to use exactly six frames then, provided frames aren't being dropped while your stimulus is presented, you will get exactly 100 ms for your stimulus.

For prolonged stimuli it probably won't matter a great deal if this decision of whether or not to run one more frame goes wrong; in the worst-case scenario you'll have a single frame too few, or a single frame too many, and that probably won't affect your stimulus. Furthermore if your stimulus duration is *very* long then you increase the potential time during which a frame might be dropped. Therefore, for long durations the most precise timing is probably to use `time(s)` settings, unless you know that your computer never drops frames during your stimulus presentation.

12.4 IMAGES AND TIMING

In the GFMT the stimuli (see Chapter 3) are presented indefinitely and the timing is not important, but in many tasks image stimuli must be presented at a precise time and for a precise duration. How well the timing occurs is specific to the machine, but when programmed correctly on a fast computer with a good graphics card then very high temporal precision of visual stimuli should occur. For images there are a couple of things to watch out for and try to optimize as follows.

Minimize the number of pixels in the image. Most cameras now take photographs with upwards of 10 megapixels. This is great for printing high-resolution images that don't look pixelated but it's complete overkill for a stimulus in your experiment. Bear in mind that on a traditional computer the entire screen might have a resolution of 1280×800 pixels (roughly 1 megapixel). Even standard HD resolution is only 1920×1080 (roughly 2 megapixels). So using high-resolution images from your digital camera probably means that you're asking PsychoPy to process 10 times as many pixels as it needs to, and that takes time.

Load images in advance if possible. When you tell PsychoPy to change the image that a particular stimulus is using, it takes time for PsychoPy to handle the request. The image needs to be loaded from the disk, which can take tens of milliseconds, and is dependent on image size. Then the image needs to have its color values scaled to the correct format and to be loaded onto the graphics card, which has separate memory. The good news is that from here onwards everything will happen extremely fast. If the stimulus needs to be rotated, flipped or changed size on the screen then this can all be done by the graphics card without recomputing the image pixels (this uses 'hardware-accelerated graphics', the key behind PsychoPy's capabilities). So the other changes can be made within a screen refresh period, meaning that we can change them whenever we like without damaging timing, though loading up the image will slow things down.

In many cases the stimulus will be loaded during a fixation period at the beginning of your trial (e.g. the 0.5 s gap before the stimuli in the GFMT, as we created it) and, if nothing critical is to be timed during that period, then all will be fine. Also, images that are constant will just be loaded at the beginning of the study, before any time-critical events begin.

For images that need to be updated on each trial (or even *within* a trial) PsychoPy additionally allows us to specify times that we call 'Static Periods', whereby we inform PsychoPy that nothing else is occurring that needs attention (e.g. no need to update the screen or check the keyboard during an inter-trial period) and this would be a good time to preload the next stimulus and put it onto the graphics card. To do this, add a Static Component to your Routine (from the 'custom' category in the Components Panel) and set the times that this should be from/to in the normal way. Make sure that no stimuli are being updated during this period and that no responses are being collected (see Figure 12.5). Then from your stimulus, instead of 'set each repeat', you should be able to select 'set during trial.ISI' from the dropdown menu for your images.

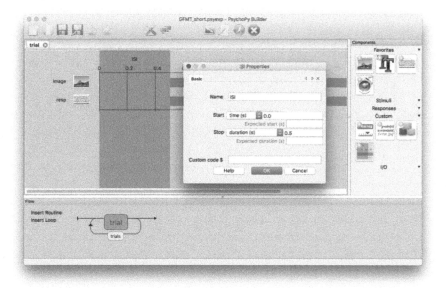

FIGURE 12.5 Adding a Static Component to our `trial` Routine indicating the period when we can safely update images.

Occasionally the computer may not be able to achieve all the necessary processing within the stated duration of the Static Component. In this case you should receive a warning message that this happened and then you need to take steps either to extend the static period or to reduce the number of images/pixels that need to be loaded/processed during that period.

12.5 RESPONSE-TIME PRECISION

The presentation of visual stimuli is just one aspect of temporal precision. Another one that scientists often need is the precise measurement of reaction times. Actually, the first part of getting precise reaction times is related to the presentation of stimuli: if you aren't managing to synchronize your stimulus presentation to the screen refresh then PsychoPy (or other software packages) will not know when the stimulus was physically presented on the screen. If we do not know when the stimulus physically appeared on the screen then we can't know very well how long after that stimulus presentation the response occurred. For this reason PsychoPy has a checkbox in its Keyboard Component settings labelled `sync RT with screen`. This indicates to PsychoPy that it should consider the start point of the reaction time to be based on screen refresh. If you start your image stimulus at `t=2.0` and your keyboard response at the same time, then, with `sync` turned on, the keyboard will consider time 0 to be the point when the visual stimulus physically appears on the screen, even if there is some timing delay (e.g. dropped frame) as that occurs.

The second issue with precision in response times, however, is one that PsychoPy can do less about. This is the problem of keyboard latencies. Unfortunately your keyboard was not designed to give sub-millisecond timing. Users of Microsoft Word do not need their keyboard to be checked for keypresses every millisecond! Even computer gamers, who do care about reaction times, do not need to check the keyboard every millisecond: given that the screen only updates 60 times per second, their character doesn't need to change position every millisecond (1000 times per second). It is pretty much only behavioral scientists that want this level of precision.

So what happens if you need sub-millisecond timing for responses (as claimed by some of the software manufacturers)? Well, in essence, you need to use a different device to record that response, namely a dedicated response box (e.g. Black Box Toolkit, Cedrus and several other companies make reaction time boxes designed for this purpose).

That said, you might want to think about whether you truly need the sub-millisecond precision that you think you need and that you've been led to believe is reasonable. Again, think about the other factors in your experiment. The biggest source of error is likely to be the participant. Humans have quite variable reaction times even when they aren't asked to 'think' about anything, just to 'respond as fast as you can'. If the sequence of neural processes from perception (see the stimulus onset) to action (respond) has a variability on the order of 50 ms then measuring it with an accuracy of 1 ms is not necessary – it's like measuring your height to the nearest micrometer.

Does this mean you can't measure experiment effects that are on the order of, say, 5 ms? No, not at all. Thankfully, by running multiple trials and averaging the reaction time across them you can actually measure rather small differences (Ulrich and Giray, 1989).

Ultimately, unless you are studying time perception (e.g. the ability to maintain a perfect beat) or studying something with the temporal precision of EEG (e.g. the neural response time-locked to a keypress) then you probably don't need your keyboard to have sub-millisecond precision!

13

MONITORS AND MONITOR CENTER

> **Learning objectives:** Understanding your monitor is not just about refresh rates. Here we teach you about monitor technologies and about calibrating your screen.

13.1 COMPUTER DISPLAY TECHNOLOGY

In the previous chapter on timing, we discussed some of the issues around monitors, namely their fixed refresh rate. There are a few additional issues around monitors that are worth knowing about, however. In particular, we get asked fairly often what sort of monitor is good for performing experiments. There are several different forms of display technology available these days, each with its advantages and disadvantages.

 Info: Graphics cards and hardware acceleration

Part of the reason that PsychoPy is able to display graphics rapidly and update them on every frame is that it uses 'hardware-accelerated' graphics to do a lot of the work. For instance, calculating what the pixels on your screen should look like, as a photograph is rotated or stretched, is all done by the graphics card. The advantage of this is that:

- the graphics card GPU (Graphical Processing Unit) is really optimized for this sort of work, which involves a lot of matrix multiplication
- while the graphics card is doing that, it leaves the CPU free to work on other things, like checking the keyboard or processing your data.

You may have heard that it's very important to have a good graphics card to run PsychoPy. It used to be the case that the PsychoPy team routinely advised against anything that contained an Intel integrated graphics chip because it tended to be both slow and full of bugs. Increasingly, however, having a powerful graphics card only matters for experiments that use lots of stimuli, or stimuli where a lot of computation is needed (e.g. a shape with many vertices that are being manipulated continuously). Even Intel integrated graphics chips are now typically fast enough and have far fewer bugs than previously.

That said, updating the drivers of your graphics card is a really good idea (especially if you have error messages to do with memory - these have usually turned out to be graphics card problems) and upgrading it to an nVidia or ATI model is generally going to make things run faster too.

CRT DISPLAYS

The cathode ray tube (CRT) is an old beast but, in its day, it was the workhorse of visual presentations. In fact vision scientists were so afraid of the poorer performance of LCD technology at first that many labs stockpiled CRT monitors for their future experiments.

For those that don't know, a CRT is the old type of not-at-all-flat monitor, a big box that was really heavy and usually a creamy beige color. The CRT contained a 'gun' that fired electrons from the back of the monitor housing to the front surface of the screen. At the screen surface the electrons would collide with a phosphor that would then glow brightly in a particular color (red, green or blue). The brightness of the glow was determined by the number of electrons, which was determined by the voltage being passed to the gun. Note that there are typically three electron guns in the CRT, one for each colored phosphor, which must be focused on each pixel location of the screen sequentially.

Each pixel is lit for a very brief period; phosphors light and return to black very quickly (on the order of a few milliseconds, depending on which phosphor is used). The entire screen is therefore effectively flashing bright and dark many times each second. As a result, CRT screens viewed in your peripheral vision (with your rods rather than cones) appear to flicker if not set to a high enough refresh rate (by 70 Hz the flicker becomes invisible for most people).

The beam typically starts at the top left corner of the screen, scans horizontally across each line and then moves down to the next line. This all happens very fast; the beam rests on each pixel for a few microseconds before moving to the next. To complete this on all the pixels of the screen, however, takes a considerable period and results in the gradual rendering of the screen image line by line from the top. The majority of the screen refresh duration is spent with the beam updating each line and then, at the end of each frame, the beam spends a further few milliseconds returning to the top left corner to start again.

What does this mean for stimulus presentation? There are several implications of this technology:

- There is a clear limitation on how often the pixels can change their values.
- The screen spends most of the time being black and each pixel is only briefly bright.
- Given the sequential updating of the lines on the screen, the bottom of the screen is updated roughly 10 ms after the top line of the screen.
- As an analog device, the CRT tube can set the brightness of the red/green/blue guns to any arbitrary level according to the resolution of the voltage control on its inputs.
- Changing the resolution of the screen does physically change the resolution on the screen, as the positions of the beam landing points can be varied

LCD DEVICES (FLAT PANELS AND PROJECTORS)

Most 'flat' screens that you encounter will be liquid crystal display (LCD) panels (there are also a few plasma screens around but those are rare as computer monitors and we will not talk about them here). Most projectors also use LCD panels and have exactly the same properties and caveats as below. LCDs work by a different technology to CRT displays. Unlike the pixels in the CRT which light up, these pixels are more like a color filter and need a light behind them (a 'backlight'). Unlike the array of pixels of a CRT that briefly flash on as the electron beam passes over them, this backlight is always on (in standard consumer systems). Also, the pixel does not have a black period in between each screen refresh – it merely switches to the next color, as needed in the next frame.

Traditionally the rate of the pixel color switching was rather sluggish compared with CRTs; it took longer for the liquid crystal to change color than it did for the CRT phosphor to light up. For many years this was a problem for scientists (particularly vision scientists) because the stimulus would 'persist' after it had been removed from the screen, and objects that moved would leave a trail behind them. Luckily those days are gone; modern LCD panels have very fast switching times and are now very suitable high-speed displays for many scientific experiments.

LCDs still have the problem that they nearly all have a fixed refresh rate (mostly 60 Hz but 120 and 240 Hz monitors are also now available) and that the screen fills downwards from the top rather than updating everywhere simultaneously.

One concern with LCD panels, though, and this can be quite a major problem for precisely timed studies, is that some of these screens don't just present the screen pixels exactly as sent by the graphics card, but perform some post-processing on them to make the colors more vivid or the blacks more black. The first problem with this is that you, the scientist, might have spent a long time perfectly calibrating your stimuli only to have them altered by the monitor. The worse problem, however, is that it might not manage to do this reliably within the frame period. This means that, although PsychoPy managed to send the pixels for your screen update in time and correctly reported the time that the computer updated its output, the screen itself was delayed in displaying that stimulus. For this reason, if the precise time that a stimulus appears matters to you then you might want to test this with some form of light detector that tells you about your stimulus timing. For example, you could test in advance with a Black Box Toolkit, or continuously monitor your stimulus onsets with a Cedrus StimTracker. On the plus side, having determined that your monitor itself is not introducing timing errors, it should remain that way; it should not, for instance, only have erratic timing when certain stimuli are presented. If you find the timing *is* poor then there may be settings in the monitor menu system (on the monitor, not on the computer) to turn off any image 'optimization'. If not, you may want to try a different monitor. PsychoPy's visual stimulus presentation should be very precise, so if you find that visual stimuli have poor timing then, for this reason, trying a different display might be a thing to do.

Another important thing to know about your LCD panel is that it has a 'native' resolution and, although it might be willing to accept other resolutions as inputs, it *must* ultimately present the screen image at its native resolution. If the monitor settings of your computer do not agree with the native resolution of the panel then it will interpolate the pixel values to fit. In extreme cases, where the aspect ratio doesn't match, this will cause the screen image to look stretched on the monitor, but in nearly all cases it will result in blurring. This will be most visible around sharp, narrow edges, such as pieces of text, but it will occur over the whole screen. To make sure your screen image is as sharp as possible, always check the native resolution of the monitor and set your Control Panel settings to match. If you use a projector or second screen to present your stimuli then make sure that the screen dimensions are set to the native dimensions of that display where the participant will view the image (not your own monitor that mirrors the stimulus display). It's no use having your display all nice and sharp if the participant is seeing something that has been interpolated and is now all blurry.

The last notable difference between CRT and LCD technology, but probably only important to vision scientists, is that LCD panels are not analog devices with a continuous range of luminance values like CRT displays. They have a fixed set of values, most commonly 256 possible levels for each color channel (this is the system with 8 bits per channel, as described below). Some LCD panels, especially on laptops, will only actually provide 6 bits (only 64 levels of each gun) and then apply fancy technology (dithering) to try and get intermediate colors. A few LCD panels allow a larger 10-bit range (1024 gray levels).

Info: What is 32-bit color?

Monitors and graphics cards cannot create any arbitrary luminance level in their range; they are restricted to a certain number of fixed values. The number of fixed values is determined by how many 'bits' of information they can provide. A single bit of information is a single binary value that can be 0 or 1. With 2 bits you have two of these binary values, and you now have four possible values (00, 01, 10, 11). With 3 bits you have eight possible values and, most generally, with N bits you have 2^N possible values. Most computers are set up to use 8 bits (256 levels) of color per 'channel' (red, green and blue), which means a total of 16 million colors. This sounds great, and for most purposes it is more than enough. It isn't quite enough for a few tasks: for instance, where we want to find the luminance level that participants can 'just' see we find that the smallest possible increment from black is already visibly different to black so, for some uses, we might want even more than 8 bits per channel. You might have heard your computer describing its color system as '32-bit color' but we've just told you that there are three channels of 8 bits (and note that 3×8 is obviously not 32)! The remaining 8 bits are stored in another channel, the alpha channel, which stores how 'transparent' the pixel is, but this doesn't ultimately alter how many colors are presented, only how the current color should be combined with others.

The CRT was necessarily tied to a particular timing procedure because the electron beam necessarily had to visit each pixel in turn with a very precise time in order to work. That absolute requirement seems less clear for an LCD panel. These obviously need a *minimum* period but could then wait an arbitrary time before drawing the next frame so the frame rate could, technically, be variable. So far, because LCD panels were built to work with computers that expected these fixed frequencies, nearly all flat panels currently do the same, but technologies like nVidia's G-Sync and AMD's FreeSync allow monitors not to refresh at arbitrary times rather than at fixed intervals. These technologies are, at the time of writing, relatively young and not widely used, but they are likely to be influential in the future.

What does LCD technology mean for stimulus presentation? In summary:

- The screen no longer flashes between black and the target color; it stays 'on' at all times and merely switches directly from one color to the appropriate color for the next frame.
- The updating of pixels still typically occurs from the top to the bottom of the screen and still takes the majority of the screen refresh period to incrementally update the lines of the screen.

- Flat panels are not analog devices; they have a fixed number of luminance levels, most commonly 256.
- Flat panels have a 'native' resolution and setting the computer to output at any other resolution simply requires the monitor to interpolate the image back to that native resolution.
- The physical requirement of the timing of frames is less strict for flat panels, but currently most monitors still have a fixed, whole-screen refresh cycle in keeping with the CRT technology they supersede.

DLP PROJECTORS

The other common form of projector technology in current usage is the digital light processing (DLP) projector. This technology is a little bit mind-blowing, but bear with us! It consists of a projector lamp that shines onto a computer chip containing millions of microscopic mirrors that can be rotated so that the light is (or is not) reflected back to the projection screen. These micromirrors become the pixels of the resulting image. Of course, being able to turn pixels simply 'on' or 'off' isn't much of a display, but they can turn on and off at a rate on the order of 30 kHz (30,000 times per second!) and by controlling the fraction of time that they are on and off they can generate a wide range of intermediate luminance values.

 Info: Texas Instruments DLP chips

The DLP processor was developed in 1987 by a Texas Instruments engineer, Larry Hornbeck, and Texas Instruments remains the sole developer and manufacturer of the chips. The TI 4K UHD, released in 2016, contains just over 4 million mirrors, which can display over 8 million pixels.

In 1999 the technology made its debut (presenting the *Star Wars: Episode 1 – Phantom Menace* movie) and is now used in 8 out of 10 digital cinema theaters worldwide, according to Texas Instruments. In 2015, Larry Hornbeck was awarded an Oscar for his contribution to the movie world. Well done, Larry!

To achieve color pixels there are two options. Some projectors use three of the micromirror chips, one for each color, and then combine these back onto the same screen. More commonly, they utilize the fact that the mirrors can turn on and off very rapidly (which means potentially high frame rates) to spin a 'color wheel' past the projector and switch the pixels to present their red, green and blue values sequentially using a single chip. In early versions this actually led to some pretty ugly color artifacts when people moved their eyes – you would perceive a rainbow of colors – but this has been solved by alternating the colors more rapidly.

The DLP projector has several advantages. It produces very high contrasts because the mirror system is excellent for not 'leaking' light when the pixel should be black (recall that LCD panels have to block the light and they never become quite opaque enough to do this). DLP projectors can also be set up to have very high frame rates (especially if the color wheel is removed, which is possible on some models).

One more thing that distinguishes this display type from the others is that it has a linear luminance profile. CRT and LCD displays need to be gamma corrected (see Section 13.5 for an explanation) but DLP projectors do not.

In summary:

- This technology is unbelievable: it uses millions of microscopic mirrors that turn pixels on and off at astounding rates. It really shouldn't be possible!
- DLP projectors have extremely high contrast: they can use a very bright lamp but still prevent it from 'leaking' to achieve very dark black pixels.
- They have a naturally linear luminance profile.

WHAT ABOUT A TV?

Most modern televisions are basically LCD (or plasma) panels, and they are often quite large and can be connected to your computer. That doesn't mean they are a good choice of display for your lab. In particular, televisions are the worst examples of performing a lot of post-processing: they try to make your image look more beautiful by playing with the colors, and getting the image onto the screen really quickly is not their main objective. If precise colors and precise timing aren't important (e.g. you just want someone's impression of some images and don't care exactly how the images look) then this is a perfectly reasonable choice, otherwise a computer monitor is probably a better idea.

13.2 MONITOR CENTER

Monitor Center is designed to make monitor calibration as painless as it can be. It's rarely painless, but we can try! Even if you don't use Monitor Center to perform the calibration itself it's worth using it to store calibrations.

Monitor Center is available from the Tools menu in either the Builder or the Coder view of PsychoPy. Selecting it brings up a new window, as shown in Figure 13.1.

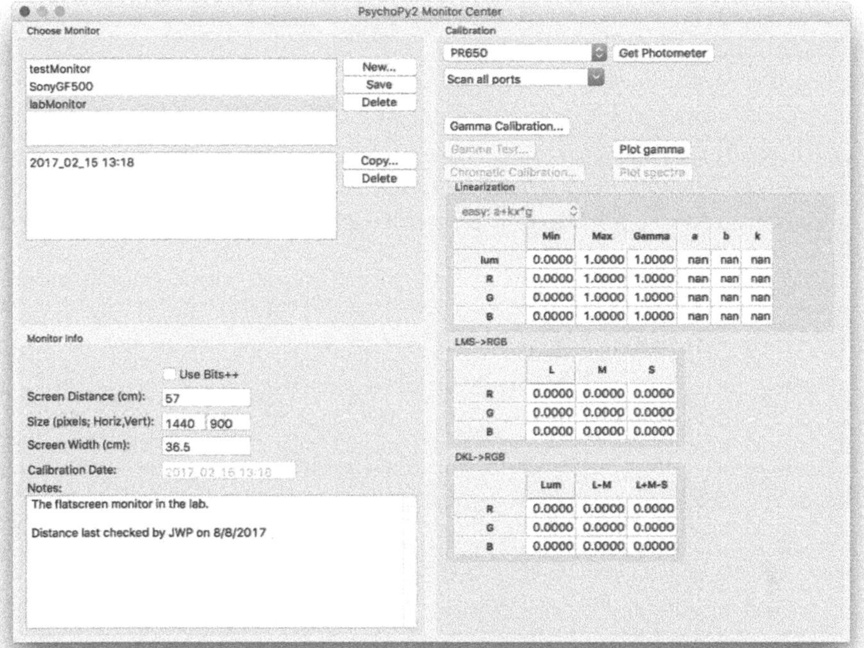

FIGURE 13.1 PsychoPy Monitor Center is available from the `Tools` menu. It can help you store multiple calibrations for different monitors. This is important if you want PsychoPy to calculate your stimulus size/position in units like degrees of visual angle. You do have to remember that your experiment also needs to know which monitor calibration to use!

13.3 MONITOR CALIBRATION

Depending on the experiment you intend to run, PsychoPy may need to know some things about your monitor in order to help you. For instance, you could prepare all your stimuli using pixel units and do the necessary maths in order to calculate what that means in terms of, say, degrees of visual angle. On the other hand, you could tell PsychoPy about the size of your monitor and distance to the participant and then PsychoPy can do the mathematics for you! Happy days!

There are three aspects to monitor calibration that may be needed, depending on what type of study you intend to run:

- **Spatial calibration** is needed if you want to set the size of your stimuli in real-world units like degrees of visual angle. This is a very easy calibration to do manually; all you need is a tape measure.

- **Gamma correction** is needed if you care about whether the mid-gray level is exactly half the luminance of the white. Surprisingly, on most screens, this is not the case and you may need to correct for it. This can be done either using a photometer or psychophysically.
- **Color calibrations** are needed to use a device-independent color space (accounting for the differences in screen colors between monitors). These calibrations require expensive hardware (a spectroradiometer).

13.4 SPATIAL CALIBRATION

Spatial calibration is very simple and allows PsychoPy to convert between coordinate systems. For instance, in order to calculate how many pixels a stimulus should span when you request '3 cm', PsychoPy needs to know the size of each of the pixels on your screen, and to know how to convert from degrees of visual angle to pixels it also needs to know how far away the participant is sitting.

To calibrate spatially, all you need is a tape measure to measure the distance and the dimensions of the visible part of the screen (i.e. the portion showing actual pixels). You also need to know the resolution of the screen, which you can determine from your computer's system settings.

13.5 GAMMA CORRECTION

Unless you're using a DLP projector then the mid-gray of your monitor will almost certainly not be half the luminance of the screen. That means you can't determine the overall luminance of your stimulus, which sensory and cognitive scientists often need to do. If you don't care about things like stimulus luminance then feel free to move along!

In general the luminance output has a gamma function:

$$L = \upsilon^{\gamma}$$

where L is the luminance, υ is the requested value (normalized to the range 0–1) and γ is the 'gamma' for the monitor, usually a value around 2. The result of this is that when we plot υ against L we get a curve that gets steeper with increasing υ. We need to 'linearize' or 'gamma-correct' the monitor so that, when we plot υ against L, we get a straight line.

There are a few ways to do this, either using a photometer or just using our eyes!

> ## 📢 Warning: Set your experiment to use the gamma-corrected monitor
>
> It's easy to forget that calibrating your monitor is only one part of the process. You also need to tell your experiment that you expect to **use** that calibration (and which one, given that you can have multiple monitors and multiple calibrations for each one). Whichever calibration method you use, you need to open your Experiment Settings and, in the `Screen` tab, type the name of your monitor calibration. If the messages at the end of the experiment include **'WARNING Monitor specification not found. Creating a temporary one…'** then your monitor calibration file wasn't found and no gamma correction was applied. Check the name of the monitor in Monitor Center.

AUTOMATIC CALIBRATION USING A PHOTOMETER

To perform a fully automated calibration you will need a device that PsychoPy can communicate with over a serial/USB port. At the time of writing the following devices are supported:

- SpectraScan PR650, PR655, PR670
- Minolta LS100, LS110
- Cambridge Research Systems, ColorCal MkII.

With these devices you can start the calibration, point the device at the appropriate patch on the screen and go and grab a coffee (or decaffeinated drink, if you are so inclined). PsychoPy will update the screen, check what value the device has measured and move on to the next level. The calibration will take anywhere from a few minutes to maybe half an hour, depending on how many luminance levels you choose to test, but you won't care if you're relaxing in the cafe while it does its thing!

PROCEDURE

Open Monitor Center and select the monitor (or create a new one) in which to save the calibration.

In the `Calibration` panel you will find various controls, including one to connect to your photometer. First select the type of photometer you have connected and turn it on, then press the 'Get Photometer' button. If all goes well you will get a message to say that the photometer has been found, and which serial port it is connected to. If you don't get this message then you may need to install drivers for your device. If you use Windows, check that it shows up in your Device

Manager, which can be found in your system settings. Most devices come with their own software to connect to them; if you have trouble then see if that works instead (if not then PsychoPy definitely can't help you).

Once you have made a successful connection to the photometer, which only needs to be done once after opening Monitor Center, you should press the button `Gamma calibration...`, which will bring up a dialog box. Select the settings you need (as mentioned in the caption of Figure 13.2). These aren't that critical; more measurements will allow you to visualize your gamma correction better but shouldn't actually make a huge difference to the quality of the calibration. The choice for the size of the patch is a matter of choosing something reasonably small, but where you can easily point the photometer just to the central stripe of the calibration screen.

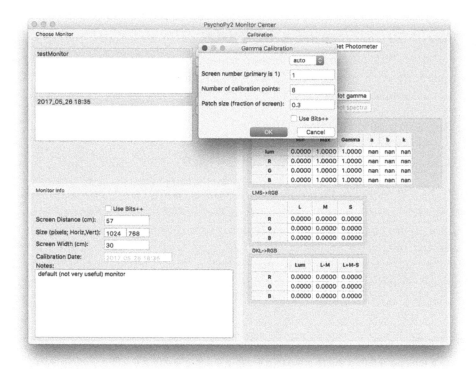

FIGURE 13.2 Selecting `auto` mode for calibration allows various settings, such as the number of levels to be measured (for each color channel), the size of the patch, and whether or not to use Bits++ (if you don't know what this is then you don't need it!).

When you press `OK` the calibration screen itself will come up (see Figure 13.3). All you need to do is point the photometer at the central stripe on the screen, ensuring that the area of measurement is not overlapping the two flanking stripes.

Once the calibration begins you shouldn't alter the lighting in the room (which should, ideally, be dark during calibration) because the luminance measurements will be affected by the ambient light reflecting off the monitor. For this reason the calibration routine also gives you a 30-second countdown, in case you want to point the photometer at the screen and then quickly leave the room before the measurements start.

FIGURE 13.3 The screen used during calibration looks like this. The critical zone is the rectangle right in the middle of the screen (it's pale gray in this image but it will change colors during the measurements).

 Info: Why is the calibration screen such a strange pattern?

For some monitor technologies the gamma correction can depend on the overall luminance of the screen. The calibration screen is designed so that, as close as possible, it has an overall luminance that matches the mean gray of the screen. This is achieved by having black and white pixels across most of the screen (recall that before calibration the middle gray value is not actually at mean gray intensity) and with stripes on either

(Continued)

side of the measurement patch that are opposing the target area in color and luminance. While you measure a black stripe the flanks will be white, while you measure a blue stripe the flanks will be yellow, etc. It probably wouldn't make a big difference if we had just a gray screen, but it's easy enough to do it this way and be sure that we have achieved mean gray.

We recommend you then test that your calibration has worked by pressing the button `Gamma Test...` and repeat the process described above. We have occasionally found graphics cards failing to apply any gamma correction to one of their output ports (if this happens to you, try plugging the monitor cable into a different output from the computer; we have never found a situation where gamma correction failed on **all** the graphics card outputs).

SEMI-AUTOMATIC CALIBRATION USING A PHOTOMETER

This approach is useful if you have a photometer but it can't be connected to PsychoPy (because it is not a supported device, or it physically can't connect to the computer). In this case you can use PsychoPy to present the various patches of different intended brightness and note down, for each brightness, what the photometer reported as the luminance.

To do this you *must* use a 'spot photometer', not a photography ambient light meter (or 'lux meter'). A spot photometer is designed to detect light coming from a small area, either by attaching to a particular place on the screen or by focusing on a particular spot as a camera would do. A lux meter is designed to detect the ambient light over a larger area and will not be useful for calibrating your monitor.

PROCEDURE

Open Monitor Center and select/create the appropriate monitor to save the calibration. In the `Calibration` panel, press the button `Gamma calibration...`, which will bring up a dialog box, as shown in Figure 13.2, but now you should select `semi` as the method instead of `auto`.

It isn't recommended that you select a large number of levels for semi-automatic calibration because it requires you to sit and record each measurement. The number of levels is multiplied by 4 for the total number of measurements (they are made once for grayscale and then once for each of R, G and B on its own) so eight levels is already 32 measurements. Especially when you first try this you might want to set only four levels!

When you press `OK` the calibration screen will appear as in Figure 13.3. You should point your spot photometer at the central rectangle on the screen (the middle of the three stripes) for each measurement and note on paper the recorded luminance from your device. Then you can press the space bar to continue to the next measurement. When all measurements are complete, the calibration window will disappear and a new window will appear for you to enter the luminance values you have recorded. From these PsychoPy will make the necessary calculations to determine your gamma value. For the measurements that ranged from black to white enter these in the row marked 'lum' and then for the others enter them in the row for the color that appeared in the central stripe.

Lastly you can give the calibration a name, but by default this is given the date and time when the calibration was made and there isn't any need to change from that. Save the monitor to make sure that the calibration is stored.

As with the automatic calibration, we recommend you then test that your calibration has worked by pressing the button `Gamma Test...` and repeat the process.

USING YOUR OWN VISUAL SYSTEM TO CALIBRATE

The third method is to calibrate your monitor using your visual system (a method that we will describe as 'psychophysical' gamma correction) to detect whether the mean gray appears lighter or darker than the average of black and white. You may have seen a method of doing this where you are asked whether a certain patch of color is brighter or darker than a set of black and white stripes. This judgment always feels somewhat hard to make and is, presumably, not very precise as a result.

PsychoPy provides a script to perform a rather precise psychophysical method (at the time of writing, this script had not been incorporated into Monitor Center but that might change). The method uses any slight luminance artifact to create a compelling sense of motion (Ledgeway and Smith, 1994) based on a logic first described by Anstis and Cavanagh (1983) to study luminance artifacts in chromatic gratings, and is described in the Info Box, 'Magical gratings for Gamma Correction'. The script works by presenting a special sequence of gratings and asking you to say in which direction the stimulus appeared to drift, and on each trial a different gamma correction is applied to the screen. If the gamma correction being applied is too strong then a clear sense of motion in one direction will occur. If it is too low, then a clear sense of motion will occur in the opposite direction. We use a staircase procedure to adjust the gamma correction on each trial until we find the point where no consistent motion is detected.

How precise is this compared with the gamma value provided by the photometer? In our experience the two techniques typically provide similar values. The photometer has the advantage that it allows us to visualize the gamma curve and look for places where the correction hasn't worked well (e.g. it might be that there are certain portions of the luminance curve that are better corrected than others). Obviously the photometer also tells you what the actual maximum and minimum luminance of the screen is (in cd/m²) which you might want to report. Conversely, the psychophysical method used here tells us whether the gamma *actually results in a perceptual effect* and this might be considered the better measure. If possible, it would be worth measuring gamma by both methods. Of course, the psychophysical method is free, not requiring you to spend hundreds, or thousand, of dollars on a photometer!

 Info: Magical gratings for gamma correction

Ledgeway and Smith's technique works by alternating visual frames of a luminance grating (bars alternate between dark and light) with a 'contrast-modulated' grating (bars alternate between uniform gray and black and white dots) and, on each switch, the phase of the grating is also shifted by a quarter cycle. The luminance grating on its own has no apparent motion (the two luminance frames are perfectly out of phase so they just appear to flash bright/dark) and nor does the contrast-modulated grating (similarly its frames are perfectly out of phase with each other). However, if there is an interaction between the gratings, caused by the contrast modulation having a luminance artifact, then motion will be apparent. If gamma is being under-corrected then the uniform gray bars will be slightly darker than the black and white dots and this will combine with the luminance grating to give an apparent motion. If gamma is being over-corrected then the gray bars will be brighter than the dots and motion will be seen in the opposite direction.

The beauty of this system is that we only need a tiny difference in luminance, between the gray field and the dots, for the motion to be quite clear and consistent, so it actually becomes quite a powerful way to calibrate a monitor.

For further details see the original book chapter by Anstis and Cavanagh (1983) and the paper by Ledgeway and Smith (1994).

PROCEDURE

To run the script you need to go to the Coder view of PsychoPy and look in the `Demos` menu for `>Demos>exp control>gammaMotionNull`. Launch the script and follow the instructions. This will actually present two staircases with 50 trials each, so 100 trials in total, taking a few minutes to run, but you could potentially edit the script to reduce the number of trials without substantial loss of precision.

In the first few trials the direction of motion should be very clear indeed – these are deliberately chosen to have quite extreme gamma values but the gamma correction should get closer and closer to the optimal value as the trials progress and that means the gratings may appear simply to flicker. Alternatively, you may find that you do have a percept that there is motion always in a particular direction (e.g. Jon always sees the grating going upwards when it is ambiguous). In fact the directions that indicate over- or under-corrected gamma are being randomized, so if you always see motion in a particular direction then this is another sign that the motion is actually ambiguous (the seemingly consistent motion is then a factor of your perceptual bias, not caused by a physical aspect of the stimulus).

When the trials have completed this procedure a data file will automatically be saved for you and this can be analyzed using the other demo, `>Demos>exp control>gammaMotionAnalysis`. By running this analysis script you can visualize the data you have just created and the graphs should tell you the optimal gamma, where you were equally likely to say up or down. This can then be applied to each of the color channels as the gamma value in the monitor gamma calibration table.

13.6 COLOR CALIBRATION

The last form of calibration is a chromatic calibration, which is needed if you want to specify a color that will look the same irrespective of monitor. Monitors, even those using the same technologies, do not have the same colors for their red, green and blue channels. CRT displays can use a variety of phosphors, for instance, and each will result in slightly different colors. To use a *monitor-independent* color space we need to be able to characterize the outputs of our monitor for each of the primary colors. This is done with a spectroradiometer, a device that measures not only the light intensity, but also its intensity at the full spectrum of wavelengths in the visible range.

To transform between different monitor-independent color spaces we need to calculate the transformation matrix to get from our desired color space for specifying the stimuli, such as the Derrington, Krauskopf and Lennie color space (1984), to the monitor's native color space (RGB).

Info: Can I just use a color meter instead of a spectroradiometer?

A *spectroradiometer* measures the light intensity across the whole spectrum, from which the color of any stimulus can be calculated in any color space. Conversely, a *colorimeter* measures the color as values in a particular color space (typically CIE space) and does not provide sufficient information for transformations to be calculated for other spaces. These devices are, therefore, only suitable for the purpose of reporting specifically the colors of your stimulus, not for calibrating your monitor to generate arbitrary colors in other spaces.

13.7 PROCEDURE

As with the gamma calibration, you need to open Monitor Center and select the monitor on which you want to perform the chromatic calibration. Connect and turn on your spectroradiometer and press `Get photometer`. Then press `Chromatic Calibration...`. This will bring up a calibration screen much like the gamma correction one. Incidentally, a chromatic calibration *without* a gamma calibration is possible but makes little sense; you should do them both but the order is unimportant. Unlike the gamma calibration, however, this procedure only needs to make three measurements: the spectrum for the red, green and blue channels, each on full intensity. There's no time for a coffee on this occasion!

14

DEBUGGING YOUR EXPERIMENT

Learning objectives: Using PsychoPy is all well and good while experiments are working. The thing that can be remarkably frustrating is when a study fails to run or when data are not being saved the way they should. This chapter will help you understand those issues.

There are several common errors that we can help you to understand, but the way to go about problem solving when something isn't working is also a general skill that can be learned. The key is, essentially, to add and remove parts of the study to narrow down the critical piece that causes the failure. Once you've narrowed the problem down to one specific Component or variable, then working out what's wrong is more palatable.

Trying Google and searching for a specific error message that you encountered is, of course, another good way to fix your study. As PsychoPy has many users, it follows that many people have encountered problems, probably including the same one that you are encountering. If so, then Google is generally very good at helping you to fix it.

Ultimately, you may need to get help by using a forum (PsychoPy's user group at https://discourse.psychopy.org is an excellent place to discuss problems) but, even so, some questions never receive an answer, so the final section of this chapter helps you to write something that gets a useful reply.

14.1 COMMON MISTAKES

There are some mistakes that won't give you an error message but the execution of the experiment won't be what you expect.

'MY STIMULUS DOESN'T APPEAR'

One of the trickier issues to handle is when a stimulus simply doesn't appear to be drawn. The problem with this is that there are *many* ways that your stimulus can fail to appear on the screen. This is a problem, however, that rarely turns out to be a problem with PsychoPy: it's usually a problem with one of the parameters set in your stimulus.

One of the most common issues here is that the stimulus position and/or size must match with the `units` that have been set for the stimulus. Having a position of `(0, 100)`, for instance, makes sense for `units='pix'` but if the units are set to `norm` then this would be a long way off the screen to the right and so the stimulus won't appear. Conversely, setting the size to be `(0.2, 0.2)` is sensible if the units are `height` (the stimulus will be a square one-fifth the height of the screen) but with units set to `pix` then this stimulus will be drawn smaller than a single pixel and therefore will not be visible.

There are additional parameters that could cause a stimulus to be invisible; an `opacity` set to zero, a color that matches the background, or a stimulus being occluded by another (take note of the order of stimuli in your Routine) all spring to mind. None of these mistakes are as common as the mismatch of units, so check that first.

THE FEEDBACK IS 'WRONG'

Many people have a feedback Routine in their experiment, whereby some feedback message is changed according to whether the response was correct. You can see how to develop such a Routine in Chapter 6.

One of the ways this can go wrong, which can lead to the complaint that 'PsychoPy's feedback is wrong!', is by incorrect ordering of the message creation and the Text Component that presents it. Remember that the order in which code gets executed is the same as it appears in the Routine. In that Routine, the Code Component updates the contents of the message and, at the beginning of the Routine, the Text Component updates itself to *use* that message. Now, if the Code Component sets the contents of the message *after* the Text Component has done its update then it won't have any effect until the *next* trial. The result is that the feedback will always lag one trial behind the responses.

Make sure your Code Component in this case executes before the Text Component (i.e. make sure it is higher in the Routine).

14.2 COMMON ERROR AND WARNING MESSAGES AND WHAT THEY MEAN

More often than not, when something goes wrong, an error message appears. Fully understanding that error message may seem too hard, but do try reading it; there will hopefully be some pointers about what might have caused the problem. If it mentions variables that you created, or particular Components from your study, then obviously you should go and look closely at these and check for settings that might not be sensible or for errors in your typing.

The fact that there are many lines is because, in programming, functions call other functions which call other functions. Sometimes it's hard to know at which level the mistake occurred that was the true *cause* of the problem, so Python provides you with all of them. Again, your best bet here is probably to look through for the line that makes some sense (e.g. mentioning a name that you recognize). It might not be at the very bottom of the error message but mid-way through it, which just means that Python was not sure that this was an error when your variable was first defined or used.

Below we consider some of the more common errors; Google will reveal explanations to many more!

xxxx IS NOT DEFINED

This is one of the most common error messages and has three principal causes:

1. You may have set a stimulus parameter to be a variable (using $ and then your variable name) but told PsychoPy that it should be `constant` rather than `set every repeat`. Go and check that anything you want to be variable is indeed set to `update every repeat` or `update every frame`.
2. You may have typed the variable incorrectly, either in the parameter or in the conditions file (or wherever you define the variable). Python cares about capital letters (so `myFilename` is not the same as `myFileName`).
3. If the variable that is 'not defined' is something that you create in a Code Component then maybe you need to create the variable earlier on. For instance, if you use the variable when a stimulus is created but the variable only gets defined once the Routine starts, then it is not defined early enough. You may also need to check that your Code Component code is being executed before the Component that uses it.

🔍 Info: Why does not setting a variable to 'update every repeat' result in 'not defined'?

The reason for this is also about the order in which code is executed in experiments. If a parameter for your stimulus is set to be `constant` then PsychoPy will try to set this just once, at the beginning of the experiment, and then leave it untouched.

(Continued)

That's the most efficient thing for it to do. Conversely, when a variable is defined in, say, a conditions file, then PsychoPy creates it only when needed, usually when the loop begins. That's handy because it means you can change values right up to the last minute.

So the problem arises when these two things occur together. When you set something to be constant but define it as a variable in a conditions file, then PsychoPy tries to use it early to create the stimulus, but only defines it later when reading the file, and so, when the stimulus is created, the variable is 'not defined'.

COULDN'T FIND IMAGE FILE

If PsychoPy complains that it can't find an image file it most often means that the file has not been placed in the appropriate location relative to the experiment file. Your images should typically be either right next to the experiment file (and then specified just as 'myImage.png') or in a folder next to the experiment file in which case the folder name must be included (e.g. 'stims/myImage.png').

One issue that sometimes crops up is that the experiment might have been saved in more than one location (e.g. you copied it to a different folder while testing and forgot which one is open) and the images are only in a single location.

This issue should *not* indicate to you that you need to type in the full path of the image. That really isn't necessary and isn't a good idea in the long run. You should try instead to work out why the shorter *relative* path does not fit with the location of the experiment.

VALUEERROR: MONITOR TESTMONITORS HAS NO KNOWN SIZE IN PIXELS (SEE MONITOR CENTER)

An error like this indicates that you have attempted to use a unit like `cm` or `deg` but you haven't told PsychoPy about your monitor and so it can't calculate the correct dimensions for you.

To fix this you need to check the Monitor Center 🖳 to make sure that the monitor has the correct dimensions set (distance, width in cm and size in pixels) and make sure in your Experiment Settings 🖼 that you are correctly specifying the name of that monitor.

WARNINGS

We often find people worrying that a warning has broken their experiment or is responsible for some other genuine error. Usually this is not the case.

Warnings are essentially there to indicate something that is important to some people, not important to others, and doesn't technically cause the experiment to crash. For instance, in some experiments it would be catastrophic to the study if the computer failed to get all its rendering done in time and 'dropped a frame' (taking more then the allotted 16.67 ms to refresh the screen). If you're studying so-called 'subliminal' processing and your stimulus accidentally appears for two frames instead of one then your results would become meaningless. Possibly PsychoPy should abort the study with an error that timing was not achieved. On the other hand, to a lot of people, presenting a stimulus with imperfect timing might not matter and they wouldn't want their study to abort if this happened. So PsychoPy reports a warning message to let you know if a frame gets dropped but does not abort your study. You can take the message or leave it; it depends on your study whether this matters.

14.3 HOW TO DEBUG AN EXPERIMENT

When something isn't working, the basic steps of debugging, in any language or software package, are either to take something that *does* work and add pieces it until it *stops* working, or to take your experiment that *isn't* working and remove pieces until it *starts* working. Sometimes a combination of the two approaches is needed. Either way the aim is to narrow down the problematic part of the code.

If PsychoPy isn't doing exactly what you want then you need to be able to work out why not. The steps here are a general skill in problem solving. Try not to take the stance of 'I'm not very good with computers so I should just ask someone else'. Even if you don't ultimately solve the problem yourself, you will hopefully narrow down the rough area in which the problem lies, which might help a more experienced colleague to fix it for you.

Also, try not to take the stance that 'My experiment doesn't work, so PsychoPy is broken'. You might be right — there are occasionally bugs in any software package — but PsychoPy is used by a lot of people so you need to think about why other people aren't having the problem that you're seeing. Have you downloaded a very, very recent version of the software (where there may be a new bug that people haven't noticed)? Are you doing anything that might be unusual in your study, such as using a piece of hardware that most users don't have, or a piece of custom code that you programmed yourself? If so then these might be the places to focus in the following steps.

START WITH A SIMPLE EXPERIMENT

Take a demo. If PsychoPy demos don't work then something is very broken. To work out what is going wrong in this case you need to try several more demos and work out which ones succeed and which ones fail. Then it probably is time to contact the users' forum and ask why this should be (explaining which demos work, which ones do not, and pasting the error messages).

If the demo is fine, but your experiment isn't, then we need to work out what the critical difference is. You could take the demo and start adding pieces until the experiment stops working. If you have some idea about where the issue *might* be, then, obviously, that would be the first addition to try and make. For each thing you add, test immediately to see if the experiment still runs without the problem that you experienced before. When you find it breaks then this is a clue about where the problem lies.

If you had to add many items before finding the one that broke the experiment, you should now go back and apply your 'break' to the original working demo, but apply it as the first step rather than the last. This will tell you whether your problem depends on just this one addition, or whether there are multiple factors contributing to one symptom.

START SIMPLIFYING YOUR BROKEN EXPERIMENT

The other approach is to try and cut out pieces of your experiment (obviously save a copy with a new name before you start cutting it up). The logic is the same as above. You're trying to find out which parts you can cut out of the study and still have it show the problem. In this instance, it's a good idea straightaway to cut the Flow down to very few Routines and Loops. Get rid of your instructions screens, for instance. They probably won't be *causing* the problem, but by removing them you speed up the rate at which you can get through the study (when debugging a study you will end up running the experiment many times, so you want each run to be quick).

 Pro Tip: Use windowed mode while debugging

While you debug the study, especially if you find it 'freezing', you should probably go into the Experiment Settings and turn off 'full-screen' mode. That way, if the experiment keeps freezing you can at least press the red 'Stop' button to kill it.

14.4 WRITING A BETTER QUERY TO THE FORUM

PsychoPy has a popular users' forum where users are very good at helping each other, volunteering their time to answer questions, though some questions never get a response. Sometimes this is because nobody knows the answer, but, often, it's because the question does not provide the appropriate level of detail.

Not enough information. For instance, if you go onto the PsychoPy users forum and simply announce that your experiment 'doesn't work' and ask for help, then nobody will be able to help you. This is like announcing that your phone 'isn't working' and hoping that somebody can tell you why. You need to give some information about roughly where the problem lies. (Does it turn on? Do you have a signal? Does it dial? Is it both speaker and microphone that aren't working? And so on.)

Too much information. On the other hand, if you give lots of information that isn't relevant (in the phone example this would be 'I was trying to talk to my grandad on the phone when it stopped working. He used to be in catering and I wanted to know how he cooked for large numbers of people…') this also doesn't help people to solve your problem and, given that people on the forum are volunteering a very limited amount of time, they probably just won't read a long post at all. Generally, in trying to solve your technical problems, the forum will need to hear the technical aspect of your problem, like what Components are involved, not the topic of your experiment.

Could you write my study? Actually, there's another type of question that typically gets no response, where somebody says, 'I'm not very technical and I want to create this complicated study. Could anyone tell me how to do it?' Asking people to spend a long time creating a study for you isn't likely to get any answers. Try to create the study and come to the forum when you have a concrete specific question about a technical difficulty.

I need it URGENTLY! If you don't get an answer to your question, then go back and try to improve the information you're providing. Writing back to the forum pointing out that you've got a deadline, and you really need to run the study URGENTLY so PLEASE COULD SOMEONE HELP, won't help. If you wrote a question that can't be answered, then it still can't be answered after begging. You need to write a better question.

Be respectful. Try not to turn your forum post into a rant. This is a place to find solutions, not to raise generalized anger. Recall that PsychoPy has been developed as an open-source, community-led project. You didn't pay anything for it and the people that wrote it are volunteers, so please be respectful of the fact that they have donated a lot of time already to helping you run experiments.

WHAT INFORMATION IS GOOD?

So, the trick to getting your question answered is to provide just enough information and just the *right* information, to give people an idea about what is needed. Don't worry if you don't get this quite right, as someone will probably ask you for further details if needed, but the closer you are the more chance you'll get an answer.

First off, say what version of PsychoPy you're using (the actual version number, not 'the latest') because some issues relate to bugs that were only present in certain versions or have now been fixed. Also, say what operating system you're using. Many issues, and some answers, are specific to one computer type, so say what you use.

The symptom of the problem is the next most important thing you need. People often write 'it doesn't work' or 'I tried various suggestions but they didn't work'. The phrase 'it doesn't work' almost never helps. In what *way* did it 'not work'? Did the stimulus not appear? Did the experiment 'freeze'? Did it crash (i.e. disappear)? Did the rest of the computer freeze as well? If you tried multiple things, did they all fail in the same way? If not, let's take the most promising one and try to fix that, but, again, you need to provide more information about *how* it failed.

The error message is also absolutely essential. Please post the entire message or explicitly state that no error message appears. The reason you need to post the entire message, not just the final line, is that the final line (e.g. `TypeError: unsupported operand type(s) for +: 'int' and 'str'`) does not tell us what *led* to this message. It could occur for multiple reasons and the rest of the message would give us a clue about what you did beforehand.

Ideally, what we need is known as a 'minimal working example' of the problem, as described below.

PROVIDE A MINIMAL WORKING EXAMPLE

Given the difficulty of finding the right balance between 'too little' and 'too much' information, either of which will get your post ignored, the best solution is to provide a *minimal working example* of the problem.

'Minimal' literally means that nothing is included unless it's necessary to demonstrate the problem. If you have 3 nested Loops and 16 Routines, then the kind person offering you their help will open the experiment and immediately close it for being too much effort to debug. If you have additional Routines that aren't needed to see the issue then remove them. If you can remove other Components within the troublesome Routine then remove them too. Ideally we want a single Routine with only two or three Components in it so we can home in very quickly on the likely problem.

'Working' means that you provide everything needed, such that the script or experiment can actually be run for testing. If you provide a demo but don't include the image files, for instance, then we can't actually see the problem occur. We *might* still be able to help, but we stand a better chance if we can run the failing experiment itself.

Nearly all posts containing such an example will get a response. If not then the example either wasn't sufficiently 'minimal' or wasn't 'working'.

Creating this 'minimal working example' is really just the same procedure as in the 'How to debug an experiment' section, above. You need to remove things as far as possible until the broken experiment starts working. This has the double benefit that it often causes you to find the problem yourself, but, if not, it will at least mean that someone more knowledgeable about the details should be able to help.

15

PRO TIPS, TRICKS AND LESSER-KNOWN FEATURES

> **Learning objectives:** There are several features of PsychoPy that you might find useful that nobody mentioned. In this chapter we look at some miscellaneous tips on how to make PsychoPy work better for you.

Some of these tips are things that you wanted to do, but didn't realize PsychoPy could take care of them for you, like expanding and shrinking the Flow panel icons, and copying Routines from one experiment to another. Some of them are things you *didn't even know* you wanted, like the ability to provide a README file that gets noticed! Let's look at that one straightaway, because it's surprisingly useful.

15.1 ADDING A README FILE TO YOUR EXPERIMENT

Have you noticed that a text document comes up in PsychoPy when you open the demos from the Builder demos menu? This is a very easy-to-use feature to provide yourself with reminders and notes about your experiments. All you have to do is drag a simple text document called `readme.txt` or README into the folder, next to the experiment file. It will pop up automatically every time you load that experiment (you can toggle its visibility really easily with `Ctrl-I`, or `Cmd-I` on a Mac, and you can turn off the feature entirely in the PsychoPy preferences).

WHY IS THIS A GOOD THING?

There are lots of reasons why you might want to use such a README file. You can use it to remind yourself of what you need to do to set up the experiment:

- Did you ever have one of those studies where you could easily forget to do something that ruined the entire study? Like, you got into the lab at the end of the session and the participant says, 'Should I have been hearing something in these headphones' and you realize you didn't turn on the audio amplifier? Well, you can leave yourself a message here about what you need to do when you load the study!

- Did you ever send your experiment to a friend/colleague but you want them to remember where they got the study in the first place, just in case they forget to credit you with the work later on?
- Did you ever change a study after some pilot stage and forget which participants were before, or after, the change? Well, this is a great place to keep a log of how your experiment developed; what dates you made changes; what dates you collected participants; and, again, the fact that it pops up every time you load the study makes it good at 'gently reminding' you to update the information.

Do it! Go and create a README file for your most recent experiment!

15.2 EXPAND OR SHRINK THE FLOW AND ROUTINE

You may not have realized that you can also expand, or shrink, the icons in the `Flow` and `Routine` panels (Figure 15.1). This is obviously handy if you plan to create complex experiments and need to fit more in. Conversely, if you have a smaller experiment and want to see more information, such as the number of repeats and conditions in a loop, then you can just expand it up. These operations can be found in the `View` menu or accessed with shortcuts (`Ctrl-+/-` for the Flow or `Ctrl-Shift-+/-` for the Routine).

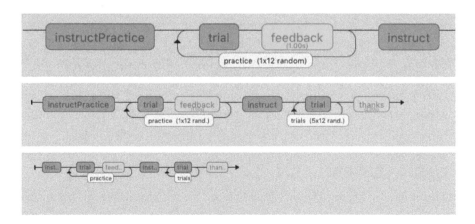

FIGURE 15.1   The Flow panel in its largest and smallest states.

15.3 COPYING AND PASTING ROUTINES AND COMPONENTS

A lot of people don't realize that they can copy and paste Routines from one experiment to another, or copy Components within a Routine.

To copy a whole Routine to another experiment, simply open a new window and then open your second experiment in that new window (don't go to your file system and double-click the file to open it because that will probably create a new copy of the application rather than opening a *new window* in the *same* application). Go to the Routine you want to copy, by selecting its tab in the Routines panel, and then go to the `Experiment` menu and select `Copy Routine`. Now you can go the experiment you want to copy this into and go back to the `Experiment` menu and select `Paste Routine....` This will bring up a small dialog asking what you want to call your Routine in this experiment.

You might even find it useful to create an experiment file that you never actually run as an experiment, but that contains your most useful Routines as templates.

📢 Warning: Be careful with copying and pasting variable names

Make sure, if you do copy Routines between experiments like this, that you adapt your variable names as needed. For instance, the feedback Routine we created in Chapter 6 refers to the Keyboard Component called `resp`, so you would need to make sure that this had the same name, or update the code for your new keyboard name in this experiment. Sloppy copy and paste behavior can lead to embarrassing errors later!

To copy a Component you need to right-click on the Component that you want duplicated and select Copy, then switch to whatever Routine you want and go to the `Experiment` menu to select `Paste Component`.

15.4 ONLINE REPOSITORIES FOR SHARING YOUR EXPERIMENTS

The `Projects` menu that allows you to synchronize a project (by which we really mean a folder on your computer) with an online repository. At the time of writing, only the Open Science Framework repository (https://osf.io) was supported for this, but there are plans to support additional venues for you to share and search for experiments. We hope there will be a gradual increase in people willing to share the materials they create in keeping with the open-source (and Open Science) ethos of the PsychoPy project and community.

Hopefully how this works is relatively straightforward; there are dialog boxes from the **Projects** menu that allow you to create projects based on a local folder and, once you've logged in, upload these to the remote repository.

WHY IS THIS A GOOD THING?

It's probably obvious why you might want to search for other people's experiments: to save yourself the effort of creating an experiment and learn the necessary coding that was required.

What might seem less clear is why it would be good to share your experiment with others. In the competitive world of modern science many scientists don't want to give their competitors any help in running experiments and feel that they spent the effort on developing the work and don't want to 'give it away'. Well, there are actually good reasons to share your work.

There are the obvious reasons about sharing being good for the science, because it's very inefficient having people constantly reinventing the wheel, and it helps make studies reproducible if we can run exactly the experiment, rather than merely get a description of it in the 'Methods' section. There are also now Open Science Badges being assigned to papers by some journals (e.g. *Psychological Science*) to highlight papers that have followed these good-for-science principles.

In addition, however, there are also good *selfish* reasons for sharing your experiment with others. The principle is that it increases the likelihood that others will develop studies based on yours and that means they will cite your paper. Having other experiments built upon your study is the *best* outcome and that won't happen if people struggle to recreate your materials and method. Make it easy for them and increase the spread of your work!

15.5 USING VARIABLES FROM THE DIALOG BOX IN YOUR EXPERIMENT

Most people have a dialog box at the beginning of their experiment where they record things like the participant ID and potentially other information (see Chapter 2 for a recap on how to change that). Often the dialog is useful merely to keep track of the information and save it for later use in the data file. Sometimes, however, the information is useful in controlling the actual experiment and, therefore, we need to access the contents of the variables. The information from this is stored in a Python 'Dictionary' called `expInfo` and you can access it by calling, for instance, `expInfo['participant']` as a variable.

For instance, if you were storing the participant's name, rather than an ID number, then you could create a message at the end of the study with a Code Component as below. If you then used that `$msg` as the text in your Text Component it would include the participant's name and appear friendly and cuddly.

```
msg = "Thanks" + expInfo['participant'] + "for your time. Have an
awesome day!"
```

 Warning: Don't store a participant's name as their ID!

Although it's a nice idea to use the participant's name in a feedback message, this would actually be in breach of most ethics proposals. By using a recognizable name in the 'participant' field you are effectively saving the name of the participant alongside their data. By doing that you aren't keeping their data anonymous. What you should be doing, in keeping with most local ethics committee policies, is providing each participant with an ID number and keeping the links between the ID and any identifiable information in a separate location from the data files (e.g. a locked filing cabinet). This way, someone with prying eyes will have to work harder to find out the personal data associated with your named participants.

Other uses for this information might be that you could set it to control your stimuli in some way. For instance, you could create a study where stimuli were presented at different orientations on different runs, and you want to control manually what the orientation is in each run. To do this you could add a parameter 'ori' to your Info Dialog, according to the Experiment Settings, and then set your stimulus to have an orientation of `$float(expInfo['ori'])`. Note on this occasion that we forced the variable to be converted into a 'float' (a number that can include decimal places) because, as the value is retrieved from the dialog box, there is no way to know whether it should be treated as a number or as characters. Our code here takes care of that by forcing it to be a number.

The contents of the dialog box might also be used to choose a particular conditions file. For instance, you could have participants assigned to group A, B or C and create three different conditions files for these (`conditionsA.xlsx`, `conditionsB.xlsx` and, you guessed it, `conditionsC.xlsx`). Now, rather than loading the conditions file in the usual way in your loop, you could refer to it as:

```
$"conditions{}.xlsx".format(expInfo['group'])
```

15.6 CONTROLLING NAMES OF YOUR DATA FILES AND FOLDERS

Experiment Settings allows you to control your filenames, including the name of the folder the files are stored in. By default, all data are stored in a single folder called 'data' and then given filenames that correspond to several values stored inside the variable called 'expInfo', such as the experiment name, the participant's name (or ID) and the date and time. All this is controlled by the setting Data filename in the Experiment Settings, as follows:

```
'data/{}_{}_{}'.format(expInfo['participant'], expName,
                       expInfo['date'])
```

This may seem complicated and scary if you have no experience of these things. Let's look at what it means. The first part `'data/{}_{}_{}'` tells us the format of how the final thing will look. The beginning of `data/` means we'll put our files into a folder called 'data' that's next to the experiment file. Each `{}` tells Python to insert a variable in these locations. The next part, looking like `.format(aThing, anotherThing, somethingElse)`, tells Python what variables it should insert into those locations. In this case we insert the participant and the date, as stored in `expInfo` (see above for what these are about), and combine it with the variable called `expName`, which you can also control in the Experiment Settings.

Note that, if the folder that you're trying to save data to doesn't yet exist, then PsychoPy will try to create it for you. As long as you have write access to the folder where this needs creating, you should be fine.

15.7 RUNNING IN WINDOWED MODE

Most experiments run in 'Full-screen mode', meaning that the window in which the stimuli are presented will fully dominate the computer screen. In this mode no other windows or dialog boxes are visible. This has the advantage that the window cannot be moved around or resized by your participant, and other windows won't peak through from the background. It also brings a performance improvement because the computer spends less time checking the other application windows or looking to see whether the mouse is hovering over another application. As a result, this mode is on by default for new experiments. On the other hand it can be annoying and you might want to turn it off. In particular, while debugging your experiment you might find that you occasionally cause your experiment to freeze (for instance, if you have a for... loop in your each frame code and that loop is never-ending, then the experiment will appear simply to get stuck). In these cases, if you have the experiment running in Full-screen mode then exiting the broken experiment can be difficult (it usually requires a force-quit procedure by using `Ctrl-Alt-Delete` on a Windows computer or `Alt-Cmd-Esc` on a Mac). On the other hand, if you had been in the more standard 'Windowed' mode instead of Full-screen mode then you could simply click on the PsychoPy window and press the red `Stop` button to get rid of the experiment. Another reason for keeping your experiment in Windowed mode is that you might want to bring up dialog boxes during the experiment to collect other responses from your participants than the standard Builder Components allow. As the Full-screen mode, by its very nature, prevents windows and dialogs from being opened in front of the window, you cannot present dialogs from this mode.

To turn off Full-screen mode for your experiment you can simply go to the Experiment Settings for your experiment and deselect that option in the `Screen` tab. Again, although it may be good to turn this off while debugging, you probably want to have it turned on again before running the experiment for real.

15.8 RECREATING YOUR DATA FILES

The main comma-separated value (csv) files are one of the most easy-to-read file formats that you can load into most analysis packages, or analyze with a Python script, but what happens if you accidentally corrupt that by making a mistake during your analysis? For instance, what if you accidentally selected a single column and pressed 'sort' such that the rows in this column now longer matched the rows in the other? Luckily PsychoPy also saves an additional file for you, the 'psydat' file. Although this file isn't human-readable, and you can't double-click on it to open it in anything (at present), it can be accessed by means of a Python script, and one nice property is that it can be used to recreate your `csv` file.

If you open the Coder view of PsychoPy and go to the `Demos` menu you should see an item there called `csvFromPsydat`. If you open it up and run it you should be able to recreate your `csv` data files as needed.

15.9 SKIPPING A PART OF YOUR EXPERIMENT

You may not have realized, but you can set a loop to have zero repeats! If you do that the loop, and all its contents, are simply skipped. This is a really useful trick to use while debugging because you can surround parts of the experiment that you don't need (like lengthy instructions or practice trials) and set them to have zero repeats while you work on another part of the experiment. Obviously, you'll kick yourself if you forget to turn a critical part of the study back on, but that's your problem!

You can even use this as a way to hack conditional exposure to certain Routines during your experiment. You can set the number of repeats to use a variable (like $showFace) and then set showFace to be 1 or 0 using a Code Component of a conditions file. When showFace is 0 the contents of that loop won't be executed. Be careful with this technique, though; it's a very easy way to create confusing experiment files with lots of Routines and loops. Usually, what you want is to think through the blocking techniques we described in Chapter 8.

15.10 TURN TIPS BACK ON

There are lots more things in PsychoPy that might not be obvious at first. It's like peeling an onion, where you find more presents inside! Or something.

Although it's annoying to have tips dialog boxes appear when you want to crack on with writing your experiment, one last tip is that it's a good idea, once in a while, to turn tips back on. You can do this in the PsychoPy preferences. You might find you'd forgotten about some of the things you can do. You might find you'd forgotten some of the awful jokes as well!

PART III
FOR THE SPECIALIST

The remaining chapters focus on certain specialized methods that are likely only to be needed by a subset of users. If you aren't in these user groups (or, maybe, even if you are) then you are likely to find these chapters rather challenging or tedious!

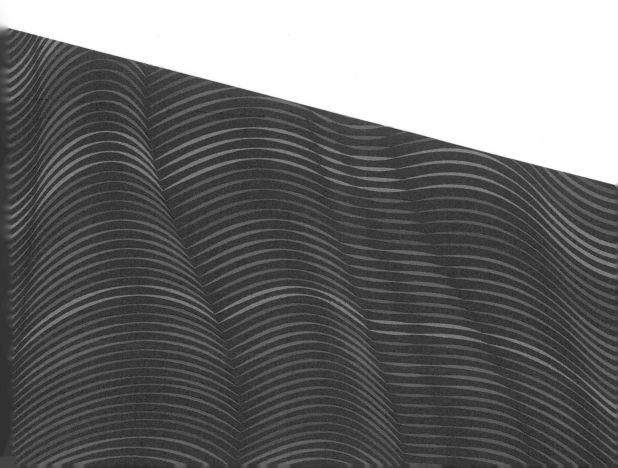

16

PSYCHOPHYSICS, STIMULI AND STAIRCASES

> **Learning objectives:** Some specific stimulus types (gratings, Gabor stimuli and Random Dot Kinematograms) and some of the special trial-handling functions, such as staircase and QUEST handlers.

Psychophysics, a term that comes from Gustav Fechner's *Elemente der Psychophysik* (1860), refers to psychological processing of physical events. It largely refers to the scientific study of the senses using behavioral measures. It is the thing that PsychoPy was originally written to do, and a lot of the machinery still reflects that. This chapter will cover some of the particular features that were developed with that field in mind.

Used correctly, the stimuli and adaptive procedures discussed in this chapter can be powerful tools but, used incorrectly, they can result in artifacts that render your results meaningless. For example, a poor understanding of the parameters in the random dot stimuli can lead to cues about the direction that have nothing to do with motion perception. For gratings, an inappropriate spatial frequency or an uncalibrated monitor can lead to artifacts in the mean contrast and luminance of your stimuli. For staircase (including QUEST) methods, poorly chosen parameters can result in staircases that never include measurements at the appropriate levels to measure the psychometric function.

This chapter will lead you through some of the common settings, the features supported by PsychoPy, and also some of the potential pitfalls of using these stimuli and methods.

16.1 GRATINGS AND GABORS

Grating stimuli, particularly sinusoidal gratings, have been the staple diet of vision scientists for decades. It is because of the grating stimulus that PsychoPy's standard color spaces are the way they are (with black being represented by −1 and white being represented by +1).

A grating is essentially just a repeating pattern, likes bars of changing color. The bars usually follow a sinusoidal pattern, so that they vary smoothly and evenly from one color back to another, but the gradient function is flexible and square-wave gratings are also relatively common.

The grating is governed by a number of parameters, such as the spatial frequency of the texture and the phase of the texture (controlling the position of the bars within the stimulus area). Obviously there are also parameters for the orientation, position, color and size of the patch, just as with any other stimulus in PsychoPy.

The **mask** of the grating essentially determines what shape the grating will have. With no mask a grating will fill a square (or rectangle) defined by its size, orientation and position. If we set the mask to be a `circle` then the circle will be the largest circle that can fit in that circle (or ellipse in that rectangle). If we want a **Gabor** (this is just a sinusoidal grating in a Gaussian mask) then we can simply specify the mask to be a `gauss`. This will result in a Gaussian profile that fits into the same rectangle as with the circle. See the section below for more information on smooth-edged mask profiles such as Gaussian profiles and, in particular, the issue that these will appear smaller than a circle with the same size settings. The third pre-defined mask is the `raisedCos`, which defines a smooth cosine profile at the edge of your stimulus. You can also use your own custom function.

Spatial frequency of a grating determines how many repeats of the stimulus there are per unit of space, so a higher spatial frequency (SF) means narrower bars. This setting will depend on the `units` of the stimulus. Vision experiments usually use units of `degrees` (of visual angle) and so the units of the SF parameter are then `cycles/degree`. If you change the stimulus units to `cm` then the spatial frequency will be refer to `cycles/cm`, and obviously for `pixels` the units of SF become `cycles/pixel` (and you need to set this to a very small number or PsychoPy will present multiple cycles of the texture within the width of a pixel).

You can also set the SF to be zero, which will result in a uniform patch of color with no change across the stimulus. In this case, phase (see below) still affects the stimulus as it controls the color that is presented.

Grating phase in PsychoPy is a little unconventional. Rather than using degrees or radians as its units, PsychoPy uses 'cycles' and the wave 'starts' in the center of the stimulus. So, when `phase` is set to 0.0, the grating will have a white stripe in the center, when set to 0.5 it will be black in the center (the trough of the wave is a half cycle from the peak); and when it reaches 1.0 it will be back to being white. This may all seem confusing, but it allows us to make the grating drift very easily by setting the phase to be a value based on time. A phase that is set to `$t` will drift at 1 cycle per second (Hz), and a phase set to `$2*t` will drift at 2 Hz.

The designated **grating color** in PsychoPy defines the color that will be in the peak of the grating. What literally happens is that the color value is multiplied by the value of the wave at each point. At the trough of the grating we then automatically get the opposite color to the one that has been set. On a gamma-corrected monitor this will be the color that, when averaged with the designated color, results in the mean gray of the screen. When you designate the color of the grating, the opposite color is not free for you to choose – it is always the negative of your designated color. If you need to have two arbitrary colors in your grating, rather than the color and its negative, then you will have to create a custom texture using a Code Component, but that will result in a stimulus that no longer has the same mean luminance as the mid-gray background of the screen.

HOW EXACTLY DOES PSYCHOPY CREATE A GRATING OR GABOR?

One of the key features of PsychoPy is its ability to use OpenGL for rendering things like gratings. In OpenGL we can upload textures onto the graphics card and tell it to perform 'operations' on those textures on the card, like moving the textures around the screen, stretching them, rescaling them and even combining them with each other. This is the essence of 'hardware-accelerated' graphics. Before this was available we had to make the calculations on the Central Processing Unit (CPU) of the computer and then upload the results pixel by pixel to the graphics card for presentation. The code for doing that was much harder to write and also much slower to run.

So, how do we use this to create a drifting grating or Gabor? Essentially all we do is provide a single cycle of the carrier grating (e.g. the sinusoid) and a single copy of the mask. We then use OpenGL calls to specify how many cycles of the grating it should use, which mask to combine these with, and the locations of the four vertices that determine the position. The calculation of the actual pixel values that result from this are then determined by the graphics processing unit (GPU) which is much faster than the CPU for these calculations and frees up the CPU for doing other things, like checking the keyboard.

The texture can be recombined, with different masks and different settings for cycles and orientation, and rendered with its new settings as many times as you like within the same screen refresh or between screen refreshes. So the process of uploading the texture (or image, because this system is the same for image stimuli but without using multiple cycles) only has to happen once.

We also don't need to change the texture if we want a new color for our stimulus. For that we just upload a new color value and the multiplication of the sinusoid by the color value is carried out by the graphics card (rather than by us before providing the texture).

All these operations performed at the level of the graphics card have extremely low overhead; they can all be carried out in a lot less than a single screen refresh. The only operation that is still relatively slow is the step where we load the texture/image data up to the graphics card. For the purposes of PsychoPy Builder, this means that the only time-consuming operation (which should therefore be done in between trials) is the setting of the texture and/or mask itself. All the other parameters can be changed instantly.

 Info: PsychoPy began with an OpenGL Gabor

The OpenGL rendering of a Gabor patch was actually the primary reason that PsychoPy was written. Jon Peirce knew how to use the OpenGL texture technique described here using C and in 2002 he discovered he could make the same calls from Python (but not from MATLAB without adding a C extension). What that essentially meant was that he could easily draw a Gabor patch with a drifting grating on it, and update its position live (according to the mouse coordinates, say). MATLAB couldn't do that in those days, without additional C code (Psychophysics Toolbox was in version 2 at the time and only added these features in the version 3 rewrite by Mario Kleiner). It was this ability to carry out precise rendering without pre-computing the stimulus that caused Jon to carry on and build the PsychoPy Python library on which all this is now based.

16.2 SMOOTH-EDGED MASKS (GAUSSIAN AND RAISED COSINE)

Gaussian and raised cosine masks are popular, especially in vision science, due to because they give a nice, smooth entry to the image rather than an abrupt hard edge. For the visual system, abrupt edges cause a great deal of activity in the visual cortex that rather dominates anything else about the image that we might be aiming to study.

Using these masks for stimuli introduces another complication, however, which is that if the image begins rather gradually such that it's hard to see where it begins, then how do we define the stimulus 'size'? What does 'size' mean for these objects? Don't worry if the rest of this paragraph means nothing to you. The take-home message is that the Gaussian-masked image looks smaller than a circle of the equivalent size (Figure 16.1). For the Gaussian mask the 'size' is the point where the Gaussian distribution would be $3\times\sigma$ on each flank of the curve. Put another way, if your stimulus had a `size=3 cm` and `mask=gauss` then your Methods section could say that your stimulus had a 'Gaussian envelope with σ of 0.5 cm'. (It has $3\times\sigma$ on each side of the stimulus, making a total of $6\times\sigma$, and this occupies 3 cm so $1\times\sigma = 0.5$ cm.)

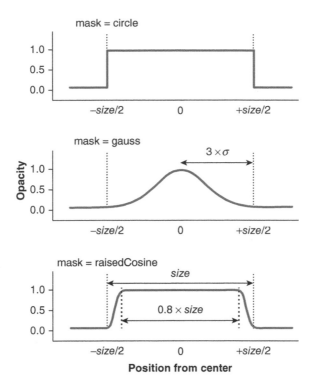

FIGURE 16.1 Profiles of the built-in masks (circle, gauss and raisedCosine). The outer dotted line indicates the stimulus 'size'. Note that the gauss profile looks much smaller for the same size but this is necessary in order that the opacity falls to essentially zero by the edge of the stimulus (otherwise a sharp edge would be visible). For the raisedCosine mask we see a smooth edge but a more rapid transition.

The 'raised cosine' mask (accessed by the name raisedCos in the mask parameter) is similar in having a smooth onset to the stimulus rather than a hard edge, but the area of onset is a little more rapid (actually it can be controlled in PsychoPy) and the size is a little better defined. The name comes from the fact that its shape is the same as the cosine function but, whereas $\cos(\theta)$ ranges from −1 to +1, this is 'raised' to sit above the 0 line ranging from 0 to +1, where 0 and +1 refer to opacity values in this case. Note, however, that it's just the edges (flanks) that have this cosine profile and the center of the stimulus is flat in its transparency.

If you specify one of the built-in named masks then the **Texture resolution** controls the resolution of that image, but, again, bear in mind that the size of the image will appear on the screen in pixels.

BLENDING RULES

As mentioned earlier (see Chapter 3) images and other visual components typically have an `Opacity` parameter. Obviously, things that are completely opaque (in the real world) are easy to see and cannot be seen through, whereas objects that are perfectly transparent (with zero opacity) are not seen at all and the object behind them is completely visible. In computer graphics this is technically achieved by applying a rule, known as a blending rule, that, in this case, takes a weighted average of the pixels of the object currently being drawn, with the pixels that are currently representing the 'background' (i.e. the combination of all the objects previously drawn). The rule, more specifically, says that the final value of the pixel should be the average of the currently drawn object with a weight set to the `opacity` value and the background with a weight set to `1-opacity`. You can see then that, if the opacity of an object is set to 0.1, then the pixels will mainly look like the background (with a weight of 0.9) and only a little like the object itself (a weight of 0.1).

The blending rule, although the most sensible rule in relation to the 'real-world' concepts of opacity and transparency, is only one of the rules we could apply. Another useful blending rule is to use *addition* instead of *averaging*. In this rule the opacity still determines how much of our current object should be added, but it does not in any way obscure the pre-existing pixels that have been rendered. This is a little like shining an image onto an existing pattern. The existing pattern is not removed or obscured by the light from your new image; rather it is added to whatever light your original is producing.

🔍 Info: Adding is not really the same as anything in the real world

There is actually a slight difference between the notion of 'adding' the textures and 'shining lights' together, which comes back to the notion of PsychoPy's 'signed' colors. Although shining a second textured light onto an existing image can make areas brighter, it can't 'take away' light to make any areas darker. Conversely, in PsychoPy, because the colors can be positive (bright) and negative (dark) they are able to accentuate any deviation from the mean gray value of the screen. If the value of the texture is bright then it brightens any pixels behind it, but if the texture is dark it *darkens* the pixels behind it. There is no true analogy to this addition of signed brightness values in the real world.

16.3 USING IMAGES AS MASKS

While we're talking about textures and masks we should also consider the fact that we can use images as masks as well. Any arbitrary image file could be used in the **mask** setting of the Grating Component (or the Image Component, for that matter). You might use that option to create your own custom smooth-edged mask, for instance, but you can also use it to generate interesting colored, or textured, shapes.

Imagine you want to create an iconic image of an apple and have it shown in different colors. You could, of course, create multiple images of your apple icon and use those images as the input to an Image Component. That isn't particularly efficient. It takes you longer to create them because you have to make multiple images, it takes more space to store them, and it takes more time to present them because loading an image and sending it to the graphics card is by far the slowest part of the stimulus-rendering process. To do this more efficiently you can use the apple image as a mask.

The other reason is that when you use an image of an apple as the image, rather than as the mask, it will probably end up with a colored square around it. This might not matter to you, and you might be able to keep the square the same color as the background so that it isn't really visible, but alternatively you can use an image as a mask to create a transparent background for your stimulus.

When you use an image file as a mask, you just give its path and filename in the same way as you do in an Image Component. Bright pixels in your mask image become pixels that are visible (opaque) when your texture is drawn and black pixels will be transparent. The mask can use the full range of grayscale and intermediate gray levels will be semi-transparent according to their luminance.

Ideally, convert your image to grayscale mode for this in your favorite image-editing software. PsychoPy will happily convert your RGB image to luminance values, but this takes more processing for PsychoPy and takes up more space on your disk than if you simply convert your mask image and save it in grayscale mode. Also remember to keep your mask image reasonably small; as with the Image Component, there's no point in having an image of 1000×1000 pixels on disk if you only present it at a size of 50×50 pixels on the screen.

OK, so how do you then use this to get a colored image? Well, when you combine this mask with a Grating Component you can set the stimulus to have a blank texture (that will just be a single, smooth color) and give it the color setting that you like, in the usual way. So now your image specifies the 'shape' of your object, including gradual transitions in opacity, and the color specifies the color of a smooth texture behind that. You could even add a texture if you like. A sinusoid might be strange on a fruit-shaped object, but you could potentially create a texture that repeats to look like fruit skin, if you wanted to.

16.4 ELEMENT ARRAYS

At the time of writing, element arrays are not directly available in the graphical interface of the PsychoPy Builder but you can add them using Code Components. These are essentially like multiple grating objects, where you can specify the mask and texture to be shared across all elements and then an array of spatial frequencies, orientations, sizes, etc., that will be applied separately to each element. As with the concept of making the graphics card do more work, and reducing the number of commands being executed by Python, these arrays allow for a much faster rendering of large sets of stimuli and you should consider them if you have more than a few similar elements to render.

Using them with a Code Component is relatively easy. Let's demonstrate by creating a visual search task using an array of Gabors with random orientations and a single target that differs in spatial frequency. The stimulus needs to be constructed with code like the following (if you Google for element array psychopy the top hit will get you the more detailed version with *all* the possible arguments):

```
gabors = visual.ElementArrayStim(win, units=None,
                elementTex='sin', elementMask='gauss',
                fieldPos=(0.0, 0.0),
                fieldSize=(1.0, 1.0), fieldShape='circle',
                nElements=100, sizes=2.0, xys=None,
                oris=0, sfs=1.0, contrs=1, phases=0,
                colors=(1.0, 1.0, 1.0), colorSpace='rgb',
                opacities=1.0,
                texRes=48, interpolate=True)
```

As always in Python, you can omit most of these arguments and allow the default setting to be used. Typically you would put code to create the array in the Begin Experiment block of your Code Component. This is because we usually only need to create it once and then we can manipulate the contents afterwards as needed. The one caveat is that we can't change the number of elements in the array afterwards; that aspect affects too many other parts of the ElementArrayStim object. If your experiment needs you to vary the number of elements on each trial, say, you would typically use this code to create the object afresh for each trial by putting it into the Begin Routine portion of your Code Component and then make sure that you leave enough time for it to finish creating before anything time-critical happens (creating the stimulus won't be instantaneous). If you need the number of elements to change *during* a trial then you will need to simulate this by creating an array large enough to handle all your stimuli and then simply making some of them invisible by setting their opacity to 0.

Some of the settings in `ElementArrayStim` apply to all the elements. For instance, all elements must share the same texture and mask (`elementTex` and `elementMask`) and `units`. Some, like `fieldPos`, `fieldSize` and `fieldShape`, apply to the entire stimulus in that they control where the array is centered, how big it is and whether it's circular or square (the latter two only have an impact if you don't manually specify the element locations using `xys`).

The arguments that are written as plurals, however, allow you to specify either a single value, which will be applied to all the elements, or a list/array of values that will be applied to the elements individually (the length of the list or array must match the number of elements). For instance, the following will give you five Gabors with different sizes but all at the same orientation (45 degrees):

```
gabors = visual.ElementArrayStim(win, units='cm',
              elementTex='sin', elementMask='gauss',
              nElements=5, sizes=[1, 2, 3, 4, 5],
              oris=45)
```

In order to see your stimulus you also need to have **On every frame**:

```
gabors.draw()
```

or you could use `gabors.setAutoDraw(True)` and `gabors.setAutoDraw (False)` when you want it to start/stop, rather than calling `draw()` each time.

Very often, you'll want to set one of your parameters to vary randomly across the array, or set a certain fraction of the array to be one value and a certain fraction to be another. There are easy functions from the **numpy** package that help us to do that. Let's create a 100-element array with random orientations and with half the set having size = 1 for half the elements and size = 2 for the other half:

```
nEls = 100

elSizes = np.zeros(nEls)
elSizes[0:50] = 1 # 1st half of array to 2
elSizes[50:] = 2 # 2nd half of array to 4

elOris = random(100)*360

gabors = visual.ElementArrayStim(win, units='cm',
              fieldSize=20,
              nElements=nEls, sizes=elSizes,
              oris=elOris)
```

UPDATING VALUES

At any point (including on every frame) you can then update the values of the element array settings; this is generally a fast procedure (it can be updated well within a single screen refresh). It is really important, however, that you **create** your updated values efficiently, using arrays to update the set, rather than a `for...` loop to update each individual element. For instance, rather than our elements always having half at `sf=2` and half at `sf=4` we change them in each trial to a variable called `lower` or `higher` which is something that varies by condition. We *could* write the update code as:

```
for n in range(100):
  if n<50:
    elSizes[n] = lower
  else:
    elSizes[n] = higher
# actually update the values in the stimulus
gabors.sizes = elSizes
```

but that code involves more than a hundred Python commands to be executed (one for each element). It would be much faster to do the same thing as we did earlier with:

```
elSizes[0:nEls/2] = lower # 1st half of array
elSizes[nEls/2:] = higher # 2nd half of array

# actually update the values in the stimulus
gabors.sizes = elSizes
```

In the example so far we used a random array for our orientations and we could very easily set that to be a new random array on each trial as well:

```
gabors.oris = random(100)*360
```

You can also take your array and gradually increment it. For instance, having set the Gabors to a new random set of orientations at the beginning of the trial, we could gradually rotate them by adding a value **on every frame**. For instance, we could add 2 degrees on every frame such that, at 60 Hz, our objects would all rotate at 120 deg/s but starting at different random positions:

```
gabors.oris += 2 # add 2 deg rotation per frame
```

If you wanted your Gabors to drift, this could be done in the same way, with `gabors.phase = random(100)` at the beginning of the trial to randomize the starting phases of the gratings, and then `gabors.phase += rate/60` where `rate` is the rate of motion you want in *cycles per second* on a 60 Hz monitor.

ELEMENT LOCATIONS

The last thing to note is about setting the element locations. You can provide your own locations for each element using the attribute `xys`, which then needs to be a 2×*n* array. Very often, however, you want your stimuli simply to be at random locations in either a circular or square field. To achieve this you can leave the `xys` as `None` and use the settings of `fieldSize` and `fieldShape` (which can be 'circle' or 'square'). With these settings PsychoPy will simply populate a random set of locations accordingly.

To repeat the process and generate further random locations with the same rules (e.g. at the beginning of each trial) you can simply call `gabors.setXYs()` or `gabors.xys = None` and both of these will have the effect of populating a new set of locations.

To access the values that have been set and used (in any of these arguments) you can simply use something like:

```
finalOris = gabors.oris
finalXYs = gabors.xys
```

OTHER USES OF ELEMENTARRAYSTIM

This stimulus can be used for various other purposes than a visual search task. One quite handy case is to use it as a set of tiles that can be individually set to transparent and reveal an image. If you open the Coder view there is a demo for this called `maskReveal` in the `Stimuli` section of the `Demos` menu.

16.5 RANDOM DOT KINEMATOGRAMS

Another stimulus that has been popular in vision sciences is the Random Dot Kinematogram (RDK). The aim of this as a stimulus is to force people to integrate motion signals from an array of dots, to detect the 'global' motion of the pattern, rather than base a decision on a single item. The stimulus is deceptive in being rather simple in concept: a set of dots is moving and the coherence of their motion (the percentage of dots moving in a 'signal' direction on any one trial) can be varied. The devil, as they say, is in the detail. There are many ways to construct the dots with different rules about how they behave. Do the dots moving in the 'signal' direction stay the same on every frame or do we randomly choose them? When the other ('noise') dots move, do they have the same speed? Do they move in a constant direction or do they meander? When dots go out of the bounds of the field, how do we replace them to keep the dot density constant across time and space?

 Warning: Reducing artifacts in RDKs

It may seem surprising but it's actually relatively hard to generate these stimuli without any artifact that could alert the participant to cheat. The most important way to minimize these artifacts is to use short dot *lifetimes* and moderately large numbers of dots.

You don't believe us, huh? You want an example? OK, for instance, if we think about what happens when we replace a dot in the field after it reaches a boundary, in nearly all implementations the dot is placed randomly back at some location in the field. Gradually, with signal dots moving in a particular direction, noise dots moving randomly, and out-of-bounds dots being placed randomly back in the field, you will find a greater density of dots towards one edge of the field, and this indicates the direction the dots are moving in.

To take another example, if we use the 'Same' rule to choose our signal dots and the 'Random Position' rule for our noise we find that the signal dots all have the same speed and could potentially be tracked, whereas the noise dots are 'jumping' and sooner or later will jump a far distance and so could be tracked; if the participant finds a dot that they can track then this tells them the global motion without their having to integrate over the dots.

The solution to these issues is to use fairly short lifetimes for your dots. In the first issue of a biased dot density in the direction of motion, the redistribution of dots by short lifetimes makes the density difference too small to detect. In the case of the observer theoretically tracking a dot, it makes it impossible because *all* dots periodically disappear and reappear. It might be nicer to debug your experiment with long-lifetime dots (precisely because you can see what they do) but **use a dot lifetime of less than five frames for running your study.**

The second consideration is to use a moderately large number of dots. If nothing else, this increases the resolution of your 'coherence' setting. If you only have 10 dots then the coherence options are obviously only 0%, 10%, 20%, etc., as you increase the fraction of your 10 dots. You may have read papers using relatively small numbers (tens) of dots but there really is no good cause for this in the modern day, where fast computers can update many elements in one frame without a problem.

There are no single approved answers to these questions (and these aren't even the only questions). There are many different versions of RDKs and all have their own different pitfalls. Scase et al. (1996) provided a way to classify these motions and PsychoPy uses that system to allow users to generate a wide range of different stimuli using Scase et al.'s method of classification. Their classification takes a little thinking about, however. The general structure is that you can have two ways to define what counts as a signal or noise dot:

1. **Same:** the decision stays constant throughout a trial, so once a signal dot, always a signal dot.
2. **Different:** when the decision about signal or noise is carried out again on every screen refresh, so that a signal dot on one frame can become a noise dot on the next

The other factor is what to do to assign the next random position to the *noise* dots, which Scase et al. call the 'noise type', with three options:

1. **Random position:** on each frame you give the noise dots an entirely new location anywhere in the field.
2. **Random walk:** on each frame the designated noise dots can move a certain distance but in any direction.
3. **Constant direction:** noise dots hold a constant direction from one frame to the next (just as the signal dots do).

These two options for choosing signal dots, and three options for the noise type, can be fully combined so there are six distinct versions of the RDK using this taxonomy. On top of these, there are decisions to be made about two fairly critical further parameters in the implementation of the stimulus, namely the `lifetimes` of the dots and the number in the array. The lifetime of the dot sets a period after which it will be randomly moved to a new location somewhere in the field, which is a very important feature to remove inevitable artifacts, as stated in the warning box on RDK artifacts. Similarly, the number of dots is relatively important in that too small a number will make it less likely that participants need to use the 'global' motion of the dots to make their decision.

Scase et al. conclude that most of these methods are fairly suitable and make little difference, but a few have since become more popular. This may be because they were easy to implement on relatively slow computers, which was a consideration when these techniques were first used. The most common method probably is to keep the *signal dots the same* from one frame to the next and to move the noise dots according to a *random position* rule (popularized by the groups of Newsome and Movshon in the 1980s).

It's a source of debate, and sometimes frustration, but PsychoPy's current Dot–Stim implementation allows you to use all of these different forms of motion, rather than providing just the common ones used by most labs (which would admittedly make the dialogs simpler and possibly reduce the chance of making bad choices). All of the options are available in PsychoPy, by selecting the Dots Component, which brings up the dialog box shown in Figure 16.2.

FIGURE 16.2   Parameters for the DotStim (RDK). Take careful note of using a short dot life to reduce artifacts, with a decent number of dots. Note also the settings for controlling the choice about the signal dots (same or different) and the method for the noise dots (random location/direction/walk). There's also a parameter called Dot refresh rule, which controls whether or not the dots are refreshed on every repeat of the Routine (usually you can leave that on).

16.6 STAIRCASE AND QUEST PROCEDURES

In many experimental designs the set of stimuli and conditions is predetermined and remains the same for all participants. This, in the world of psychophysics, is referred to as the Method of Constants. It works very well when we know what range of values is relevant (e.g. what range of contrasts you need to test to find someone's detection threshold). If you don't know in advance where the threshold value is likely to be and, especially, if it is likely to differ from one participant to the next, then you may end up having to test an awful lot of different values in order to find the point where a participant *just* detects a stimulus. It seems inefficient, and frustrating, to collect large numbers of trials where a participant can very easily see the stimulus, or where they have no chance of ever seeing it. We want to focus our trials predominantly in the region close to the participant's threshold.

This is where *adaptive* methods come in. The idea with these techniques is that they automatically adjust the stimulus level according to the previous responses and gradually home in on the value of interest (typically the detection or discrimination threshold). If you aim to find a threshold for detection, say, then you start with something detectable, you decrease its intensity in steps until the participant fails to reliably detect it, then you make it more intense until they clearly detect it again, etc. You still collect a range of responses at various stimulus intensity values but the choice of the values that are used is essentially optimized for the participant by centering them around the participant's threshold. This procedure is referred to as an adaptive staircase.

Even then it can be frustrating if the staircase doesn't home in *quickly enough* on the region of interest. If you make the step size small to make sure that you don't jump *past* it, it can then take a long time to get down from your initial easily detectable level, so there has also been a lot of time and effort spent trying to identify more *optimal* staircases.

THE TECHNIQUE IS NOT JUST FOR DETECTION THRESHOLDS

Although these techniques were designed for measuring detection thresholds, they needn't only be used for that. Or, thinking about it in a different way, we can rewrite many experiments to be about measuring thresholds. The concept can be used in any experiment where:

- the stimulus condition can be determined by a number
- getting a trial 'wrong' or pressing 'no' will cause the number to go up and getting it 'incorrect' or pressing 'yes' will cause it to go down.

For instance, you might measure sensitivity to changes in facial shape by creating a set of photographic morphs from one face to another. You can then measure how far apart a pair of faces have to be on this continuum for you to reliably detect that they are different. You are essentially measuring a threshold for discrimination of faces, but this is not probably how you thought about the study!

A staircase could also be used to measure a point of subjective equality. Say you're studying a size illusion and you ask participants which of two objects looks bigger. You could manipulate the size of one of the objects up and down, and use the staircase to home in on the point where they appear the same.

STANDARD UP–DOWN STAIRCASES IN PSYCHOPY

Setting your stimulus to use a value from a standard, simple staircase in each trial is quite easy in PsychoPy. Create your trial as usual and insert a loop around it. Now, when the loop dialog comes up you should select the `loop type` and set it to be `staircase`. When you do this the options of what you control will change, as you can see in Figure 16.3. There will no longer be an option to insert a conditions file because the conditions are being determined for you by the staircase. You simply specify the characteristics like `start value`, `step size`, `nReps`, etc., as needed to control your staircase. These choices are described below.

How do you then **use** the value that the staircase is generating? Once a staircase has started, a variable called `level` is created and updated in each trial. You can simply use this value `$level` to control your stimuli. Note that the value is always going to be pushed upwards on a wrong answer and downwards on a right answer, so make sure you use that appropriately. This makes sense if you use `level` to

FIGURE 16.3   The options available to control a standard up-down staircase in PsychoPy. These result from inserting a loop and setting the loop to be 'staircase' rather than 'random'.

control the duration or intensity of a stimulus (a longer duration or higher intensity makes the stimulus easier to see) but it could be counterintuitive if you want a correct answer to increase something (e.g. the intensity of a mask). In such a case, you might need to set the mask to be `1-level` rather than using `level` directly.

The standard adaptive staircase has a rule about how many answers have to be wrong/no before the value returned by the staircase goes up, and how many right/ yes answers before it goes down. The former is nearly always 1 and the latter depends on the particular value you want to home in on. The most common options are the 1-up/3-down staircase, which homes in on the 79% correct level (common for a two-alternative-forced-choice task in which the expected chance performance is 50%) and the 1-up/1-down staircase, which homes in on the 50% point (useful to measure the point of subjective equality).

Choosing step sizes and step types. There is also a choice to be made about how big each step is along the staircase. As mentioned above, setting the step size to be too small results in the staircase taking too long to get to the desired location, but setting it too large will result in a poor resolution of your measurements, with data not being collected closely enough to the actual threshold value of interest. A common solution to this issue is to start the staircase with relatively large step sizes and gradually make them smaller. PsychoPy allows you to decrease the step size on each 'reversal': that is, when the staircase has been making the trials harder and then starts making them easier (because the participant got a trial wrong). The question of **step type** revolves partly around whether you think each step should be an *additive* or a *multiplicative* step. You might think intuitively that you want to add or subtract a value (every five step we add or subtract 0.1, say) but, in many things that we vary, the more appropriate rule is to increase by a certain ratio (every five steps we double the size). The former rule is easier and so you should set the `stepType` to be `lin` (for linear).

If you want a ratio increment/decrement then set the step to use `log` units or `db` (decibels). 'But how big is a log unit (or a decibel)?' I hear you ask. Specifically we're using log base 10 here and so *1 log unit* means that the value will change by a factor of 10, either up or down. That's quite big for most things you'd want to vary. If contrast were set initially to 0.5 and then dropped by a factor of 10 (to 0.05) it would be a very big step. So we want something smaller. Fractions of a log unit indicate how many steps will be needed to make that factor-of-10 jump. If we request *0.2 log units* (i.e one-fifth of a log unit) then we will jump by a factor of 10 (1 log unit) over a series of five steps. If we start at 0.5 our sequence will be 0.5, 0.315, 0.199, 0.125, 0.079, 0.05. As we tend to use rather small steps in *log units* many people then switch to using *decibels* simply to make the numbers nicer: *20 db* is the same as *1 log unit* so rather than specifying a step of *0.2 log units* we could take *4 db* and, well, it just sounds nicer! It confuses everyone else that you talk to, but it sounds nice. With this in your pocket, you'll fit in beautifully with vision/ auditory scientists. They love a good *decibel* unit!

Choosing start values. Often, we choose starting values so that the stimulus is clearly visible, as this helps settle the participant into the task and encourages them in knowing exactly where to focus their attention, etc. In some cases (e.g. in measuring points of subjective equality) we might be concerned that this would introduce a bias by always starting on one side of the expected threshold. A common solution is to run staircases with multiple starting values, such as having one deliberately well above the target value and another well below the expected target. Often these staircases would be set to run *interleaved* trials (see below), whereby the staircases maintain separate histories and, on each trial, the staircase that is used gets randomized.

Choosing when to terminate. You also need to decide when you have enough trials to be able to make an estimate of the threshold. You might set this based simply on the number of trials (e.g. 50 trials per run) but very often people set the staircase to terminate after a certain number of reversals. This has the advantage of ensuring that the participant spent a reasonable number of trials around the level of the threshold (they didn't, for instance, spend 40 trials just reaching the threshold region and only 10 trials once there). The key thing here is to inspect the raw staircase data in a plot to make sure that the staircase is converging on a threshold as expected, and that you are indeed collecting enough trials once converged.

We should note that there are many further derivatives of these systems, such as staircases where the size of the step *up* differs from the size of the step *down* (García-Pérez, 2001) and, at the time of writing this book, PsychoPy does not support those options.

INTERLEAVED STAIRCASES

Very often we want the staircase procedures to be *interleaved*. For instance, if we were trying to test the threshold of detecting a circular as well as a star-shaped target (no idea *why* we'd want to do that, but it's amazing what people want to do) we could measure the threshold for one and then the other, though this could introduce an order effect or something could happen during the second block that didn't happen in the first, etc. Ideally we would interleave trials for our different conditions.

An interleaved staircase allows us to do exactly that. Interleaved staircases are a like a cross between a method of constants (where we need a conditions file to specify how the trial varies) and a staircase. Each staircase can be controlled by different parameters (like different start values, and different step sizes). Those values must be specified in a conditions file, with appropriate columns. Each staircase can also be given additional variables that can be used in the stimuli, which are specified in additional columns, just as in standard conditions files. Columns that specify names related to the staircase are automatically used to create it, and additional variables are simply available to Routines within the loop as before.

For example, Table 16.1 shows the conditions file that would specify the interleaved staircases set up for an experiment testing high and low spatial frequencies, each using two staircases, starting below and above the expected contrast detection threshold.

TABLE 16.1   Possible conditions file for four interleaved standard staircases.

startVal	stepSizes	sf	label
0.01	[2, 2, 1, 1, 0.5, 0.5, 0.25]	2	lowSF_lowStart
0.01	[2, 2, 1, 1, 0.5, 0.5, 0.25]	4	hiSF_lowStart
0.20	[2, 2, 1, 1, 0.5, 0.5, 0.25]	2	lowSF_hiStart
0.20	[2, 2, 1, 1, 0.5, 0.5, 0.25]	4	hiSF_hiStart

In these conditions we have set the staircases all to have 40 trials and different start values (0.01 and 0.2 will be used as contrast values by our stimulus) and we have also specified a spatial frequency variable, `sf`. That `sf` value won't be used in the staircase per se but we will use it within our stimulus. We can then simply set up our stimulus to have:

- spatial frequency = `$sf`
- contrast = `$level`

and our experiment will correctly use the values from the staircases. On each trial one of our four staircases will be randomly selected and the next `level` extracted from it. Data (from a keyboard that has been set to `store correct`) will be recorded and set to update the appropriate staircase for its next level. Any additional staircase settings over which you need control should be added to the file (for instance, `stepSizes`, `minVal` and `maxVal` are all commonly needed).

The `label` column is convenient merely to give each staircase an identifier so that we can easily sort the data according to the staircase in our analysis.

BAYESIAN METHODS (QUEST)

One of the most major steps forward in developing the staircase was the introduction of Bayesian-optimal methods of choosing the next level. Watson and Pelli (1983) reasoned that the optimal level at which to run the next trial was at the current estimated value of the threshold. The procedure therefore conducts, after each trial, a maximum likelihood search to estimate the threshold and updates its `level` for the next trial based on that estimate.

Advantages: The procedure is designed to home in very quickly on a threshold, which in many cases is the aim. One of the other things in QUEST is that you don't have to specify the step sizes (and therefore you don't have to wrap your head around nasty things like *decibels*)! You need an estimate of the threshold and an estimate of how wide a range might be useful (technically the standard deviation of the fitted curve), but that's all you really need. It will automate the rest based on responses.

Disadvantages: At other times you might want to characterize the full shape of the psychometric function (the curve that relates the stimulus intensity to the response probability across the full range) rather than home in very quickly to focus attention entirely on the threshold value. Also, with QUEST you tend to start your trials around the expected threshold value, rather than at a comfortably visible level. Therefore, it might be more important here to run some practice trials first to get the participant comfortable with the stimuli.

In QUEST you need to give starting values (there are further options, which you can find on the PsychoPy documentation pages, but these are the key ones that typically need setting):

- startVal: this is your initial guess of what the threshold might be
- startValSd: this is your initial guess as to the spread of the psychometric function
- pThreshold: this is the threshold value that you want to home in on, expressed as a fraction (e.g. 0.8 for an 80% threshold target).

In PsychoPy Builder, the QUEST algorithm has been implemented and is available via the interleaved staircase, as above, but does not appear as a single staircase option in the loop dialog. To use it, therefore, you need to select **Interleaved staircase** and then, for your **stairType**, select **quest**. Now you can specify your conditions file, as before, with one or more independent, interleaved QUEST procedures. For example, your conditions file might look like the one shown in Table 16.2.

TABLE 16.2 Possible conditions file for four interleaved QUEST staircases.

startVal	startValSd	pThreshold	sf	label
0.5	2.0	0.8	2	lowSF
0.5	2.0	0.8	4	hiSF

ANALYSIS OF STAIRCASE DATA

Just as there are several ways to run a staircase procedure and almost every psycho-physicist seems to have their own preferred method, there are also several ways to analyze the data that result from them. As with most measurements, however, it's a really good idea to look at the raw data to make sure that the measure you use represents what the individual responses appear to be showing. Too often people rely on some calculation, such as one of the options below, without first checking whether the staircase appears to have converged. Maybe it never reached the target threshold, or ran straight past. Maybe it got stuck in some zone of impossible values that the participant didn't report as looking strange, and you need to go back and restrict the minimum/maximum values in your staircase.

The general forms of staircase analyses are as follows:

1. To take the average of the final few reversals (for a standard up–down staircase, QUEST doesn't have 'reversals' as such). The logic of this is that the staircase should have been oscillating around the threshold value in the latter part of the staircase and in relatively small jumps at this point, so these values should provide a good approximation of the threshold. Make sure you only average the reversal values, however, not *all* values, because those are biased 3:1 in favor of the value above the threshold (in a 1-up/3-down staircase). The advantage of this method is that it's rather easy to calculate and always gives a sensible value (assuming the staircase converged).

2. To take all trials, bin them into groups of trials that had the same intensity level, and calculate the percentage correct for that group of trials. You can then fit a psychometric function to this full data set which allows you to extract values from any part of the function. The advantage of this is that all the data are used in informing us about the threshold, not just a few values where reversals occurred. On the other hand, fitting curves to data, especially noisy data, can be hazardous, so check that the fits are working correctly and not spitting out garbage threshold estimates.

3. For QUEST, we can simply look at the final values of the fitted function, the standard deviation and the value of the staircase, because these have been updated all the way along as maximum likelihood fits. This is a little like performing the same calculation as in option 2, except that you haven't visualized the data along the way. We strongly recommend you do that as well.

Exactly how you calculate these values from the data files we will leave up to you. It can be done in Excel (at least option 1 is relatively easy) but you might like to use your own analysis script in R, MATLAB or Python.

If you do want to see how the analysis might be done in a Python script, you can see an example on the companion website to this book. The script should be loaded into the Coder view of PsychoPy and you can launch it from there to find a data file. We've provided a couple of example files for you to play with as well.

17

BUILDING AN FMRI STUDY

> **Learning objectives:** In this chapter we will consider the special considerations for fMRI studies. The biggest question here is how to synchronize with the scanner and ensure that good timing is maintained through a (potentially long) scan, but we also look at options for how to calibrate your display.

Functional magnetic resonance imaging (fMRI) has some particular considerations for experiment construction and stimulus presentation. In particular, fMRI studies typically have a lesser need for timing precision within a single trial because a sluggish hemodynamic response means that sub-millisecond precision is really not needed here. Conversely, it is more important in fMRI studies that timing *across* trials is consistent. For example, if in each trial we overshoot the intended times by 10 ms (i.e. by half a screen refresh period) then after 100 trials the stimulus timing is now delayed by 1 second, which could have a major impact.

17.1 DETECTING TRIGGER PULSES

In experiments using fMRI you usually need some method to detect when the scanner has acquired a volume and this is usually done by the scanner sending out a trigger pulse of some sort. The nature of that pulse is up to you and your hardware, and you may need to get the technical help of the scanner operator to find out what signals your system provides.

Generally the scanner itself emits triggers as TTL (Transistor–Transistor Logic) pulses, where a single wire is switched briefly to/from 5 V. If that is your system then you could use a parallel port or a USB interface device (such as a LabJack) to detect the change. To do that detection will probably require you to insert a simple code component into your experiment that will search for the trigger signal, on the necessary input port, and not advance until it is found.

Very often, however, laboratories convert that signal to something easier to use by means of an additional box. Current Designs Ltd (www.curdes.com) fiber-optic response boxes, for instance, provide a controller that can convert the signal to a range of other options including simulated keypresses. Simulated keypresses, whereby the trigger simply looks like a regular keyboard event, are obviously extremely easy to handle in PsychoPy: you can simply add a Keyboard Component to your experiment with the only 'allowed key' being the one that the trigger box will send. Often you would do this by creating a separate Routine called something like 'waitTrigger', which comprises a Keyboard Component set to last for ever and set to **Force End Routine** when the key is pressed. Set the **Allowed keys** to be just what the trigger converter will send and you should be all done! Oh, you might also want to show something on screen, like a message that explains to your participant that we're waiting for a trigger pulse, or maybe you just want to put a fixation cross on the screen.

The potential downside to converting triggers into simulated keypresses is just that, if you aren't careful, you can find that you have corrupted your experiment (or some other document) by filling it with trigger pulses because there's no way for your computer to know that these *weren't* actually keypresses.

It's usually a good idea to include one of these 'waitTrigger' Routines at the beginning of the experiment because most scanners take a few seconds to get started even when you tell them to start. By doing this you can start your experiment, which will then wait for the scanner to start collecting actual data before advancing to your first real 'trial'. The options for how you ensure good timing for the rest of the study are outlined below.

17.2 NON-SLIP TIMING

The most common way to go about timing stimuli, but which is not recommended for fMRI, is to use logic along the lines of:

- start a clock (at zero) when the trial/stimulus begins
- for each screen refresh, check the time on that clock and see if it exceeds your intended duration
- if duration has not been exceeded then present the stimulus for this screen refresh as well.

The above logic seems sensible and would be reasonable in many study designs. It would typically overshoot the intended stimulus duration, however, by up to one frame (e.g. 16 ms). The reason is that we have set up the decision to require the time to be *over* our stimulus duration so that we always reach *at least* that time. If we want a 2-second stimulus and our clock gets to 1.998 seconds (i.e. only 2 ms from our target duration) then, using this logic, we will present another frame and our total stimulus duration will be 2.014 seconds.

Although this wouldn't be a problem for many studies, it would be bad for our fMRI study to have an overshoot on every trial. We could, alternatively, time our stimulus by number of frames to make it more precise, but that would not be effective if we occasionally drop frames on our system because, again, this would cause us to overshoot by however many frames were dropped. Another solution would be to set our time threshold to be the target duration minus a fraction of a frame (e.g. half a frame) so that the result is not *always* an overshoot; this would often be a better solution, but it doesn't guarantee that the overshoot is corrected for.

PsychoPy has a solution that essentially corrects for the overshoot in one trial by altering the presentation time in the next. This is done using a countdown timer that is not reset according to the following logic:

- use a countdown clock that is *not* reset at the beginning of each trial
- instead, take whatever its residual value was at the end of the previous trial and *add* the intended duration of your next trial
- for each screen refresh, check whether your countdown clock has reached zero
- if it has got to zero then go to the next trial and add the next duration.

The key here is not resetting the clock to zero, but leaving it at its previous value, including whatever over/undershoot remained. This solution is what we refer to in PsychoPy as **non-slip timing**. When it is in use the timing error is going to be at most one frame by the end of the study, with no gradual slippage.

Non-slip timing is only possible if the end of a Routine is to occur at a known point in time. If a response is required and this ends the trial then it cannot be used. If the trial is going to end on the basis of some equation or other event then non-slip timing cannot be used and you *may* need some other way to synchronize with the scanner. For instance, you might want to start every trial at the same point in time, relative to a scanner pulse, but then have variable-length trials. If so, you would simply create an additional Routine ('waitTrigger'), as described above, but now insert it into your loop preceding each trial, rather than just at the start of the experiment.

Even if the trial has a pre-designated duration but this has been set to use number of frames instead of a time-point, then this cannot be used, as it would lead to problems if the computer were dropping frames or if the experiment were run at a different refresh rate than the one used during development.

In the Builder view, the Flow panel identifies any Routine that is able to use non-slip timing by showing it in green rather than red. So, if your experiment is for fMRI, then check that your Routines are correctly showing in green.

17.3 HOW TO CALIBRATE A MONITOR FOR FMRI

The other issue that often crops up with performing fMRI experiments is how to calibrate the monitor. This is a bit different to most other setups because the screen is often at a distance from the participant and viewed via a system of mirrors. It is also hard to gamma-correct the screen because it is next to a massive magnet and you really, really can't take your photometer into the room with it!

 Warning: Shared labs

One additional problem with running experiments in fMRI is that in nearly all circumstances an fMRI facility is a shared facility, so somebody else has likely been in and used it after you, for a completely different type of study. The concern here is that you may have spent an hour carefully calibrating everything and then another user decides to turn down the brightness of the projector/monitor so now your calibration is meaningless.

Whenever you use a shared lab like this you should check that:

- the resolution of the screen hasn't changed (in the computer's Control Panel)
- the screen hasn't been moved to a different position
- the settings on the monitor itself (e.g. the brightness settings) haven't been altered. Ideally, you should try and prevent these from being changed, either by locking them or with a bit of sticky tape and a passive–aggressive message!

SPATIAL CALIBRATION OF SCREENS IN MR

The issue of spatial calibration isn't so very different from systems in a standard laboratory with a flat-panel display. To measure degrees of visual angle (which is definitely the most general way to refer to your stimulus size) you need to know the width of the screen in cm and in pixels. In this case the width of the screen is literally the width of the area where pixels are actually visible (i.e. don't include any border), just as it is with the regular monitors. You also need to know the screen width in pixels and you should check that this hasn't been changed;

people very often seem keen to change the resolution of displays in shared laboratories and often they don't know the rule that a flat-panel or projector should always be running in its native resolution (as explained in Chapter 13).

The last part of the spatial calibration concerns mirrors and how they affect the distance to the screen. Assuming your mirror is flat, then the 'distance' in cm that you need to provide to PsychoPy Monitor Center is simply the distance that the light has to travel to go from the eye, bouncing off the mirrors, to reach the screen. For example, if you have a 45-degree dog mirror that is 5 cm from your participant's eyes and that reflects down to a screen 3 m from the mirror, then you need to tell PsychoPy that the distance to the screen is 305 cm.

 Pro Tip: Are participants at different distances?

In many studies in psychology laboratories, participants place their head on a chin/headrest such that all participants have the same distance to the screen. In fMRI this is not generally the case and participants are moved back and forth slightly to get their brain into the sweet spot of the scanner. Depending on the level of precision you need in your study, you may then need to measure the distance from the mirror to the screen for each participant. If so, you might want to do something to remind yourself of the need to update the distance setting in PsychoPy at the beginning of the session (e.g. you could leave a message for yourself as the experiment waits for the scanner like 'Jon, did you remember to set the screen distance?!' or you might use the system of README messages described in Chapter 15). Also, you'll quickly realize that passing a tape measure inside the scanner to the position of the mirror for each participant is awkward, especially with a person lying on the scanner bed. How about, instead, measuring the distance from the mirror to some known position on the sliding part of the scanner bed (near the participant's feet) and then, for each participant, you just measure from that mark to the screen and calculate the total distance from there?

GAMMA OR CHROMATIC CALIBRATION OF A SCANNER MONITOR

Hopefully you've never done anything silly, like taking a metallic object into the scanner room with you and getting it stuck to the very expensive scanner. For your photometer there's an additional potential concern, which is that photometers typically cost about £1000 and spectroradiometers (e.g. PR655) cost upwards of £10,000! Not only could you get the object stuck to the scanner, requiring a quench of the system, but also you could cause damage to the delicate circuitry of the photometer (we have no evidence that these devices are damaged by high magnetic fields, but I wouldn't want to be the first to find that they are!).

If you can't take the photometer into the scanner room then how do you perform a gamma calibration on your system? Luckily, there are a few options.

Calibrate through the window. One solution is to use a spot photometer, like a Minolta LS110 or a Spectrascan PR655, and point it at the screen remotely, from inside your shielded control room. Don't worry too much that there might be a mesh in the window between the control room and the scanner: although this may reduce the brightness coming back from the screen it should only scale it, so the gamma correction will not be affected even if the measurement of the maximum luminance may be a slight underestimate. With your device safely housed in the control room and pointing at the projector screen in the scanner room, you can then run your calibration routine as described in Section 13.5.

Bring your projected image into the control room. If you can't point the photometer at the projector screen through any window then maybe you can move the screen into the projector room or, failing that, simply turn the projector to point at a plain wall in the control room? The measurement of the absolute luminance (and chromaticity) will definitely be only rough estimates using this method but, again, the linearity of the projector output can still be assured.

Measure the gamma correction psychophysically. If you have no means to point the photometer at the screen, because of the layout of your scanner and control room, then you may have to resort to a simple psychophysical gamma correction method, also described in Section 13.5. Now you obviously don't have *any* estimate of the screen luminance, but the technique is a good way to linearize the projector without needing any device. Note, of course, that although the control room may well have a 'copy' of the projected screen showing on the computer monitor, the one you need to look at is the projector image, not the monitor. This is really important as they will likely have different gamma values and it would be an easy mistake to gamma-correct the wrong display using this technique.

Buy a DLP projector. Of course, the other option for linearization of your screen is to buy a device that is inherently linear in the first place, as are DLP projectors (see Section 13.1 for further information).

18

BUILDING AN EEG STUDY

Learning objectives: Using the parallel port to send trigger pulses, and making sure that the timing of everything is tightly linked to the trigger pulse.

When conducting neuroimaging experiments (EEG, fMRI, MEG) we typically need to send signals somehow between the computer presenting stimuli and the neuroimaging hardware. In the case of EEG the usual expectation is that the stimulus computer is what controls the start of each trial and simply informs the EEG hardware that a trial (or some other event) has occurred, by means of a trigger. We therefore need to be able to *send* trigger events to the EEG system. Conversely, for fMRI studies (as described in Chapter 17), the scanner normally sends the trigger pulses and it is up to the stimulus computer to *receive* these and start a trial accordingly.

We will not be looking at specific EEG hardware options; we expect you to know enough about your own hardware and what it needs (put another way, we don't have one of each EEG system to test trigger methods on).

18.1 WHAT IS SPECIAL ABOUT EEG STUDIES?

We have sometimes suggested that the timing of your system doesn't need to be at the sort of sub-millisecond precision that you might expect (because, for example, the screen takes several milliseconds to perform its refresh and the variability in participant responses can be on the order of tens of milliseconds). EEG is the place where that is no longer true. Some of the components in an event-related potential (ERP) can last only a few milliseconds and might have a small amplitude, so, without precise synchronization, these components might be smeared in time and may become undetectable. Also, although participant responses have quite a variable latency, some parts of their ERP waveform are really extremely consistent in their timing.

It is therefore essential that timing is made very precise in these experiments, depending slightly on what events your ERP is intended to measure. If the ERPs are related to a visual stimulus onset then marking the beginning of your stimulus (with millisecond precision) is critical, and means you should use a fast computer and check the timing of your monitor carefully using a photodiode. If your study needs ERPs relating to participants' keyboard responses then you need to be able to record these also with a high temporal precision (that means not using a keyboard!). Essentially, whatever event you are intending to use for your 'event-related' potential, you need to be able to record that very precisely and this probably means using specialized hardware, at least to begin with.

18.2 SENDING EEG TRIGGERS

There are many different EEG systems and each has its own method of communicating. We often get asked, 'Can PsychoPy communicate with my EEG system?', to which the answer is almost certainly 'Yes'. Or the question is '*How* do I make PsychoPy communicate with my EEG system?', to which the answer is 'Tell us what your EEG system wants'.

Many systems use parallel ports to receive triggers, or a USB device like Lab-Jack, to send digital signals. This is relatively straightforward for PsychoPy to communicate with. Builder has built-in support for parallel ports and LabJack, as explained below, so you might not have to write any code at all for these systems.

Other systems allow communication over a computer network protocol (TCP/IP). Python has network communication libraries built in as well, so this is also possible. Some systems have a library to implement the communication for you and, generally, someone will have written a Python equivalent library, which means you should be able to communicate with the system using a Code Component. Electrical Geodesics Incorporated (EGI), for instance, supplies a library as NetStation and this has been ported to the Python library as PyNetStation (provided within PsychoPy).

We can't tell you what your hardware expects in terms of a trigger signal, so you'll need someone (preferably someone local to your department) with knowledge of the system. If not, then the first thing to do is read the documentation of your system and/or contact the manufacturer to find out what the hardware expects.

18.3 COMMUNICATING BY PARALLEL PORT OR LABJACK

This is probably the simplest way to send and store sync signals from the experiment. Parallel ports are simple communication systems with a series of pins that can each be set to 'high' or 'low', together representing the current state of the port.

There are typically eight or more pins available and so we often think of these as storing an 8-bit number (i.e. any integer value between 0 and 255). There is no memory, or buffer, for this system. It just has a current state that can be read at frequent intervals by the EEG system and can be updated (with sub-millisecond latencies) by the host computer.

Increasingly it's hard to find computers with real parallel ports but you can still buy them as add-ons for Windows/Linux desktop systems and for laptops and Apple Macintosh computers you can use USB devices, like the LabJack U3 as a similar (more flexible) alternative.

If one of the channels of your recording system is designated for storing trigger signals and this trigger channel can take some arbitrary value (say, 0–255, in keeping with the parallel port) then you can use the port to send information about the current state of the stimulus or trial. To some extent the way you code this information is up to you, although you might want to think about what your analysis software (e.g. EEGLAB or FieldTrip) will find most easy to decode and analyze.

The most common option is probably to send brief pulses on the parallel port to indicate some event occurring. For instance, you could designate an ID for each of your stimulus onsets and 'send' this number to the parallel port. As mentioned above, a parallel port doesn't have any memory or buffer, only a current state, so when we 'send' a pulse, what we actually do is set the parallel port to that value and, after a brief pause, we simply set it back to zero to end the pulse. The duration of the brief pause, is up to you, but you need to leave it long enough that the receiving system has time to detect it. There probably is no disadvantage to leaving the pulse on for too long so you could, for instance, leave it for one screen refresh period, or 10 ms, or even 100 ms, to be certain. Under this coding system you would also want to send another (different) event to indicate the end of your stimulus. So, for instance, you could send a pulse of value 2 (for 100 ms) to indicate the start of a 'fearful face' condition, a value of 3 to indicate the end of 'fearful face', a value of 4 to indicate the onset of 'happy face', etc. (actually you might want them to have consecutive numbers, but there's no technical reason that you can't). Then your analysis pipeline would need to search for events of each type to create the average waveform surrounding each event occurrence (e.g. fearful face onsets, offsets, etc.).

Another coding system might be to set the stimulus to a particular value at the onset of the stimulus/trial and leave it there *for the duration of the epoch* and then set it simply back to zero to indicate the stimulus finishing. This is, of course, very simple to code, but may not be the preferred system for your analysis package.

Hopefully you, or someone near you, is already running and analyzing EEG experiments and you can base your method on what they do. Once you understand how the communication between your stimulus computer and the EEG recording hardware works, actually implementing it in PsychoPy is probably relatively painless.

TO USE A PARALLEL PORT FROM PSYCHOPY BUILDER

You need to insert a Parallel Out component ☟ , which you'll find under the tab marked I/O (for Input/Output) in the Components panel. This Component supports both traditional parallel ports and LabJack devices. For the former you need to find out the 'address' of your port. To do that you can look in the Device Manager in your system settings. Some common options are built in to PsychoPy, and show up as a drop-down menu in the ParallelOut Component dialog box, but you can add additional port address options using PsychoPy's preferences settings (in the General tab). For Microsoft Windows systems you need to use the format 0x0378 for the address (0x is the way to tell Python to treat this as a hexadecimal value). The address of the parallel port in Linux systems is treated simply as a file path (e.g. /dev/parport0) to which you may also need write-permissions.

The ParallelOut Component has settings to control the start/stop time, just as any other Component, and also a setting for Start data and Stop data which are simply the values that the port will be set to at the start and stop times. If you want to send a particular value of brief pulse to indicate stimulus onset then you could set the Start data to, say, 32, set the Stop data to 0 and set the duration to be one frame (one screen refresh should be sufficient to have the pulse detected by the receiving hardware). You may also want to set the expected duration to 0.016 so that the pulse shows up on your Routine's timeline.

SYNC YOUR TRIGGER TO THE SCREEN REFRESH

If your trigger is related to a visual event (e.g. a visual stimulus onset/offset), then you probably want to synchronize the trigger to the physical screen refresh. With this setting the command to change the parallel port value will be sent *immediately after* the screen refresh signal is sent from the graphics card. Timing precision of this should be very good; it should be limited only by the speed at which we detect the screen refresh (which you can measure, as discussed in Section 12.2).

If the screen does not refresh at the time we requested (e.g. because rendering couldn't be completed in time and a dropped frame occurred) then this synchronization will take that into account (the stimulus will appear a frame later than you intended but the trigger will still give the correct onset time). The only problem is if your monitor itself suffers from erratic frames due to performing 'post-processing' (see Section 13.1); such timing errors cannot be detected or accounted for by PsychoPy and if your stimulus display suffers from this you will need hardware to detect stimulus onset.

If your stimulus is not based on a visual stimulus (e.g. the signal is identifying an auditory onset instead of a visual one) then make sure you set the `Sync to screen` setting to be `False`. An auditory stimulus will start as soon as possible (although how quickly this occurs is strongly hardware dependent) so you will want the trigger signal to be sent *immediately* rather than having it wait until the next screen refresh.

18.4 SENDING EEG TRIGGERS BY NETWORK CONNECTIONS

If you need to send trigger signals by some other means, such as a custom library or a network connection, then you will need to use a simple Code Component to send the triggers. For network signals Python provides relatively easy access to TCP or UDP using the `socket` library.

Let's set up the code for an experiment where we send the value `msg` to our device, yoked to the onset of a visual stimulus called `target`. We'll do this using the `status` attribute, which nearly all PsychoPy Components have and which is used to test whether an object is `NOT_STARTED`, `STARTED`, `FINISHED` or `PAUSED` (videos or sounds). By using this we don't need to worry about the specific timing of the experiment; if we change the start time of the target, the start time of the trigger will change accordingly.

 Warning: Remember the importance of Component order

Recall that Components in a Routine execute in the order that they appear. If you want one thing to base its onset on another stimulus starting then make sure the main stimulus comes first in the Component order. In the current case of using this for triggers, swapping the order so that the Code Component comes *before* the `target` would result in the trigger being sent one frame late. It would be very precisely one frame late but we could make it more exact than that!

We could set the value of `msg` to vary on every trial as part of our conditions file or it could be some fixed value, according to the needs of our experiment. Note that, unlike a parallel port, network protocols don't need to be restricted to sending 8-bit integers; `msg` could be 'bananaface' and, although that might be strange and not very useful, the system would be able to send and receive it.

For the sake of the following code examples, we'll imagine your EEG system's IP address is 128.333.444.555 and it receives inputs on port 11111. Both of these are exceedingly unlikely to be correct so you'll need to find out your own hardware port address for the system.

USING TCP/IP

To use this you would add a Code Component to your trial with the following in its 'Begin Experiment' section to set up the connection:

```
import socket
triggers = socket.socket(socket.AF_INET, socket.SOCK_STREAM)
triggers.connect( (128.333.444.555, 11111) )
```

We need to (re)set a value at the start of each trial to indicate that the trigger has not yet been sent, so set this as the **Begin Routine** code:

```
triggerSent = False
```

Then you need something to change the signals when the stimulus starts. You could do this with something like the 'Each Frame' tab. The value of **msg** is something you could set in your conditions file to make it stimulus specific, or it could be a constant value like **"STARTED"**:

```
if target.status==STARTED and not triggerSent:
    win.callOnFlip(triggers.send, msg) # synched method
    triggerSent = True # trigger is now on
```

The reason we have the value **triggerSent** is that we only want to send our trigger value once, but this code is going to get executed every screen refresh so, without checking whether we've sent the trigger, we'd end up sending the value **msg** in a constantly (every 16.7 ms). So we set it to **False** at the start of the trial and then **True** when a single trigger has been sent. If you need to send multiple different trigger signals then this is totally possible, but you probably need multiple variables to track what has/hasn't been sent.

In the code above we're assuming that **target** is a visual stimulus, so we're synchronizing it to the screen refresh. You could avoid that synchronization by calling the function **trigger.send(msg)** directly instead of passing it as an argument to **win.callOnFlip()** as we did in the code above.

If your hardware expects a **UDP connection** then the code looks very similar, and the concepts are all the same, but this protocol has a concept where we don't maintain a 'connection': we simply send the data to a specific location each time. Here's the full code for the **Begin Routine** section of your Code Component:

```
import socket
triggers = socket.socket(socket.AF_INET, socket.SOCK_DGRAM)
```

Note above that the type of socket switched from **socket.SOCK_STREAM** to **socket.SOCK_DGRAM** and we didn't use a **connect()** function. The **Begin Routine** code is exactly the same as for the TCP/IP code:

```
triggerSent = False
```

For the **Each Frame** code the logic is exactly the same as for TCP/IP but for UDP we have to specify where each message is being sent to (because we don't have a fixed connection to a single location):

```
if target.status==STARTED and not triggerSent:
    triggers.sendto(msg, (128.333.444.555, 11111))
    triggerSent = True # trigger is now on
```

Again, if you don't want to synchronize your pulses to the screen refresh then change the line:

```
win.callOnFlip(triggers.sendto, msg, (128.333.444.555, 11111))
```

to be:

```
triggers.sendto(msg, (128.333.444.555, 11111))
```

18.5 USING CUSTOM LIBRARIES

The final option is that some systems recommend you use their custom library to communicate with the EEG hardware. Hopefully they have already written a Python library in that case (most hardware manufacturers are aware that Python is the language of choice for any scientist, so just ask them). It would be beyond our scope of this book to show you how to use arbitrary third-party libraries with PsychoPy but the following are the key steps that are common to all the options:

- make sure that the version of Python supported by the library matches the version of Python that PsychoPy provides (at the time of writing we were switching PsychoPy to use Python 3.6, but a Python 2.7 distribution will be maintained for some time in order to support manufacturers that only have Python 2.7 libraries)
- place the library in some accessible (readable) location
- go to PsychoPy preferences and add the location to the library to the `paths` setting in the `General` tab (e.g. `['C:\\Users\\jwp\\libs', 'C:\\AnotherLocation']`)
- add the code you need for the library using one or more Code Components.

19

ADD EYE TRACKING TO YOUR EXPERIMENT

> **Learning objectives:** Learn how to interface with an eye tracker so that your Builder experiment can use real-time gaze or pupil data from your participants.

Eye tracking can be used to make stimuli gaze contingent (such as an on-screen cursor or mask that appears precisely where the subject is looking). Alternatively, we might want to record the movements of the eyes or the dilation of the pupils as dependent measures. PsychoPy can connect to a range of eye-tracking systems and other hardware using integrated software called *ioHub*. This chapter can only provide a brief introduction to using ioHub. We will show how to connect with and calibrate your eye tracker, and then how to access real-time eye-position data. We will use this to ensure that the participant is looking at an initial fixation target before commencing each trial of our visual search task. Once you know how to do that, it is very simple to make stimuli that are controlled by the position of the eye.

 Warning: Code ahead!

Because eye tracking is such a useful and well-utilized technique, we felt that we really needed to at least introduce it in this book, even though Builder doesn't (yet) have a graphical eye-tracker component. So at present, to incorporate eye tracking into your Builder experiments requires you to roll up your sleeves and use some code to communicate with your eye-tracker hardware.

Don't worry, we'll hold your hands along the way!

19.1 EYE TRACKING IN BUILDER

Eye tracking is a great tool for probing the brain and behavior. Measuring eye movements, fixations and pupil diameter are each fascinating fields of research in their own right. But eye tracking can also be used for more mundane purposes, in studies where gaze control or pupillometry is not the topic of interest. For example, you might simply want to ensure that each participant is fixating the same stimulus location on screen before each trial starts. So we'll revisit the visual search experiment from Chapter 9, adding a routine so we can check that the participant is fixating at the center of the screen before proceeding to the experimental task. Once you can access the gaze data from an eye tracker, we'll then be able to show how easy it is to control your stimuli using real-time gaze coordinates.

IOHUB: ONE THING TO RULE THEM ALL

There are many different models of eye trackers, provided by different companies. There are also many different technologies that can be used to do the eye tracking (although most modern systems have converged on using image processing of video to extract the center of the pupil and one or more reflections from the surface of the cornea). Each manufacturer has its own ways of interfacing with and controlling its trackers, and those methods can vary even across different models from a single manufacturer. This has traditionally made it challenging to integrate eye tracking with experimental control software. You had to become an expert in the communication protocols of your particular tracker, and hope that they were compatible with the software used to control your stimuli.

PsychoPy seeks to simplify this situation somewhat by incorporating a single software system that can control multiple eye trackers in the same way. This should make it easier to teach people how to control their eye trackers, as it will reduce the proliferation of techniques. It also should make experiments more portable from lab to lab, or to adapt to upgraded eye trackers. This is achieved through the ioHub software package.

ioHub is designed to provide a single, common, software system for controlling eye trackers from a variety of manufacturers. Each of those manufacturers also has its own proprietary data storage formats, which makes it challenging to analyze data across labs in a consistent and comparable way. So another key feature of ioHub is that it can also record data in a common file format (HDF5), regardless of which eye tracker you use. This then also allows you to use the analysis and visualization tools provided by ioHub, rather than the inconsistent proprietary software provided by each manufacturer.

ioHub was developed by Sol Simpson, who was originally commissioned by the international Eye Movement Researchers' Association, on behalf of the wider eye-tracking community. Like PsychoPy, to maximize its use, it was decided to make ioHub open source, freely available and cross-platform. Collecting and analyzing eye-tracking data is only part of what is required to run an eye-tracking experiment, however: there also needs to be a system for precisely controlling and presenting stimuli. Sol saw that PsychoPy could fulfil that need, and so ioHub became integrated within the PsychoPy project, as the `psychopy.iohub` Python package.

TRACKER SUPPORT

`ioHub` currently supports many models from the following eye-tracker providers:

- SR Research *(EyeLink)*
- SMI SensoMotoric Instruments *(iViewX)*
- Tobii Technologies
- LC Technologies *(EyeGaze* and *EyeFollower)*
- EyeTribe.

Don't be too disconcerted if your particular eye tracker doesn't appear in the list above. Because ioHub is open source, support for additional eye trackers (and other sorts of hardware) can be added. Manufacturers generally (although not always) provide documented software interfaces (*APIs*) to their systems, and so ioHub device support will hopefully be extended to new and existing systems.

IOHUB RUNS ASYNCHRONOUSLY TO THE REST OF PSYCHOPY

You will have noticed that there is generally a sort of rhythm or cycle to a PsychoPy experiment: routines are repeated within loops (say, every few seconds) and, within routines, stimuli are drawn and responses checked on every screen refresh (typically at, say, 60 times a second). Although some eye trackers measure eye position and pupil diameter at similar or even slower rates (25–60 Hz), high-end systems sample at up to 2000 times per second. How can PsychoPy code, generally running in a cycle with the screen refresh rate, possibly keep up with that? The answer is: it can't. Instead, ioHub interfaces with the eye tracker by running as a separate software process, independent of the rest of PsychoPy. In technical terms, this is known as the two programs being *asynchronous*. That is, they run in parallel: ioHub will run at whatever speed required to allow it to keep up with the stream of data being sent to it by the eye tracker. It isn't constrained by the display-based cycle usually followed by the rest of PsychoPy. Conversely, our Builder script doesn't need to try to keep up with ioHub. The two processes just communicate with each other when required. For example, let's say that ioHub is collecting and storing gaze data samples from the eye tracker in real time at 500 Hz. Our Builder script, meanwhile, is updating visual stimuli in time with an LCD display running at 60 Hz. If one of those stimuli has its position controlled by the current gaze position, our experiment code just asks ioHub for that value once on every screen refresh. That is, ioHub is happily receiving and storing data at 500 samples per second, but we only need to tap into that data stream periodically, to control the stimulus at the much slower refresh rate of the display.

MONITORING OTHER HARDWARE AT A FAST RATE

In Builder we (usually) only check for responses from our participants (such as key presses and mouse movement) once per screen refresh rate. This is usually sufficient, as there is often no point in trying to deal with inputs faster than we can update stimuli on screen in response. However, you might be concerned that this imposes a certain minimum granularity on response-time measurements, as we can collect responses only once per refresh. (For a variety of reasons, this isn't usually actually as much of a problem as it might appear to those seeking the mythical 'sub-millisecond accuracy' of reaction time measurement (Ulrich and Giray, 1989).) ioHub, however, can collect data from a variety of hardware, not just eye trackers (such as the keyboard, mouse, gamepads, and LabJack hardware interfaces). Because ioHub is not locked in to the screen re drawing loop, it can collect such responses at a higher frequency than typical Builder code. We won't cover it further in this book, as it is really a feature for programmers rather than Builder users, but bear in mind that you can, for example, use ioHub in place of PsychoPy's standard keyboard and mouse checking functions, to get higher resolution reaction time measurements.

19.2 CONFIGURING IOHUB

In the absence of a graphical Builder component for an eye tracker, how do we tell ioHub what settings to use? The easiest way is by editing a text file that contains all the parameters needed to control your particular eye tracker, and telling ioHub to read in that file (a bit like how we use a .csv format text file to specify the conditions for a loop). These configuration files need to be specially crafted so they can be interpreted correctly by ioHub, but fortunately Sol chose to use the YAML format, which is also designed to be easily readable and editable by human beings.

 Info: What is YAML?

The official definition of what YAML stands for has changed over time and is a topic only of interest to train-spotters and stamp-collectors.

To have any credibility though, ensure you pronounce *YAML* so that it rhymes with *mammal*.

YAML FORMAT

To give you an idea of the format, below is a very small extract of a YAML configuration file providing settings for an EyeLink tracker:

```
runtime_settings:
    # sampling_rate: Specify the desired sampling rate to use.
    # Actual sample rates depend on the model being used.
    # Overall, possible rates are 250, 500, 1000, and 2000 Hz.
    sampling_rate: 250

    # track_eyes: Which eye(s) should be tracked?
    # Supported Values: LEFT_EYE, RIGHT_EYE, BINOCULAR
    track_eyes: RIGHT_EYE
```

Within the file, we provide a valid value (such as 250) for each of a number of specifically named keys (such as **sampling_rate**). Keys are separated from their values by a colon. YAML files have a hierarchical structure, which, like Python code, is governed by white space. For example, in the extract above, the keys **sampling_rate** and **track_eyes** are both clustered under the heading of **runtime_settings**. When editing these files, it is important to preserve the levels of indentation so that the hierarchy is maintained. It pays to make a copy of one of the bundled example files, to ensure that you can always refer back to the unchanged original in case your editing causes problems.

Notice that YAML files can contain comment lines (prefixed with a # character, just like in Python code), which explain what the various parameters mean and the possible values they can take. There are a variety of example YAML files bundled with Builder's ioHub demos. You can view files which contain all of the possible values that can be set for each supported eye tracker at the PsychoPy GitHub repository: https://github.com/psychopy/psychopy/blob/master/iohub_docs/iohub/api_and_manual/device_details/default_yaml_configs/.

 Warning: Tabs are dangerous

In Python, for consistency with other code, we *recommend* you use spaces rather than tab characters for white space. In YAML, however, white space *must* consist of spaces: tabs will cause errors when parsing these files.

You might want to use a text editor that makes white space characters visible. This makes the presence of any errant tabs obvious, and allows you to count how many spaces are present in an indent. There are heaps of free text editors out there: don't be tempted to use a word processor. They can *really* muck up what should be simple text files.

AN ACTUAL IOHUB CONFIGURATION FILE

Below is an actual ioHub YAML configuration file, containing settings to control an SMI iView X Hi Speed eye tracker. For brevity, we've omitted all of the useful comment lines which would otherwise explain what the keys mean and what valid options they can take. So don't worry if you don't understand all of the details (some of which will be very specific to this model of eye tracker). For example, we communicate with this particular eye tracker using messages that get sent over the network, so ioHub needs to know the IP address of the eye tracker computer to send to (192.168.110.63 on port 4444), and the same details for the computer running PsychoPy, where it will listen for messages and data coming back in response.

Hopefully you can see the hierarchical nature of the file. First, we need to specify what hardware devices we want ioHub to monitor. At a minimum, we need to tell it about two devices: the eye tracker (naturally), but also the display being used to show our stimuli. Just for completeness, we've left in some references to the keyboard and mouse, but you can leave these out if you only intend to use the standard Builder keyboard and mouse components.

Lastly, we also need to specify some options about how ioHub will store the eye-tracking data. In this case, we have enabled ioHub's own common data file recording system, but this is optional if you prefer to just use your eye tracker's proprietary data recording format.

```
# specify what devices to monitor
monitor_devices:
    - Display:
        name: display
        reporting_unit_type: pix
        device_number: 1
        physical_dimensions:
            width: 1574
            height: 877
            unit_type: mm
        default_eye_distance:
            surface_center: 1649
            unit_type: mm
        psychopy_monitor_name: DLP

    - Keyboard:
        name: keyboard

    - Mouse:
        name: mouse
```

```
    - Experiment:
        name: experimentRuntime


# SMI iView eye tracker configuration
- eyetracker.hw.smi.iviewx.EyeTracker:
    name: tracker
    save_events: True
    stream_events: True
    event_buffer_length: 1024
    monitor_event_types: [BinocularEyeSampleEvent]
    network_settings:
        send_ip_address: 192.168.110.63
        send_port: 4444
        receive_ip_address: 192.168.110.65
        receive_port: 4444
    runtime_settings:
        sampling_rate: 500
        track_eyes: LEFT_EYE
        sample_filtering:
            FILTER_ALL: FILTER_OFF
        vog_settings:
            pupil_measure_types: PUPIL_DIAMETER
        calibration:
            type: FIVE_POINTS
            auto_pace: Yes
            pacing_speed: FAST
            screen_background_color: 20
            target_type: CIRCLE_TARGET
            target_attributes:
                target_size: 30
                target_color: 239
                target_inner_color: RED
            show_validation_accuracy_window: False
        model_name: HiSpeed


# specify data storage options
data_store:
    enable: True
    experiment_info:
        title: Visual search with eye tracking
    session_info:
        code: SUBJECT01
```

19.3 PROGRAMMING IOHUB

We've seen that configuring ioHub to use our particular hardware is a relatively straightforward process of simply editing a text file. But as noted in the warning at the beginning of this chapter, to actually establish communications with your eye-tracker hardware, control it, and get it to send eye-position data back to PsychoPy, will all still require some Python programming. Although there isn't yet a graphical component that will do these tasks for you, they all fit neatly within the different tabs of a Builder Code Component. Given the time at which code in each of those tabs runs, this is the basic scheme we will be using.

'BEGIN EXPERIMENT' TAB

Here we need to do some initial set up tasks that are required before the experiment can commence, such as:

- Establish communications with the eye tracker.
- Send the eye tracker some configuration information (such as which eye or eyes to record, what sample rate to measure at, the participant's study ID, and so on).
- Calibrate the eye tracker so that the measured eye position can be mapped to gaze coordinates on the screen.

'BEGIN ROUTINE' TAB

Here we typically do things that need to occur at the start of each trial. For example:

- Tell the eye tracker to start recording/sending data.
- Send any required stimulus-related information to the eye tracker (such as the filename of the currently displayed image). This may be needed for the eye tracker's own proprietary data file, or to allow real-time display of gaze over the image within the eye tracker's own operating software.

'EACH FRAME' TAB

This is where 'real-time' tasks happen. That is, each time the screen re-draws, we might need to:

- Read the current gaze position to check if the participant is fixating at the right place.
- Update the position of a stimulus so that it becomes gaze contingent (such as moving a gaze cursor, or masking the currently fixated word in a text).

- Check whether the participant is currently maintaining a stable fixation, is making a saccade (rapid gaze shift to another location), or is blinking. For example, we might implement a change-blindness task by manipulating stimuli only while the eyes are saccading and vision is suppressed.
- Send some event-related information to the eye tracker that may need to be recorded in its own data file (such as when changes in stimuli occur or when the participant makes a response).

'END ROUTINE' TAB

- Tell the eye tracker to pause or stop recording/sending data.
- Tell the eye tracker to save the data for this trial (if you aren't relying on ioHub's own data storage).
- Add any required variables to the PsychoPy or ioHub data files (such as whether the participant was correctly looking at the fixation point at the start of the trial).

'END EXPERIMENT' TAB

Depending on the eye tracker, you might have some 'tidying-up' tasks to do here, such as:

- Tell the eye tracker to save the data file (if that wasn't happening in chunks at the end of each trial).
- Close the connection to the eye tracker.

19.4 ADD EYE TRACKING TO THE VISUAL SEARCH TASK

We've spent quite a lot of time describing ioHub. Let's finally get our hands dirty and actually put it to use. Rather than start from scratch, we'll extend the visual search task we created in Chapter 9 to incorporate real-time eye tracking.

What will we use the eye data for? In Figure 9.1, we saw that as the number of distractors increased, the time taken to find the same-colored target also increased, at about 200 ms per distractor. Perhaps not coincidentally, 200 ms is the typical length of a human saccade/fixation cycle. If the stimuli are far enough apart that each must be fixated and inspected individually until the target is found, we should inspect an additional increase in search time of about 200 ms per distractor. In Chapter 9, however, we had no way of controlling where the participant was looking at the start of the trial. If the participant just happens to be fixating where the target stimulus appears at the start of the trial, then we should expect an unusually low reaction time even in the presence of a large number of distractors. This sort of trial-by-trial noise could be accounted for if we could control where the participant is fixating, prior to the appearance of the stimuli.

So our first eye-tracking amendment will be to only allow any trial to commence once we know that the participant is steadily fixating an initial fixation stimulus. This is actually very simple to implement. Before we get to that stage, however, we have a bit of housekeeping to do to configure and set up our eye tracker.

CONFIGURE IOHUB FOR YOUR EYE TRACKER

We saw above that we can configure ioHub for a given eye tracker just by editing a YAML file, and that example files can be found in the demos bundled with PsychoPy or online at the PsychoPy GitHub page. You'll need to work through a file specific to your system, consulting the documentation provided by your eye-tracker manufacturer to enter the appropriate values. You'll need to specify things like how to communicate with the tracker, what calibration procedure to use, which eye(s) to measure, and what eye information you want to receive (whether it be simple gaze position or pupil diameter; or classifications of whether the eye is currently making a saccade, fixating, blinking, etc.).

 Warning

Realistically, this first hurdle of getting the configuration details correct will likely be more troublesome than anything that follows in this chapter.

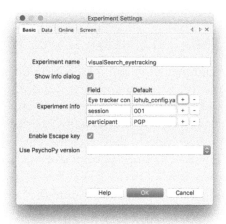

FIGURE 19.1   The *Experiment Settings* dialog. A new *Eye tracker config* field has been added, with a default value of *iohub_config.yaml*. This YAML filename will be used for ioHub to read in its required configuration information to control the eye tracker.

Once you have crafted your YAML configuration file, you need to let ioHub know where it is. A convenient way to do this is to add a field in the ExpInfo dialog that appears at the start of each experiment. Do this by clicking the `Experiment Settings` icon in the Builder toolbar, and clicking the + button to add a new field (Figure 19.1). Put 'Eye tracker config' as the name of the field, and paste the name of your YAML file into the corresponding default text field. If the YAML file isn't in the same folder as your Builder .psyexp file, you should also include its relative path.

We now need to tell ioHub to read in your configuration file, which requires a little code. Because we have a few housekeeping tasks to do (like connecting to and calibrating the eye tracker), you should insert a new routine in the Flow panel, before the loop that controls the actual experiment procedures. We'll call it `tracker_setup`. Simply insert a Keyboard Component on it, set to last indefinitely, and to force the end of the routine when any key is pressed. This means that the experiment won't proceed until we've completed the necessary setup procedures. Perhaps also insert a Text Component saying something like 'Please wait while we set up the eye tracker' so the participant knows what is happening.

Now let's start the magic. Insert a Code Component in that routine, and put some code like this in the `Begin Experiment` tab, to tell ioHub to read in your configuration file:

```
# keep track of we manage to connect:
tracker_connected = False


# get the name of our YAML config file from the expInfo dialog:
config_file = expInfo['Eye tracker config']


# load some useful libraries
from psychopy.iohub import util, client


# now import the config file
io_config = util.readConfig(config_file)
```

If the code above runs correctly, then ioHub will have read in all of the configuration details from the YAML file, and placed them into a list contained in the variable called `io_config`.

CONNECT TO THE EYE TRACKER

The next step is for ioHub to take the configuration information and attempt to establish a connection to the eye tracker (the YAML file should contain the details of how to establish a communication channel with your particular eye tracker). If we can't connect, we will terminate the experiment immediately. So continue the code above as follows:

```
# attempt to connect to the devices in the config file:
io = client.ioHubConnection(io_config)


# check that we can specifically get the details
# for the eye tracker device (named 'tracker' in the
# YAML file):
if io.getDevice('tracker'):
    # give it a name so we can refer to it:
    eye_tracker = io.getDevice('tracker')
    tracker_connected = True


if not tracker_connected:
    print("Quitting: we couldn't connect to the eye tracker.")
    core.quit()
```

SET UP AND CALIBRATE THE EYE TRACKER

Each eye tracker has its own setup procedures and calibration mechanisms. Fortunately, ioHub has learned how to do this for us. So, regardless of what system we are using, we set them up in the same way, by issuing just this one command (we show exactly where to insert it shortly):

```
eye_tracker.runSetupProcedure()
```

When we do this, ioHub will display a dialog box containing options as shown in Figure 19.2. In this example, we have pushed **E** to enable a live view of the eye being tracked. We can also use this dialog to conduct a calibration of the eye tracker and then a validation of the quality of that calibration.

ioHub manages the calibration process automatically, by displaying a calibration target on screen, and moving it to the next position only when the eye tracker signals that a valid fixation was measured. All we have to do is specify the relevant

FIGURE 19.2 *Left:* The common eye tracker setup procedure window displayed by ioHub. *Right:* The live streaming eye image window.

parameters of the process in the YAML file (such as how many calibration targets to show, what size and color they should be, how rapidly they change, whether they are accepted manually or automatically, and so on).

ioHub creates its own window to draw the calibration targets, rather than drawing in the standard window that Builder uses to display display stimuli. So before starting the calibration, we need to minimize the Builder window (which is always called **win**) so that the ioHub window can come to the front. Once the calibration process is complete, we need to maximize the Builder window again. To run the calibration process in this way, append the new lines from the code below:

```
if io.getDevice('tracker'):
    # give it a name so we can refer to it:
    eye_tracker = io.getDevice('tracker')
    tracker_connected = True

    # minimize the Builder window to get it out of the way:
    win.winHandle.minimize()

    # show ioHub windows for running the calibration:
    eye_tracker.runSetupProcedure()

    # allow keypresses to go back to the Builder window:
    win.winHandle.activate()

    # and maximize it to continue the experiment:
    win.winHandle.maximize()
```

```
if not tracker_connected:
    print("Quitting: we couldn't connect to the eyetracker.")
    core.quit()
```

ENSURE GAZE IS ON A FIXATION POINT

Now it is time to actually use some gaze data. As discussed above, let's insert a check that the participant is correctly fixating at the center of the screen before allowing each trial to commence.

First, insert a new Routine, between the **instruct** and the **trial** routines, which we call **fixation** (see the Flow panel in Figure 19.3). In that routine, insert a Polygon Component to act as the fixation target. We specify that its position is (0, 0) (the center of the screen), that it is (20, 20) pixels in size and has 99 vertices (so it appears as a circle). You can specify the fill and line colors on the Advanced tab of the Polygon Component dialog. Most importantly, leave the duration field blank: we want this target to be displayed indefinitely, as the routine shouldn't end until we know the participant is fixating it correctly.

Now we need to actually start monitoring the stream of gaze data to detect a stable fixation. This needs to be done in code, so insert a Code Component. In its **Begin Routine** tab, we put the code that needs to run every time this routine starts. First, we tell the eye tracker to start sending ioHub the continuous stream of gaze data and eye events. We also set a variable to keep track of whether we have detected the onset of a fixation on the target: this has to have an initial value of **False**, as we have not done any checking yet:

```
# tell the tracker to start streaming eye data to ioHub:
eye_tracker.setRecordingState(True)

# keep track of whether we have detected the onset of
# the fixation yet:
fixation_started = False
```

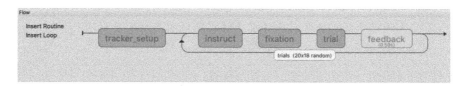

FIGURE 19.3 The Flow panel for the visual search task, revised to incorporate eye tracking. A *tracker_setup* routine has been added to the beginning of the experiment, to connect with and calibrate the eye tracker. A new *fixation* routine has been inserted between the *instruct* and *trial* routines. This ensures that on every iteration of the loop, the trial does not proceed until gaze is maintained steadily on the central fixation target.

Now that we have started the eye data stream, we need to begin monitoring it to detect whether a valid fixation has occurred. A fixation has two key characteristics: a stable *position*, maintained for a minimum *duration*. We will define the minimum duration to be 300 ms (or `0.3` in our code, as PsychoPy does its timing in seconds). This is so we are confident that the eye is fixating the stimulus, and not just being detected as it briefly saccades across the target on the way to another location. We define the threshold for a stable position as being continuously within 30 pixels of the center of the fixation stimulus, for the entire period of our 300 ms duration criterion. We've chosen this threshold rather arbitrarily. The most suitable value for you depends on a number of factors, which can be technical (such as the variability of the signal from your eye tracker) or physiological (the stability of the participant's fixation control, which can be impaired by nystagmus, square wave jerks, drift due to fatigue, and so on). So you might want to vary this threshold from session to session rather than hard-code it into the experiment, and you might also wish to express it in degrees of visual angle, which are generally more meaningful to eye-movement researchers than arbitrary units like pixels.

To find the distance of the *x* and *y* coordinates of the current gaze position from the screen center, we make use of Pythagoras' Theorem. (If that particular geometry lesson has become buried in the darkest recesses of your high-school memories, then refer to Appendix A for a spot of quick revision.)

The first step is to request the current gaze position. Remember that ioHub is receiving a firehose of eye-position samples, at the full rate produced by the eye tracker – we just ask it for the current value, once every screen refresh:

```
# ask ioHub for the current gaze coordinates:
gaze_pos = eye_tracker.getPosition()
```

If ioHub gives us a valid eye position, it should be in the form of a Python list or tuple object (i.e. a pair of *x* and *y* coordinates). If ioHub can't get a valid sample from the eye tracker, it will return just a single value (like the Python `None` object, or a single number representing an error code). So we need to check that we have received a list or tuple before attempting to do anything that requires a pair of values:

```
# check that we got a pair of gaze coordinates:
if type(gaze_pos) in [list, tuple]:

    # we did, so split the list into individual x and y values:
    gaze_x, gaze_y = gaze_pos
```

```
# compute the distance of the gaze position from the
# centre, using good old Pythagoras (taking the square
# root of the sum of the two squared coordinates):
distance_from_centre = sqrt(gaze_x ** 2 + gaze_y ** 2)

# check the eye is within 30 pixels of the centre:
if distance_from_centre <= 30:

    if not fixation_started:
        # this is the first sample close enough
        # to the target to qualify:
        fixation_started = True

        # record the time when the fixation began:
        fixation_start_time = t

    # else the fixation is already underway, so
    # check if it has exceeded the duration criterion
    # of 0.3 seconds:
    elif t - fixation_start_time > 0.3:
        # the fixation is complete, so move on to
        # the rest of the trial:
        continueRoutine = False
else:
    # even if a fixation had started, the eye must
    # have moved away, so start searching again:
    fixation_started = False
```

MAKE A STIMULUS GAZE CONTINGENT

In some tasks, we want to make the position of a stimulus gaze contingent. For example, you might display a stimulus whose position is continuously updated with the current coordinates of the participant's gaze. This could function as a gaze cursor, moving on the screen like a mouse pointer, indicating where the participant is looking. Or it could function as a mask or artificial scotoma, occluding whatever information is at the current gaze location. Creating a gaze-controlled stimulus isn't really needed in this particular experiment, but we show how to create one anyway, just as an example of how easy it is.

So let's make a gaze cursor, which will allow us to monitor how well our fixation detection is operating, and where the calibration (at least at screen center) is still accurate. On the `fixation` routine, add another circle stimulus (a Polygon Component with 99 vertices). We'll make it a bit bigger then the stimuli (a size of (0, 0)), and give it no fill color so that it doesn't obscure the stimuli underneath it (i.e. it will appear as a hollow ring). The key step in making the stimulus gaze contingent is simply to set the position to equal the current gaze coordinates. This is just a matter of entering this in the Position field, `(gaze_x, gaze_y)`, and setting that field to update every frame.

You should now have a circle that automatically moves to match the real-time position of the participant's eyes. We only include this on the fixation routine, as we don't want it to distract the participant during the main part of the trial.

POINT WITH THE EYES INSTEAD OF THE MOUSE

In the original visual search task in Chapter 9, the participants looked around the screen for the target. Once found, they moved the mouse pointer to that target, and then finally clicked the mouse button to end the trial. If we are recording eye movements, then we can stop using the mouse to give a secondary, indirect spatial response. Instead we can use gaze position as a direct indicator of the selected target position, as well as recording the actual search process itself that leads to finding the target.

That leaves the question of how to end the trial by indicating that the target has been found. That can be done purely with gaze data: for example, we set a 'dwell time' threshold for fixating on the target, and end the trial when it is exceeded. This isn't always a good idea, though: just because the participant is fixating on the target doesn't necessarily imply that they have recognized that it *is* the target (it's quite common in visual search tasks to look directly at the target and yet erroneously move on and continue the search). This is known in the eye-tracking world as the *Midas touch* problem: fixating on something is not always sufficient evidence to take an action. For example, imagine an eye-tracking interface to a computer operating system: we wouldn't want to interpret every fixation on a control as a click on that control. Instead, we need some additional response to indicate that the currently fixated stimulus is something the participant wants to take action upon. This could be an another ocular response (e.g. a prolonged blink), or a manual response, like a keypress or mouse click.

We'll avoid the Midas touch problem by only checking if the participant's gaze is on the correct stimulus if they have pushed a key:

```
# get the current gaze position:
gaze_pos = eye_tracker.getPosition()

# check that it contains a pair of x & y coordinates:
if type(gaze_pos) in [list, tuple]:
    gaze_x, gaze_y = gaze_pos
    have_valid_gaze = True
```

```
else: # must be None or an error code:
    have_valid_gaze = False

# avoid the Midas touch by only checking if the target
# is selected if a key is pressed:
keys = event.getKeys()

if keys: # if the list of keys isn't empty..
            # we're hogging the keyboard, so need to manually
            # check for the escape key:
            if 'escape' in keys:
              core.quit()

            # only proceed if we have current gaze coordinates:
            elif have_valid_gaze:

                # if the target is being fixated:
                if target.contains(gaze_x, gaze_y):
                    # record RT and end the trial
                    thisExp.addData('RT', t)
                    continueRoutine = False

                else: # participant is looking somewhere else
                    # so give feedback:
                    wrong_sound.play()
                    # and continue with the trial
```

Note that above, instead of using Pythagoras' Theorem to check if the participant was looking at the target, we used this method:

```
if target.contains(gaze_x, gaze_y):
```

Most PsychoPy visual stimuli have a `.contains()` method. There are pros and cons to using this technique versus the Pythagorean distance check:

- The `.contains()` method takes into account whether the response occurs within the boundaries of the particular shape of the stimulus (e.g. an Image stimulus is rectangular, and a Polygon stimulus could be triangular). By contrast, the Pythagorean approach tests only whether the response coordinates are within a certain radius of a central location. So the effective 'hit zone' it tests for will be circular, regardless of the shape of the target stimulus.

- With the Pythagorean approach, we can easily alter the radius threshold to allow a tolerance for error (such as a calibration offset in the eye-tracker data). The `.contains()` method, however, will return `False` if the response coordinates are even a single pixel away from the boundaries of the stimulus.

For small stimuli such as the shapes used in this search task, the Pythagorean technique is probably the better one to use, as it doesn't require absolutely perfect calibration. You should adopt whatever works for your particular requirements.

END OF ROUTINE

Once the target in the visual search task has been found, the Routine ends. We put this small snippet of code in the **End routine** tab to stop recording eye data at that point (remember, it restarts at the beginning of each fixation routine):

```
if eyetracker:
    eyetracker.setRecordingState(False)
```

END EXPERIMENT

In most PsychoPy experiments, we seldom need to put any code in the **End Experiment** tab of a Code Component, as Builder takes care of most of the 'housekeeping' required when the experimental session is coming to an end. In an eye-tracking study, however, we have other things to consider. First, we're connected to some external equipment and software (the eye-tracking system). We should politely disconnect from it, so that it is ready to use again and has a chance to do any of its own housekeeping processes. Second, since ioHub runs in a separate software process from the rest of PsychoPy, it's good practice to tell it to shut down as well, just in case it fails to do so itself:

```
# terminate communications with the eye tracker:
if eyetracker:
    eye_tracker.setConnectionState(False)

# tell ioHub to close and tidy up:
io.quit()
```

19.5 DATA STORAGE VIA IOHUB

So far, we've covered how to access real-time eye movement data, first to check that central fixation was achieved prior to the trial, and then to check if the correct target was found during the trial. This level of eye tracking may be sufficient for running many studies where eye movements themselves aren't the topic of interest (i.e. they are just being used to assess task compliance or gather a response). But if the eye-movement data are themselves of interest to examine and analyze offline, then we also need to store all the data permanently on disk. The storage of high-volume device data (such as a stream of eye-tracker samples) is something that ioHub can provide for us. This feature is simple to enable, by including something like these settings in the ioHub configuration YAML file shown earlier:

```
# specify data storage options:
data_store:
    enable: True
    experiment_info:
        title: Visual search with eye tracking
    session_info:
        code: SUBJECT01
```

Why should we use ioHub's data storage rather than the standard PsychoPy data output? Eye-tracking studies can generate high-throughput data (> 1 kHz). PsychoPy would struggle to handle that: it is optimized for displaying stimuli with temporal precision, and having to store large volumes of data at the same time would jeopardize that primary duty. ioHub *is* optimized for streaming high-throughput events (from multiple devices) to a single, unified data file on disk. So ioHub runs in a parallel, asynchronous process to the main PsychoPy software. That way, ioHub and PsychoPy each do what they are best at, and we get to enjoy the best of both worlds.

HDF5 FILES

PsychoPy primarily uses a simple .*csv* tabular data file format, where each column corresponds to a variable and each row contains the values of those variables for a single trial. This format isn't really compatible with storing raw eye-movement data. Each cell in a .*csv* file typically contains just a single value (say, a reaction time). But even just a few seconds of eye tracking can generate thousands of values, for say, eye-position coordinates. So to effectively store eye-movement data along with other variables, it can be more useful to move away from a single-table format, and shift to something more flexible.

ioHub uses HDF5 files, a sophisticated data storage format, optimized for handling large, multi-dimensional scientific data sets in an efficient manner. Rather than being a tabular text file, it is a database format, which can contain multiple tables of differing dimensions. For example, it can contain a table with one row per trial, effectively the same as PsychoPy's standard data output. But it can also include separate tables at the rate of one row per eye tracker sample, which can be thousands or millions of rows long. The various data tables can be linked, as they use a consistent time-stamp. For example, you can send your own event messages to ioHub, such as indicating when a trial starts or ends. Those messages go into their own table and can be matched to other streams of device data to see when they occurred relative to mouse, keyboard or eye-tracker events, as they are all time-stamped on a common basis.

Because the data format is hierarchical, we also get the advantage that subsequent sessions can be added to the same file. We just need to provide distinct subject identification codes for each session. PsychoPy, by contrast, generates a new *.csv* data file for each session, so we need to collate all of these data together at the analysis stage.

 Pro Tip: Viewing HDF5 contents

To analyze data stored in HDF5 files will generally require some coding. They are specially structured hierarchical database files: unlike common old *.csv* files, they can't just be opened in regular spreadsheet software. There is, however, a freely available program that will allow you to graphically open and explore the structure of the HDF file, export data to simpler tabular formats, and even do some rough plotting of time-series data. Google The HDF Group the organization that maintains the HDF format, and download their free HDFView software (Figure 19.4).

EMBED THE CONDITIONS FILE IN THE HDF5 DATABASE

Even if you are using ioHub's HDF5 data storage, Builder will still save its own *.csv* data files (unless you tell it otherwise in the *Experiment Settings* dialog). But is is useful to get some of that information also embedded within the HDF5 file. We do this by linking ioHub to the loop surrounding our experimental routines. The loop itself is connected to an external conditions file. So we need to connect ioHub to the loop, so it can create a table within its data store that contains the variables in the conditions file:

```
# only do this once:
if trials.thisN == 0: # on the first trial,
    # connect the ioHub data store to our TrialHandler
    # (i.e. to the loop called 'trials'):
    io.createTrialHandlerRecordTable(trials)
```

FIGURE 19.4 An ioHub-generated HDF5 file, as seen when opened with the HDFView software. Unlike PsychoPy's standard *.csv* flat, single-table output, HDF files have a hierarchical structure, containing many related tables. Here, the primary eye-movement table is highlighted in green, with the panel to the right showing some of the variables it contains. Such a table could contain millions of data points, while other tables could be very simple. For example, the *experiment_meta_data* table contains just a single row of information pertaining to the study, such as its title and description. Rows in the various event tables are labelled by a common time-stamp, so keypresses, mouse movements and custom messages can be linked temporally to the eye-movement data stream.

 Info: For the curious

In PsychoPy Python code, the object that runs a cycle of trials is a *TrialHandler*. It handles a lot of the housekeeping required to repeat trials (such as reading a conditions file, controlling randomization, keeping track of how many trials remain, and storing data on disk). In the Builder interface, however, to make things more straightforward, we simply label this a 'loop'. So when you see a function like `.createTrialHandlerRecordTable(trials)`, you can translate this in your mind to 'this function will create a table to record the variables in my loop trials'.

At this stage, the conditions table in the HDF file contains only the names of the variables. At the end of each trial, you should then call this function:

```
io.addTrialHandlerRecord(thisTrial.values)
```

This will actually fill in the row of values for each variable in this particular trial.

EMBED OTHER MESSAGES IN THE HDF5 DATA

We can also embed custom messages in the ioHub data store, for information which isn't specified in advance in the conditions file. For example, you might want to indicate the time at which certain events occur, so you can divide the continuous stream of eye-movement data up into its corresponding periods. So at the beginning of the fixation routine, we can embed this message:

```
io.sendMessageEvent('fixationtask_start')
```

Similarly, at the beginning of the trial routine, we can embed this message so we know the time at which the eye-movement data begin to correspond to the actual search task rather than the preceding fixation period:

```
io.sendMessageEvent('trial_start')
```

19.6 SAVING IMAGE STIMULI TO DISK

Our visual search task uses dynamically generated stimuli. That is, instead of displaying a static image file from disk, in each trial we draw randomly scattered polygon stimuli over the screen. This approach can create a bit of problem for the analysis of an eye-tracking study, as we often want to display gaze data superimposed upon the information the participant was examining. This is tricky to do if the information disappears at the end of each trial. Fortunately, PsychoPy has a hidden superpower: the window has a function called **getMovieFrame()** that

grabs what is currently displayed and stores it in memory. Another function called
{saveMovieFrames()} will save that information to a file on disk.

Let's add this to the *End Routine* tab of the Code Component in the trial
routine so that at the end of each trial, whatever was being shown gets saved to
disk, in a uniquely named file. Because the generated stimuli in this experiment
are randomly created, we need to ensure that each file gets named with the details
of the subject and the trial number, so that the images can be matched back to the
data later:

```python
# get the subject ID and the current trial number:
subject = expInfo['participant']
trial_num = trials.thisN

# insert that info into a filename:
image_file = 'subject_{}_trial_{}.png'.format(subject, trial_num)

# get the image displayed on the screen:
win.getMovieFrame()

# save it to disk, in .png format:
win.saveMovieFrames('stimuli/' + image_file, codec='png')

# add it to the data for this trial:
thisExp.addData('image_file', image_file)

# and store it in the HDF file:
io.addTrialHandlerRecord(thisTrial.values())
```

Note that the HDF file is only set up for storing variables associated with the loop
if they are specified in the conditions file. So to be able to store the image_file
variable, make sure there is a column with that label in the conditions file. The
column will be empty in the conditions file, as it is only during the experiment
that we know what image name will be associated with what trial.

Figure 19.5 shows the results of this: for each trial, the dynamically generated
stimulus display has been saved to a bitmap image. This image can then be used by
eye-movement analysis to overlay the corresponding eye-movement data for that
trial, showing the spatial sequences of fixations required to complete the task.

PSYCHOPY AS A STIMULUS GENERATOR

The win.saveMovieFrames() function can be used for more than just docu-
menting the displays that occurred within an experiment. For example, we can

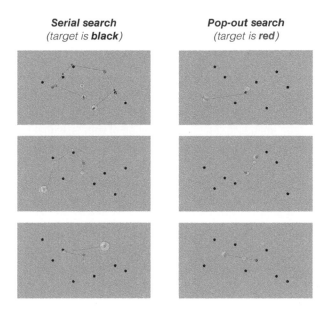

FIGURE 19.5 Some scanpaths from individual trials in the visual search task. The background images were saved by PsychoPy at the end of each trial and used to superimpose the corresponding fixation data. The left column shows data from three trials with a black hexagon target. A serial search of varying lengths was required to locate the target among the similar black pentagon distractors. In the right column, the hexagonal target was red, popping out from the black distractors. This led to a much shorter sequence of fixations to reach the target.

use PsychoPy not to run an experiment, but simply as a program to generate bitmap stimuli that are then used by an actual experiment. For example, text stimuli are sometimes rendered differently on different computers. A given font may be missing and replaced with another, and even the same font can be rendered differently across operating systems. Particularly for eye-tracking studies, if you want the stimuli to be pixel-identical across different computers, it can be worth generating static bitmap images to ensure this. That is, create your stimuli in PsychoPy as normal, using whatever Builder components are needed, then save the entire screen to a bitmap file. In the experiment itself, all of the visual stimulus components can be replaced with a single `Image` component, showing the entire rendered display.

Another reason for saving to a bitmap file is when the stimuli you're creating are so complex that they can't be created dynamically without causing timing issues. For example, you might be composing a display that is constructed by layering hundreds of component stimuli. By rendering the entire window to a bitmap file, you can reduce the process required to show the stimuli at just the time required to open and display that single bitmap.

Pro Tip: Become a presentation pro

Stand out from the crowd with their boring, bullet-point-laden, text-only PowerPoint slides! Often the best way to explain a dynamic task is to actually show it in motion, rather than just describe it verbally or with a static diagram. You can use PsychoPy's ability to save screen images to create an animation of your task: that is, gather a series of exported bitmaps and use your software of choice to stitch them together into a movie file or animated GIF.

Even journals are increasingly encouraging submission of stimulus animations to appear in online versions of Methods sections, or even in 'graphical abstracts' to entice readers.

Task animations can also spice up your website, or be shared on sites like www.figshare.com And nothing will get you more followers on social media than showing off your favorite rotating grayscale Gabor patches superimposed on a random dot kinetogram.

19.7 CONCLUSION

Phew, you've made it to the end of what may be the most complicated chapter in this book: well done. Of necessity, we had to introduce quite a bit of code here, which we've tried to minimize in the other chapters. Hopefully you've now gained some appreciation of what Builder does for you with its components: it hides a lot of complexity and code generation behind a graphical interface, allowing you to concentrate on the design of your experiment. For the moment, however, eye tracking in Builder still requires us to get our hands dirty with some Python code. But that does open a whole new and powerful set of options for conducting exciting experiments.

APPENDIX A

MATHEMATICS REFRESHER

This is where you might be wishing you could remember some of your basic mathematics from school! Lots of the simple geometric functions you learned about turn out to be useful if you want things to move and change in interesting ways.

A.1 SINE AND COSINE

Do you remember $\cos(\theta)$ and $\sin(\theta)$? They are useful calculating the height and width of a triangle from an angle but it turns out these functions have another neat use: they produce waves that vary smoothly between -1 and 1. Why is that useful? Well, if we want something to move backwards and forwards (or do anything else rhythmically) then `sin()` and `cos()` are usually the easiest ways to achieve it.

The functions `sin` and `cos` can be thought of as defining a circle. Imagine a circle of radius 1 (any unit you fancy!) and say that θ is the angle of a point going around that circle. By convention θ starts at zero when the point is to the right of the circle (i.e. at the 3 o'clock position) and increases (in units of *radians* if you're an engineer) as the point rotates anti-clockwise around the circle.

So how do sine and cosine relate to this? In this case, $\sin(\theta)$ gives the vertical height of the point from the center of the circle and $\cos(\theta)$ gives the horizontal distance from the center (Figure A.1). As you can imagine, the vertical distance is initially 0 but as the point rotates towards the top of the circle (the 12 o'clock position), the value of $\sin(\theta)$ increases. At the top, it reaches the maximum of 1 and then starts to decrease again. When it gets to half way around the circle (the 9 o'clock position, or 180°), the vertical distance is again 0, and as it reaches the bottom of the circle (6 o'clock, or 270°) it is -1. So $\sin(\theta)$ is a wave that starts at 0 and varies smoothly between +1 and -1 (Figure A.2). The equivalent for $\cos(\theta)$ is the same, except that the horizontal distance from the center starts off at its maximum when $\theta = 0$ (the right most edge) and gradually goes down to 0 at the top.

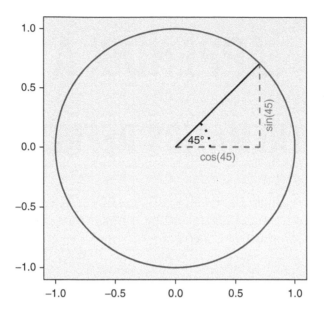

FIGURE A.1 A circle of radius *1*. Any point on the circle has its position defined by its angle from the starting position at 3 o'clock (in this case, 45°). As the point sweeps around the circle, the sine and cosine functions tell us how far it is vertically and horizontally from the center.

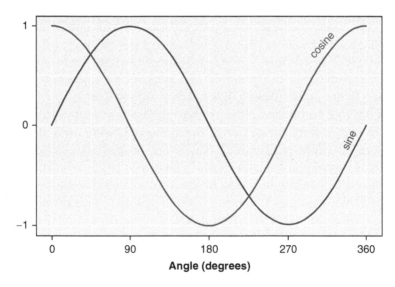

FIGURE A.2 The values of the sine and cosine functions for a complete revolution around the unit circle. For example, at 0° (3 o'clock), the radius line is completely horizontal, so its horizontal component (cosine) is 1 and its vertical component (sine) is 0. At 45°, halfway between being perfectly horizontal and perfectly vertical, the two components are equal, so the sine and cosine lines intersect (at ≈ 0.707).

So we could make a stimulus that moved in a circle around our screen. All we need to do is set the position to `$(sin(t),cos(t))` and this stimulus would move around in a circular trajectory, depending on the units ('normalized' units will result in an ellipse due to the aspect ratio of the screen, but you could set the stimulus to 'height' units to get a better circle).

 Pro Tip

Most programming languages deal with angles in terms of radians, but most humans are happier thinking in terms of degrees. There are $2 \times \pi$ radians in a circle, compared with 360 degrees. So we can convert angle values from degrees to radians by multiplying by π and dividing by 180. For convenience, Builder imports a couple of useful functions from the *numpy* library: `deg2rad()` and `rad2deg()`. It also imports a variable named `pi`, so you don't need to show off how many of its digits you know by typing them out literally.

A.2 RESCALING AND CHANGING START POINTS

Increasing/decreasing the magnitude of any variable is usually handled by multiplying or dividing a value. Changing its start value is done by adding and subtracting. If we want the amplitude of a circle to be larger (maybe our stimulus units are in pixels so we want the circle to have radius of 200 rather than 1) then we need to take a position of `$(sin(t) * 200, cos(t) * 200)`. Alternatively, if we want to change where the variable starts (in this case altering the circle center) then we should add or subtract something. If we add 100 to the x value and subtract 100 from y, to give `$(sin(t) * 200 + 100, cos(t) * 200 - 100)`, then we get a circle more in the lower right quadrant of the screen.

Note that computers do care about conducting mathematical operations in a specific order. Possibly you remember at school you were taught the word 'BODMAS' to give you the correct order (Brackets, Orders or pOwers, Division, Multiplication, Addition, Subtraction). The key is that multiplication and division get performed before addition and subtraction. The order that they get written is largely irrelevant. So `-4 + t * 5` is the same as `t * 5 - 4`. The multiplication by 5 always occurs before the subtraction of 4 (or the addition of negative 4). If you need an addition to occur before a multiplication or division then you need to add brackets: `(-4 + 2) * 5` is `-2 * 5` which is `-10`, whereas `-4 + 2 * 5 = +6` because the multiplication occurs first. If you go into the Shell panel in PsychoPy (switch to the Coder view and look in the bottom panel) then you can try typing in some equations with and without brackets to find out what the results are.

A.3 PYTHAGORAS' THEOREM

Pythagoras was the first to discover that the length of the hypotenuse (i.e. the long edge, usually denoted c) is related to the lengths of the other two sides (a and b) by the equation:

$$a^2 + b^2 = c^2$$

and so:

$$c = \sqrt{a^2 + b^2}$$

This equation is really useful in working out how far apart two objects are. For example, if we want to know the distance from the current mouse position to the center of the screen then we can use Pythagoras' Theorem. If you have a mouse object in your Routine (let's assume you got creative and called it `mouse`) then you can extract the position of that mouse at any time with the code `x, y = mouse.getPos()`. Now you have two values `x` and `y` giving the position relative to the center of the screen, in the same units as the screen itself (see Experiment Preferences). Then, the *distance* from the center is simply given by `sqrt(x**2 + y**2)`. Note that, in Python syntax, `**` refers to raising a value to a power, so `sqrt(x**2 + y**2)` is the Python syntax for $\sqrt{x^2 + y^2}$.

To get the distance between two objects instead of the distance from the center of the screen (which is $(0,0)$) you need to subtract the x and y positions of the two objects first. So if we have `x, y = mouse.getPos()` as above and `stimX, stimY = stim.getPos()` then we can measure the distance between them with:

```
dist = sqrt((stimX-x)**2 + (stimY-y)**2)
```

which is simply the Python code for the equation:

$$\sqrt{(stimX - x)^2 + (stimY - y)^2}$$

There are lots more simple mathematical equations out there to help save you time and/or make your life more interesting. Go and find them. Embrace them, even!

APPENDIX B

EXERCISE SOLUTIONS

In addition to the solutions presented here you can find working examples of all the relevant code in the online materials: https://study.sagepub.com/psychology.

2.1: CHANGE THE SCREEN COLOR (FROM PAGE 41)

All you need to do to change the screen color for the experiment is go to the **Experiment Settings** and take a look in the tab that says **Screen**. In that tab you'll find a setting for color. To start with it's in PsychoPy's RGB format but you can also just type in a color name or you can *right*-click and select a new color from the colors system dialog box.

2.2: CREATE THE FRENCH STROOP (FROM PAGE 41)

All you need to do to change the words that appear is alter the conditions file. If you need to keep both available then you might want to rename the conditions file to have **conditions_en.xlsx** and **conditions_fr.xlsx** and then you can have different versions of your experiment that select these. The chapter on sections on blocking and counterbalancing will give you more information about how to control those further, but that's a more 'intermediate' topic.

2.3: MEASURE THE 'REVERSE' STROOP EFFECT (FROM PAGE 41)

Done correctly, this is unbelievably simple. As with Exercise 2.2 this is just a matter of changing the conditions file so that the **corr_ans** refers to the **word** instead of the **word_color**. You might be tempted, however, to go and recreate the **trial** Routine or something more complex. One of the skills you'll improve during this book (hopefully) is learning how to think of the *easy way* to do things.

2.4: CHECK OUT THE FULL EXPERIMENT (FROM PAGE 42)

If you haven't looked at the demos yet for Builder then note that the first time you use the demos you have to unpack them to a folder of your choosing so that you keep your own copy outside of the application. To do this go to the **Demos>** menu and select **Unpack....**

In the Extended Stroop demo, the **feedback** Routine uses some Python code to create some text (in a variable called **msg**) and that **msg** variable is then used in the Text Component to be drawn on the screen. Take a look at the code that is used in this box (it's a fairly basic Python `if...else...` statement).

3.1: ADD INSTRUCTIONS (FROM PAGE 55)

You could recreate the Routines from scratch for this, but you just created an `instructions` Routine for the Stroop task that will be very similar in structure to this one. You could copy and paste that to here and then just change the contents of the Text Component so that the instructions make sense for this study. For the 'Thanks and goodbye' Routine you probably don't need to edit anything at all!

Once you see the menu items `Copy Routine` and `Paste Routine`, in the `Experiment` menu, this task will probably seem straightforward. The thing that could potentially be confusing is that you need both experiments to be opened in the same instance of PsychoPy in order to do the paste step. If you double-click two experiments from within Windows then they might open in two different instances of PsychoPy. To get around this, you might need to go to the PsychoPy window with your Routine to copy, then open a new window (`Ctrl-N`) and open your other experiment in that window. This way you make sure that they are both in the same PsychoPy and can talk to each other.

3.2: ADD PRACTICE TRIALS (FROM PAGE 55)

To get this to work you want to create a new conditions file for your practice trials, with the same columns as the main conditions file but with fewer rows (and probably not pointing to the same images, so that your participants don't have any pre-exposure to the stimuli).

4.1: GAZE CUEING (FROM PAGE 68)

To do this you obviously need to fetch an image file of some eyes (looking either to the left or the right). You can use that image file as a stimulus, as described in Chapter 3. To control whether the eyes look to the left or the right you could use two different image files (you could flip the image in your favorite image editor and save another copy) and then set your conditions file to refer to the appropriate image file ('eyesLeft.jpg' or 'eyesRight.jpg') or you could get PsychoPy to do the flipping for you by setting the size of the stimulus to have a negative width on some trials (because negative width or height values are like flipping the stimulus in the X or Y dimensions, respectively).

Make sure in this version that you have equal numbers of trials where the eyes point at the target and when they don't because we want the eye gaze not to be informative in order to see whether it affects the behavior *instinctively* and automatically.

4.2: MEASURE THE EFFECT FOR DIFFERENT SOAS (FROM PAGE 69)

Posner and colleagues studied the attentional cueing effects for a variety of time differences between the cue and the probe (stimulus onset asynchronies or SOAs) and found some interesting characteristics. One of the surprising effects is that when the cue is *not* informative about the location of the probe, we can measure both positive and negative effects of cueing (a speeding up or a slowing down of reaction times) according to which SOA was used. With very brief SOAs (say 100 ms) and an uninformative cue we often still find a faster reaction time when the probe is in the cued location, but with longer SOAs (say 300 ms) we see the opposite effect where participants are actually slower to detect the stimulus if it lands at the previous cued location. This is thought of as an 'Inhibition of Return', whereby inhibition prevents the attentional mechanism from revisiting the previously attended location, leading to a decrease in reaction times at that location.

As a participant it takes some time to run the cueing experiment with multiple time-courses to map out this effect, but you might find it an interesting task to create the experiment with valid and invalid cues as in your Posner cueing task, but now with multiple SOAs built into your conditions.

5.1: REVEAL AN IMAGE BY CHANGING OPACITY (FROM PAGE 83)

Note that opacity is a parameter that varies from 0 (completely transparent, so invisible) to 1 (completely 'opaque', so fully visible). You could take an image and gradually reveal it using opacity in two ways. You could have an image that gradually *increased* its opacity. For instance, if you set the opacity to have a value of $t/5$ then it will become visible over a period of 5 seconds. Alternatively, you could draw a stimulus followed by some sort of mask that gradually *reduced* its opacity to reveal the stimulus behind (a value of $1-t/5$ would take 5 seconds for the mask to disappear). Either way, when you set the opacity to an equation remember that it needs to **update every frame**.

5.2: ROTATING EYEBALLS (FROM PAGE 83)

To make a pair of simple eyeballs you need four objects; two white eyes and two pupils. Position them on either side of the fixation and make the pupils move in a sinusoidal pattern left and right. You'll need to play with scaling the amplitude of the motion (using multiplication) and with the center of the motion (addition and subtraction). Some handy tips for this exercise:

- Don't use normalized units for this because drawing the circular pupil is hard with those. Use 'height', 'pix' or 'cm' depending on what you feel most comfortable with.

- Make sure you draw the white elliptical part of the eye first and the pupil second (by having the component for the pupil *below* the component for the white of the eye in the Routine view).
- Start with just one eye while you get the settings right. When you've done that you can right-click the Component and 'Copy' and 'Paste' it back in ('Paste Component' is in the Experiment menu of the Builder or **Ctrl-Alt-V**). That way the settings for the second eye will all be done and the only thing that will need changing is the position.

6.1: PERFORMANCE-BASED TERMINATION OF PRACTICE TRIALS (FROM PAGE 95)

Really, all you need to do to make this work (once you've learned how to track performance, following Chapter 6) is to add the following lines to the end of the 'Begin Routine' section in your Code Component (i.e. just after you update the value of **nCorr**):

```
if nCorr >= 4:
    practice.finished = True
```

This causes the loop called **practice** to terminate at the point that it next goes around the loop. It won't cause the current Routine to terminate, so participants will still get the feedback as in other trials. The code won't even abort other Routines that immediately follow this one (if we had any). It only affects the experiment when we next try to go around the loop.

6.2: SHOW PROGRESS ON THE SCREEN WITH TRIAL NUMBER (FROM PAGE 96)

Use a Code Component, **trackProgress**, to create a variable, **msg**, and then use this with a Text Component that updates according to the value of the **msg** just as you did in previous examples.

The easy solution to this, if you know how many total trials you will run and never change this, is to 'hard-code' the total number of trials with something like:

```
msg = "{}/30".format(trials.thisN)
```

but that isn't recommended. What tends to happen is that you change your study and forget to update the number and then your participant gets annoyed that at doing 38/30 trials! It's a better idea to insert this from PsychoPy:

```
msg = "{}/{}".format(trials.thisN, trials.nTotal)
```

7.1: FIND OUT ABOUT RATING SCALE'S MANY ADVANCED SETTINGS (FROM PAGE 108)

This one's easy, at least to get started: Google it! One of the key lessons here is that, because PsychoPy is used by lots of people, Google has experienced lots of people asking questions about it, and this means that Google has a pretty good idea by now of what pages are useful for you.

A search for `psychopy rating scale` will take you straight to the correct page in the online documentation. The top two suggestions from Google are both reasonable. One takes you to the documentation for the Rating Scale Builder Component and the other takes you to the documentation for the RatingScale object in the underlying Python library (i.e. the version you would typically only use if programming rather than using Builder). The latter is actually the one we want on this occasion, because using `Customize everything` is actually just a sneaky way of going straight to the code. Don't worry though: if you *had* gone to the Builder Component document you would have scrolled down and found the entry for `Customize everything` and this would simply have directed you to the other page anyway.

Now, at the top of this programming documentation page you'll see the following (the line wrapping will be different, though):

```
class psychopy.visual.RatingScale(
    win, scale='<default>', choices=None,
    low=1, high=7, precision=1, labels=(),
    tickMarks=None, tickHeight=1.0,
    marker='triangle', markerStart=None, markerColor=None,
    markerExpansion=1, singleClick=False, disappear=False,
    textSize=1.0, textColor='LightGray', textFont='Helvetica Bold',
    showValue=True, showAccept=True, acceptKeys='return',
    acceptPreText='key, click', acceptText='accept?', acceptSize=1.0,
    leftKeys='left', rightKeys='right', respKeys=(),
    lineColor='White', skipKeys='tab', mouseOnly=False,
    noMouse=False, size=1.0, stretch=1.0, pos=None,
    minTime=0.4, maxTime=0.0, flipVert=False, depth=0,
    name=None, autoLog=True, **kwargs)
```

The meaning of each of those items is explained further down on the same page, but you might still be wondering how you use them in the `Customize` box.

Basically, you can insert any of those, separated by commas, and any that you *don't* specify will revert to the default value above. For instance, you could write `precision=10` and you would get all the settings above, except that in between each tick there are now 10 subdivisions that participants could select. Or you could insert `high=5, precision=10, noMouse=True` to get a 5-point scale with 10 subdivisions and the participant is only allowed to respond by pressing the left/right keys (not using the mouse).

To see the text better you can use new lines after the commas, so this is valid:

```
low=1, high=7,
precision=10, labels=("Hate it", "Love it")
```

but it will cause a 'Syntax error':

```
low=1, high=7,
precision=10, labels
=("Hate it", "Love it")
```

7.2: USE MULTIPLE RATINGS AT ONCE (FROM PAGE 108)

At first glance, inserting multiple Rating Scales seems easy enough. Hopefully you got as far as inserting a text stimulus, being fed by a variable **word** in a loop, and a pair of Rating Scales. Hopefully also, you moved your two ratings and your stimulus to positions on the screen where they were all visible. So the task *sort of* works, but there are several settings we could change for it to work more smoothly:

1. By default PsychoPy allows you to keep making changes and then press the 'accept' button to confirm your rating. That could be tiresome if you've got several ratings to make, so we turn it off by unticking 'Show Accept' and ticking 'Single click' (both in the **Advanced** settings of the dialog).
2. The next problem is that the trial is ending when either of the ratings is used because, by default, 'Force end of Routine' is ticked. Let's untick that for both our ratings.
3. Now, of course, we don't have *anything* that causes the trial to end! We'll add a Keyboard Component, accepting the **space** key with **Force End Routine** turned on. So, at this point, the participant can respond on each of the scales and then press <space> to move on to the next word.
4. Unfortunately they probably don't know how that should work, so you might also want to add a Text Component to the top of the screen with some instructions like, 'Click on the ratings and press space to move on.'

That should work more smoothly. There is another solution, where you could present the ratings one after the other, each in its own Routine. You could have put your word onto each Routine, at the top, say, and presented the relevant rating underneath. In a sense the settings for the Rating Scale are then more natural and all you lose is the ability to see the ratings all at once while making them (do you care about that?). As with all things, sometimes you have to decide whether there are tweaks to the experimental design, like this, that weren't how you originally imagined it but that make it easier to build.

8.1: BLOCK DESIGN WITH FACES AND HOUSES (FROM PAGE 122)

Obviously, the first step in this task is to create a Routine that presents the images, but make sure you create a *single* routine that doesn't care whether the image is a house or a face (just using a variable name like `filename`).

Create a pair of conditions files (`faceTrials.xlsx` and `houseTrials.xlsx`) to specify the face filenames and another for the house filenames.

Create an outer loop for your task that controls the conditions file to be used by the inner loop (`faceTrials.xlsx` or `houseTrials.xlsx`) needed for each block. Specify this as a variable in a conditions file called `blocks.xlsx`.

To get three blocks of each you could create `blocks.xlsx` with:

- Six rows and set your outer loop to be **random** with one repeat
- Two rows and set your outer loop to be **fullrandom** with three repeats; the effect of this will be exactly as in the previous solution, except
- two rows and set your outer loop to be **random** with three repeats. This will be slightly different in that the randomization of the blocks will be more constrained (you can't get three of the same block in a row).

8.2: COUNTERBALANCE YOUR FACE/HOUSE ORDER (FROM PAGE 122)

Create two conditions files for your outer block: `groupA.xlsx` specifying the houses conditions file first and `groupB.xlsx` specifying the faces conditions first. In the outer loop make sure you set this to be **sequential** rather than **random**.

Then set up a **group** variable to appear in your Experiment Info and set the conditions file of the outer loop to have the value `$"group{}.xlsx".format (expInfo['group'])`.

Now the *group* conditions files is selected according to the dialog box, and the conditions file for each block is determined by this *group* conditions file.

9.1: CHANGE AN IMAGE'S CONTRAST BY HOVERING THE MOUSE OVER IT (FROM PAGE 142)

The solution here is very similar to the example in the chapter where we showed how to use the mouse to magnify a stimulus when the mouse pointer was hovering over it. Again, it will require a little code inserted into a Code Component, in the **Each Frame** tab. Let's say you have a pair of image stimuli called **image_1** and **image_2**, and a Mouse Component called **mouse**:

```
# check if the mouse pointer coordinates lie
# within the boundaries of each of the stimuli:
if image_1.contains(mouse):
    image_1.contrast = 0.5 # decrease its contrast
else:
    image_1.contrast = 1 # reset it to normal
if image_2.contains(mouse):
    image_2.contrast = -1 # totally invert it
else:
    image_2.contrast = 1 # reset it to normal
```

9.2: USE THE MOUSE TO MOVE A STIMULUS AROUND THE DISPLAY (FROM PAGE 142)

It is actually pretty straightforward to click and drag a stimulus. The **isPressedIn()** function of the mouse tells that a mouse button is currently pressed and that the pointer is within the boundaries of the stimulus. So we simply set the position of the stimulus to be equal to the current mouse pointer location. As this gets updated on every screen refresh, the stimulus can be dragged smoothly around the display in real time:

```
if mouse.isPressedIn(image_1):
    image_1.pos = mouse.pos
```

BIBLIOGRAPHY

Anstis, Stuart M. and Patrick Cavanagh. 1983. 'A Minimum Motion Technique for Judging Equiluminance'. In *Colour Vision*, edited by L. T. Mollon and John D. Sharpe, 156–66. Academic Press, London.

Burton, A. Mike, David White and Allan McNeill. 2010. 'The Glasgow Face Matching Test'. *Behavior Research Methods* 42 (1): 286–91. doi:10.3758/BRM.42.1.286.

Carpenter, Roger H. S. 1988. *Movements of the Eyes,* 2nd rev. edn. Pion Limited, London.

Dahl, Christoph D., Nikos K. Logothetis, Heinrich H. Bülthoff and Christian Wallraven. 2010. 'The Thatcher Illusion in Humans and Monkeys'. *Proceedings of the Royal Society of London B: Biological Sciences* 277: 2973–81.

Derrington, Andrew M., John Krauskopf and Peter Lennie. 1984. 'Chromatic Mechanisms in Lateral Geniculate Nucleus of Macaque'. *Journal of Physiology* 357 (1): 241–65.

Elwood, Richard W. 1995. 'The California Verbal Learning Test: Psychometric Characteristics and Clinical Application'. *Neuropsychology Review* 5 (3): 173–201.

Frischen, Alexandra, Andrew P. Bayliss and Steven P. Tipper. 2007. 'Gaze Cueing of Attention: Visual Attention, Social Cognition, and Individual Differences'. *Psychological Bulletin* 133 (4): 694.

García-Pérez, Miguel A. 2001. 'Yes–No Staircases with Fixed Step Sizes: Psychometric Properties and Optimal Setup'. *Optometry & Vision Science* 78 (1): 56–64.

Johnson, John A. 2014. 'Measuring Thirty Facets of the Five Factor Model with a 120-Item Public Domain Inventory: Development of the IPIP-NEO-120'. *Journal of Research in Personality* 51: 78–89.

Ledgeway, Timothy and Andrew T. Smith. 1994. 'Evidence for Separate Motion-Detecting Mechanisms for First-and Second-Order Motion in Human Vision'. *Vision Research* 34 (20): 2727–40.

Lejuez, Carl W., Jennifer P. Read, Christopher W. Kahler, Jerry B. Richards, Susan E. Ramsey, Gregory L. Stuart, David R. Strong and Richard A. Brown. 2002. 'Evaluation of a Behavioral Measure of Risk Taking: The Balloon Analogue Risk Task (BART)'. *Journal of Experimental Psychology: Applied* 8 (2): 75.

MacLeod, Colin M. 1991. 'Half a Century of Research on the Stroop Effect: An Integrative Review'. *Psychological Bulletin* 109 (2): 163.

MacLeod, Donald I. A. and Robert M. Boynton. 1979. 'Chromaticity Diagram Showing Cone Excitation by Stimuli of Equal Luminance'. *Journal of the Optical Society of America* 69 (8): 1183–6.

Peirce, J. W. 2007 'PsychoPy – Psychophysics Software in Python'. *Journal of Neuroscience Methods* 162 (1–2): 8–13.

Posner, Michael I. 1980. 'Orienting of Attention'. *Quarterly Journal of Experimental Psychology* 32 (1): 3–25.

Preston, Malcolm S. and Wallace E. Lambert. 1969. 'Interlingual Interference in a Bilingual Version of the Stroop Color-Word Task'. *Journal of Verbal Learning and Verbal Behavior* 8 (2): 295–301. doi:http://dx.doi.org/10.1016/S0022-5371(69)80079-4.

Scase, Mark O., Oliver J. Braddick and Jane E. Raymond. 1996. 'What Is Noise for the Motion System?' *Vision Research* 36 (16): 2579–86.

Stroop, J. Ridley. 1935. 'Studies of Interference in Serial Verbal Reactions'. *Journal of Experimental Psychology* 18 (6): 643.

Thompson, Peter. 1980. 'Margaret Thatcher: A New Illusion'. *Perception* 9: 483–4.

Ulrich, Rolf and Markus Giray. 1989. 'Time Resolution of Clocks: Effects on Reaction Time Measurement – Good News for Bad Clocks'. *British Journal of Mathematical and Statistical Psychology* 42 (1): 1–12.

Watson, Andrew B. and Denis G. Pelli. 1983. 'QUEST: A Bayesian Adaptive Psychometric Method'. *Attention, Perception, & Psychophysics* 33 (2): 113–20.

INDEX